EQUITY:IN

EQUITY:IN

—— A HITCHHIKER'S GUIDE TO ——
INVESTING IN INDIAN EQUITY MARKETS

ANSHUMAN KHANNA

Notion Press

Old No. 38, New No. 6
McNichols Road, Chetpet
Chennai - 600 031

First Published by Notion Press 2016
Copyright © Anshuman Khanna 2016
All Rights Reserved.

ISBN
Hardcase: 978-1-946129-91-8
Paperback: 978-1-946280-44-2

This book has been published with all efforts taken to make the material error-free after the consent of the author. However, the author and the publisher do not assume and hereby disclaim any liability to any party for any loss, damage, or disruption caused by errors or omissions, whether such errors or omissions result from negligence, accident, or any other cause.

No part of this book may be used, reproduced in any manner whatsoever without written permission from the author, except in the case of brief quotations embodied in critical articles and reviews.

DEDICATED TO MY CHILDREN – AARUSH AND RIDHIMA

THANK YOU, RASHMI KHANNA

DISCLAIMER

1. This book is intended to be a discussion on the approach for investing, typical to the Indian economy and stock markets. The approach suggested imbibes subjective elements and normative judgement on the part of the investor and the efficacy thereof is thus dependent on the judgement of the investor. The author does not warrant any results or outcome with respect to the recommended strategies contained in this book.
2. The author does not intend to recommend any particular stocks to be invested in by the investor via the medium of this book. Any and all investment decisions which may be made by the reader whether by applying any of the principles recommended in this book or otherwise would be at the sole risk of the reader without recourse to the author or publisher hereof.
3. Due care and diligence has been made in relation to the figures and data taken in this book in relation to markets, companies and the stocks discussed. However in no case do the author or the publisher warrant the accuracy or completeness of the data. The reader is suggested to undertake their own analysis and independent verification of the companies, financials and the stocks and make investment decisions based on their findings rather than relying on figures and data contained herein.
4. While many companies, promoter groups and stocks have been discussed in this book, such discussion is by way of illustration only and not meant to be treated as the basis of investment decisions by the reader.
5. Any views expressed herein regarding the business prospects or future prospects of any company or sector are subjective views of the author for discussion purposes as illustrations only and ought not to be considered as recommendations by the author or the publisher. The projections

Disclaimer

provided in relation to the financials of the companies are illustrative only and ought not to be relied upon or considered as accurate by the reader.

6. Any views expressed regarding promoter groups or the business prospects of the companies are by way of illustration only and not be considered as a view of the author or the publisher on the promoter group or company in question. The reader is advised to undertake their own analysis and due diligence before taking a position in any stocks as such.

7. All case studies and projections in relation to companies undertaken in this book are by way of illustration only and are not meant to be actual or projected guideposts in relation to any company or stock. The reader is advised to undertake their own independent analysis of companies and stocks before taking any position therein.

8. Data in this book in relation to companies and stocks may not be up to date at the time of publishing of this book. As such the author or the publisher do not warrant that the information or figures contained in this book are up to date. The reader is advised to undertake their own independent analysis and verification to ascertain correct and up to date data.

9. The author has not expressed any view in this book regarding any promoter group or management of any company. All discussions in this regard are on a hypothetical basis and should not be considered as a basis for investment. The reader is advised to form their own view regarding the company, its promoter group and management before undertaking investment therein.

10. All trading strategies and ideas discussed in this book are indicative in nature and the reader is advised to carry out their own independent assessment before undertaking any strategy or trade discussed.

CONTENTS

Preface .... *xi*

CHAPTER 1	INTRODUCTION 1
CHAPTER 2	SELECTING A STOCK TO INVEST IN – WHAT'S RELEVANT AND WHAT'S NOT 15
CHAPTER 3	MAIN CRITERION ONE: PROMOTER GROUP PROFILE 35
CHAPTER 4	MAIN CRITERION TWO: BUSINESS PROSPECTS 63
CHAPTER 5	MAIN CRITERION THREE: VALUATION 87
CHAPTER 6	SECONDARY FACTORS 151
CHAPTER 7	TIMING YOUR ENTRY AND EXIT 171
CHAPTER 8	PORTFOLIO ALLOCATION 181
CHAPTER 9	REGULATORY FRAMEWORK 191
CHAPTER 10	INFORMATION BASED INVESTING 201
CHAPTER 11	TECHNICAL CHARTING AND TRADING IDEAS 215
CHAPTER 12	CLOSING SUMMARY 239

Acknowledgements *255*

PREFACE

The stock market has been a source of attraction for millions of investors and traders since time immemorial. It feeds into our speculative desires and yet offers the opportunity for expending intellectual capital in our endeavours to succeed. The room for application of mind and determination of outcome in equity investing is superior to the opportunity to do the same in case of casinos or betting on horses, though the rate for success may not similarly correlate.

The stock market has seen success stories which have been aggrandized by many, with legendary investors of the likes of Warren Buffett being emulated and people trying to replicate their rags to riches story by studying their investment or trading approach and attempting to adopt the same. For every success story in the stock markets there are multitude of failed investors and traders. The level of public attraction and coverage that has been seen in case of successful investors has not been echoed in case of the failures, although it may be argued that the causes of failure are a much more telling guide for any new initiate to the markets than the legendary successes.

Even before I turned 20, I delved into Indian equity markets when I was studying for my Chartered Accountancy. Like any youngster initiated to equities, I felt I had the superior intellect and ability to pick the winning stocks and outperform not only the markets but also my peers. More so, given the subjects of financial management, accountancy, costing, and taxation that formed an integral part of my formal training coupled with my avid interest in the success stories of legendary investors such as Buffett and traders such as Soros, it was thus a natural occurrence that I took a deep dive into the equity markets.

I continued to pour money into the markets while I did my law, and this time my presumed financial expertise was supplemented by a broader understanding of the regulatory framework of our country, which has a bearing on any and every company transacting business in India.

Preface

I also supplemented my formal education with avidly reading some of the bibles of stock market investing ranging from Benjamin Graham's discourse in the intelligent investor, to books elaborating the approaches of greats such as Warren Buffett, George Soros and others. Each of these books were very enlightening and did go a long way in shaping my views and approach to the equity markets in India, though I would not reckon any single book to have had a decisive influence.

One book that I read, which stayed with me, was "Reminisces of a Stock Operator" by Jesse Livermore. Jesse Livermore was one of the original speculators, taking positions of multi million dollars in the US stock markets way back in the 1920's. While it is a different story that he did not end up in the best of the circumstances in his life, the book chronicling his thoughts and approach is a brilliant read for any person interested in the equity markets. This being so not for the fact that the book necessarily offers any winning formula to investing but due to the fact that the book offers valuable insights on the pitfalls and mistakes which often take down many with them. As they say, experience is the best teacher. Mr. Livermore has shared his experiences in the most engaging manner and one gets to learn a lot from his experiences.

As for my experience of equity markets in the last 15 plus years, alas, things seldom pan out as you may envisage. While I have not been a winner in the equity stock markets in the legendary fashion as everyone sets out to achieve, it has been a pleasantly exciting journey nonetheless with few regrets and many learnings.

I have tried my hand at many approaches, ranging from value investing to technical charting to day trading to futures and options trades. Each experience has taught me valuable lessons. More than teaching me what I should be doing, I have learnt what one must avoid. If you know what pitfalls and temptations to avoid in the stock market you have more than half the battle won. What then remains is a simple and common sense oriented approach which, if applied correctly and with strictly enforced discipline and patience, can see you making money in the markets at a fairly reasonable pace of outperformance to the market.

It is thus, that I recommend any one with the desire for earning a return on their capital, superlative to the benign debt market returns, and to participate in the India growth story at the same time, to take a head on plunge into the Indian equity markets. There has not been a better time, given the point of inflexion that the country stands on today, and given the fact that equities have hands on been the best performing asset class when one considers returns over long term period such as three to four decades.

This book attempts to encapsulate my learnings from my experiences of trading and investing in the Indian stock market over the years. It provides an approach to investing which I have developed by combining the prescriptions of various global market legends with the learnings from the mistakes made and adapting the entire approach to the peculiarities of Indian markets. While the resultant prescription may not be unique or novel, an attempt has been made by me to make it simplistic and common sense oriented so that it may be adopted in part or whole by the lay investors who look to enthral themselves with the jamboree of the Indian equity markets, and also serve as a seeding ground for thoughts and introspection by regular Indian market players and experts alike.

This book is not written from the perspective of being a text book on the theories and fundamentals surrounding stock markets and companies. Moreover it assumes a basic level of knowledge regarding companies, financials and the markets on the part of the reader. It does not adopt a ground up approach of elaborating basic principles of financial management or valuation, rather it looks to flesh out the critical factors and considerations while leaving the irrelevant considerations on the way side.

While I have tried to expound on my prescriptions for the newly initiated market investor, this book is not an attempt to capture a new approach to investing or any novel ideas that you wouldn't have heard of or read before. It is an attempt to lay out a systematic approach to picking the correct stocks by an investor in the context of the Indian markets. The approach advocated here is a simplistic common sense oriented approach with emphasis on areas that are important and also covering aspects which make investing in the Indian markets unique.

Preface

I hope it emerges as an interesting read for the reader with aspects staying with the readers for long after as they venture on in their quest for equity market glory in India. I also hope that after reading this the readers would be able to adopt the approach propagated here if not on the whole, then at least in part, or be able to use the pointers given in this book to suitably modify or improve their approach to investing in the Indian markets.

CHAPTER 1

INTRODUCTION

> *Indian equity markets and India as a country, are unique in certain ways, which mandates a tailor-made approach to investing in Indian equities.*

The Indian stock markets present an attractive destination for varying category of traders and investors, ranging from foreign and domestic institutions, to hedge funds and retail investors.

India as an emerging market has always been a big draw for the foreign investors, given it's growth potential of unparalleled proportions owing to the population base and trailing economic indicators such as per capita income. Indian companies have been seen as the proxy play for the India growth story and investors have made a bee line for stocks seeking to find and benefit from multi-baggers over the years.

As such, the Indian equity indices have seen a commendable performance in the 21st century with the Indian benchmark index, Nifty rising from 1482 in 2000 to 7946 in 2015.

Below is the chart showing Nifty's rise from 2000 to 2015.

With the liberalization of the foreign exchange norms on the back of the introduction of Foreign Exchange Management Act in 1999, the flows by foreign investors in India have augmented the liquidity flow. It has not only aided the returns being generated by the Indian equities but has also taken the entire market into a whole new tangent in terms of corporate governance, financial reporting and investor activism.

Over the last five years, the interest in India has developed even more, with the country emerging as one of the fastest growing economies in the world and the demand and infrastructure deficit driven story unfolding before our eyes.

In their efforts to successfully operate in the Indian markets, investors and traders alike, tend to adopt well known techniques for investing or trading as have been used globally for a long period of time. The techniques adopted range from value-based investing to technical charting and hedging based strategies.

It has been seen that there are certain peculiarities in the Indian market which do not allow for a cookie-cutter prescription, as available in US-centric authored books, to be applied to the Indian markets. While for the large part an approach to investing as provided in the 'Intelligent Investor' may hold true for Indian markets, it cannot be applied without adaptation. Similarly, books on technical charting do not necessarily hold good for the large part of Indian market movements for reasons discussed subsequently.

It would be evident to any investor or trader participating in the Indian markets that in fact India is a unique country with equally unique stock markets and business environment which exhibit certain features which distinguish it from the markets of developed economies. It is important to recognize these differences in order to be able to tailor your approach to Indian stocks and companies and not be caught at the wrong end of the proverbial rifle at the risk of losing your capital.

So what is it that makes Indian markets unique or different? Some of the factors are discussed in this chapter.

1. MARKET DEPTH – OR THE LACK THEREOF

Indian markets do not boast of the level of depth that is present in US markets or any other mature market. While volumes in the Indian stock markets have grown over the years, especially with the opening of the Indian economy to foreign direct investment (FDI) and foreign institutional investors (FII) in the 1990s, the volumes and market capitalization of Indian markets still lags behind those of developed markets such as USA and Europe.

This lack of depth is even more pronounced at the individual stock level with various mid cap and small cap stocks in India seeing volumes and turnover levels which are so low that any mid-size investor may be able to influence the price movements in the stock by virtue of his concerted buying or selling orders, a practice that is patently illegal under Indian laws as it is in developed markets. Moreover such low volumes negate big positions being built or liquidated at a given market price and thus throw off analyst findings based on a quoted price of the stocks.

The inevitable consequence of the lack of depth and maturity in the Indian market is that at any point of time large and erratic price movements in the equity prices or even at index level may be precipitated by the action of few large investors. The corollary of this phenomena is that the market, being at the mercy of few numbers, would not always act in a perfectly rational manner and may be subjected to the whims or manipulation by select players. Thus many theories, especially those of technical chartists, which may work perfectly in mature markets such as US and Europe, may not work in Indian equity markets.

As a consequence, a stock which may make a compelling investment target owing to its apparent undervaluation may still suffer adverse price movements and not see its market price reflecting its intrinsic value. This is so purely on account of the lack of depth and the price movement being influenced by few large players. Thus such stocks may seem to belie the fundamental approach to investing in the short to medium term.

Similarly, stocks which may appear undervalued may not in reality be undervalued as the quoted price of the stocks would not be supported by substantial volumes. As such transacting in such stocks at the 'quoted' price with a view to build a reasonable size of a position would not be feasible and when the investor would start building a position he would end up paying a price per share which may be the perceived intrinsic worth of the share in the first place, thereby negating any attempt to reap gains on the stock.

The volume and depth at the stock as well as market level thus has to be kept in mind by the investor when considering India specific investment strategies.

2. REGULATORY SENSITIVITIES

Indian markets tend to react very erratically to any regulatory action, especially any perceived negative moves.

Whether it be the action of the tax administration to go after any foreign multinational group company or the infamous Vodafone centric retrospective amendments in tax law or even levying of a tax on the foreign institutional investors. It may be an adverse judicial pronouncement affecting the business prospects of a company, or an action of the regulators taking steps to penalize or even ban products or services of companies.

At any given point of time, for any particular sector, the investor is a sitting duck where the regulatory action or even the smell of any such action may lead to wild movements in the stocks of the companies that are in such sector. While this may hold partly true for mature capital markets as well, the level of impact that such regulatory moves and rumours tend to have on Indian equity markets is far more emphatic.

Add to this the level of regulatory complexity prevalent in India. From the plethora of legislation at the Centre and State level, the regulatory framework imbibes delegated legislation in the form of rules, regulations and notifications. There is a multitude of authorities and approvals that any company needs to interface and liaise with. Moreover, at any given point of time there are a large number of regulatory considerations which could end up furthering or adversely affecting the business prospects of a company. The differing political ideologies of the many political parties, regional as well as national, also affect the business activities of the companies in different and unexpected ways.

For any investor to navigate the expanse of the Indian stock markets, it would be inevitable that they gain insights into the unique regulatory landscape present in the Indian economy and particularly familiarize themselves with the sector specific regulations that govern the investee company's business.

Apart from affecting the price of stocks, regulatory events and actions can have the effect of decimating the entire business model of companies and for this reason also the understanding and tracking of the regulatory framework as a part of the investor's activities is required in India.

For example in 2005, post the demerger of Reliance Industries into various entities, the Ambani brothers had formed a company by the name of Reliance Natural Resources Limited (RNRL) with the objective of purchasing gas from Reliance Industries from its KG Basin block and selling the said gas to Reliance Power for use as feedstock for its proposed power plant in Dadri. At the time, RNRL was considered as a hot favourite in the Reliance stable of stocks, as it was viewed to be having a fairly certain and stable business model with the margins on purchase and sale of gas locked in with long term purchase and sale contracts. The stock was lapped up by the investors.

However, regulatory action intervened, in the form of steps taken by the ministry as well as the courts striking down the proposed arrangement as being unlawful and contrary to the terms of the public policy and production sharing contract governing Reliance's KG Basin block. There was thus a total decimation of the business model of RNRL and the company ended up remaining a shell company which was ultimately merged into Reliance power.

Such regulatory actions and developments, though not unique to India, are nevertheless pronounced in their effect when it comes to Indian equity markets and specific company stocks. The regulatory actions and changes are moreover frequent, complicated and cascading in nature and the complexity of the regulatory framework in India coupled with the foregoing, sets the Indian market apart.

3. POLITICAL STRUCTURE

Not only is India the world's largest democracy, it is also unique insofar as the federal structure of the political setup under the Indian constitution. This when combined with the fact that there is no restriction on the number of political parties which may contest in an election, it results in the inevitable fallout that we see different political parties governing in the different states as well as the Centre thereby creating a methodical chaos.

Consequently, there is a divergence of political ideologies and policies prevailing from state to state. Any company transacting business in India in multiple states not only has to deal with the respective state governments but also the particular party in power in the Centre.

Understanding the political ideologies of the different (and changing) political parties and tweaking the business prospects of companies based on the same is thus peculiar to the process of investing in the Indian equity markets. Diverse political ideologies range from the conservative and pro-labour policies of the Communist parties in States such as West Bengal and Kerala, to the pro-business liberal policies in states such as Gujarat and Maharashtra.

Not only do these ideologies and policies influence the working at the level of the State Governments but also at the Centre especially where the ruling government is comprised of a coalition of parties, which is the often the result of the imperfect working of the world's biggest democracy. In fact, for an investor to have a real sense of the leanings of the Government and the expected business environment, it becomes necessary to have a sense of the relative strength of the different political parties in the coalition set up. As has often been seen, a relatively strong conservative coalition partner ends up stalling the reform agenda of a progressive coalition lead party.

It would thus be seen that the diversity of the political ideologies and how these come into play in the unique democratic setup of India to affect the business prospects of companies, is yet another distinguishing feature of the Indian equity markets.

4. STAGE OF MATURITY

The Indian markets are also unique in terms of their stage of maturity.

Unlike the markets in US or Europe which have been operating for decades and have evolved sophisticated systems and regulations to govern their operations, the Indian markets only started to find their feet post 1990's liberalization measures announced by the Narasimha Rao – Manmohan Singh government.

Even in the 1990's the Indian markets were susceptible and fell prey to major stock market scams amidst manipulations by the likes of Harshad Mehta and Ketan Parekh. Accordingly, dematerialization of securities was brought in during the 1990's and the Securities and Exchange Board of India (SEBI) was constituted as the market regulator to bring in the new century in place of the draconian Capital Controller of Issues.

With the advent of the liberalized foreign exchange regime under FEMA 1999, the markets were opened up to foreign investors albeit under a regulated and monitored route of FDI and FIIs. This, in turn yielded newer problems for the Indian markets in the form of controversies behind participatory notes (P-notes) and the suspected round tripping of black money by resident Indians using the P-note mechanism. Amendments were made on a repeated basis to check the menace and even today the regulators keep a close eye on the FII route for investment. To the extent that every time there is even a whiff of the regulators banning issuance of P-notes by the FIIs or otherwise restricting them, the market goes into a tizzy of a downward spiral.

In parallel, the SEBI regulations for disclosure and investor protection have been refined and spruced up, bringing greater transparency and disclosure to the investors, affirming minority rights and tightening corporate governance.

SEBI insider trading regulations have been implemented and amended from time to time to restrain inside information based trading and other malpractices. SEBI has also actively developed the Takeover regulations and delisting regulations to address the need for a systematic framework for corporate takeovers and delisting exercises at par with international markets.

The corporate law and foreign investment regulations have also been continuously upgraded by the Central Government of India with a view to align these to policy objectives such as minority protection and greater participation of foreign companies in various sectors such as insurance, retail and manufacturing. The approval systems have been eased over a period of time with increasing number of inclusions under the category of automatic approval to aid ease of investing in India by the foreign business houses.

The tax treaties of India with various countries have been put in place to provide the framework and tax benefits for foreign nationals and corporates investing or doing business in India.

While many steps have been taken towards the development of the Indian markets, there have also been many regressive elements or unaddressed issues which still continue to dog the markets and the participants. This includes retrospective taxation of profits on sale of shares, tax litigation on equity transfer such as Vodafone case, and uncertainty around approvals for foreign investment and takeovers.

As such the Indian markets still have a long way to go to achieve a matured framework for the investors and promoters alike, yet the initiatives taken have been directionally affirmative.

The aforesaid plethora of developments and uncertainties add to the uniqueness of the markets in India.

5. STAGE OF ECONOMIC DEVELOPMENT

The Indian economy and the markets are also unique insofar as these present a one of a kind amalgam of size and potential for growth.

While there exist large economies such as that of the USA with high GDP and per capita income levels, these economies do not exhibit a growth curve which may excite an investor looking for multi-baggers. This is primarily due to the fact that these economies are matured and demand saturated.

Again there are economies such as China which have a large population base, yet these also do not exhibit potential for sustained growth in their GDP levels owing to the fact that there has been rapid pace of economic development and infrastructure planning by the Government. There is equitable level of income distribution and the potential for demand based growth remains limited.

As opposed to these, India is a unique proposition of a country, with a large population base, infrastructure deficit, low per capital income and huge demand based growth spurts in various sectors of the economy. Any product or service which is yet to penetrate the rural population of India yields exponential growth prospects for the companies.

The liberalised and pro-business environment with the transparent procedures and systems, aided with the governmental initiatives puts India in a unique position, perhaps incomparable to any other country, when it comes to the business prospects and potential for returns.

6. SENSITIVITY TO GLOBAL DEVELOPMENTS

It is a fact that in today's age all the international markets are inter connected and exposed to each other when it comes to price movements, especially in the case of currency markets, commodity markets and equities.

Similarly with the opening up of economies to global trade and investment, there is greater susceptibility of markets to the flow of liquidity.

However the vulnerability of certain markets to international events, price movements and liquidity flows tends to be more than the others. This is especially the case with the Indian equity markets.

The Indian equity markets are characterized by a high degree of sensitivity to various external events and global developments. This is so for a number of reasons. The primary reason is the fact that Indian markets still depend, to a large extent, on foreign liquidity flows and consequently, the buying or selling activities of foreign institutional investors tends to impact the markets significantly. This impact is two-fold, first the foreign inflows and outflows affect the Indian currency which in turn affects the financials of the companies which are having forex exposure, and secondly the foreign inflows and outflows in the form of buying and selling of stocks affects the price levels of the stocks as well as the broader market.

Thus, in a situation where the sentiment of the foreign institutions changes from a long to short based on international developments and they pull out funds from the Indian market, we see the Indian markets react strongly to such an eventuality.

Similarly the Indian markets tend to react strongly to developments in other countries such as recession in the USA for instance. Being exposed to other countries in terms of export and import trade, the Indian economy is affected by changes in the international economic scenario.

Thus in 2008, when the sub-prime crisis hit the USA, the Indian market took a massive tumble with the benchmark Nifty index falling 50% from 6000 levels of January 2008 to 3000 levels in second half of 2008.

Furthermore, changes in the monetary policies of the central banks of other countries also affect the exchange rate of the Indian rupee vis-à-vis the major foreign currencies and has a strong reaction from Indian markets in terms of the stocks of companies exposed to foreign currencies, as well as from bonds.

Again the movement in global commodity prices such as coal and crude oil also evinces strong reaction in the Indian markets given our high dependence on import thereof.

The high beta of the Indian markets to global macro-economic events is yet another unique feature of the Indian capital markets which requires an investor to tailor the investment methodology to countenance such aspects.

7. PROMOTER GROUPS

The Indian corporate diaspora is comprised of a unique confluence of promoter groups. Prominent amongst the Indian promoter groups are the government owned public sector companies such as Indian Oil Corporation, Oil & Natural Gas Corporation, Steel Authority of India and Shipping Corporation of India. The Indian Government, both Centre as well as State have taken it upon themselves to participate in private business and even list such businesses in the Indian equity markets.

Then there are the family owned companies, with a major business presence in diverse areas, such as Birlas, Tatas and Ambanis and plethora of other household names that are put on a pedestal and idolized for their business acumen and empires. Many of these family groups have spawned multiple generations and have seen the businesses being split and multiple groups being formed with differing or even overlapping business interests. For instance, the Ambanis saw a split in the first decade of the 21st century and the erstwhile Reliance empire got sub-divided into two Reliance Groups. Similarly the Jindals as a family also find themselves running different business groups with the Sajjan Jindal Group, Naveen Jindal Group and others. The family owned promoter group is a dominant category in the Indian equity landscape with a large number of companies falling under the same.

The third category of promoter groups found in India are the multinational corporates, comprising of companies owned by MNC groups such as Nestle, Holcim, Gilette, and Unilever.

Lastly there are companies which are 'promoter less' such as HDFC Bank, ITC and L&T.

The diversity of the promoter groups is augmented by the fact that the promoter families as well as MNCs themselves prevail from different geographical and cultural backgrounds and operate businesses with totally different mind-sets from one another.

The diversity and implications of the promoter groups on the investee companies are discussed in depth in a subsequent chapter of this book.

8. RAMPANT TIPS AND SPECULATION

Tipsters are everywhere and information 'tips' are there for the asking in any country. But unlike the mature western markets, in India, so called 'tips' which are posed to imbue inside information and promised as a sure shot road to money making, are rampant. So much so that one would almost forget that such information sharing and access is patently illegal and bound to land someone even in jail – at least in theory in India, but for real in other countries a la Rajat Gupta in the USA.

In such a situation the uninitiated lay investor has to skilfully navigate the waters of Indian equity markets keeping in mind the pitfalls of such information based investing and filtering the extent and nature of the information to be relied upon. Even where the information provided is genuine and not falling within the ambit of inside information, the investor needs to be aware of how to, and to what extent, make use of such information for purposes of his investment activity.

Information comes in many forms and areas and need to be dealt with based on multiple factors. This unique aspect of the Indian market is also discussed in depth in subsequent parts of this book.

Keeping the above peculiarities of the Indian capital markets in mind, this book endeavours to share with you some insights on the approach of investing in the Indian equity markets, by adapting the various well known principles of investing and trading to the India centric circumstances.

This book deals with the approach to be adopted by an investor in building a portfolio with a medium to long term perspective in the Indian capital markets. It does not provide short term trading or intra-day strategies though these have also been discussed briefly at the appropriate places.

This book considers the various factors that may come up before an investor for his consideration during the course of the above exercise. It also tries to filter out the factors that are relevant from those that are not relevant for consideration and the weightage that may be ascribed to each of the relevant factors.

The main approach to picking stocks for investment has been reduced to three main factors or criteria that a stock must fulfill for it to be considered worthy of investment. These three criteria are discussed in detail along with examples of companies from the Indian markets.

Thereafter we discuss secondary factors which though not the mainstay for picking or rejecting stocks, still have a bearing on the stock selection such that, a stock which may fulfil the three main criteria may still be rejected on account of certain secondary factors.

Once the stocks fulfilling the three basic criteria and also satisfying secondary factors have been selected by the investor (answering the question 'which stock to invest in?'), we go on to discuss the aspects relating to the allocation of capital amongst these stocks i.e. portfolio allocation as well as the timing of purchases and sales of the portfolio stocks by the investor i.e. 'how much to buy and when?.'

We then go on to discuss some of the other relevant aspects of the Indian stock markets i.e. the regulatory framework and how the investor should understand the relevant regulatory aspects affecting his investee companies as well as how he should keep a track of changes therein. We also discuss the so-called 'tips' in the Indian markets, the different types of information floating around and how these should be dealt with by an investor if and when he stumbles upon information which may be pertinent to his investee companies.

We have also discussed aspects relating to technical charting and trading strategies in a separate chapter. While these are not core to the practice of building a fundamentals based portfolio, these have nevertheless been discussed by way of ideas particular to the Indian markets which may be adopted by an investor to supplement his long term portfolio.

The discussion on the various aspects as above has been illustrated with real life Indian companies' examples including the price charts and financials wherever pertinent.

CHAPTER 2

SELECTING A STOCK TO INVEST IN – WHAT'S RELEVANT AND WHAT'S NOT

> *It is more important to know what to ignore than what to rely on, when evaluating factors affecting an investment in an Indian stock*

The market is the temptress that will lure you with the dream of quick and easy gains and snatch away your purse and along with it your dignity so that you stand forlorn stripped naked on the proverbial street with the mask of your pride in your hand.

One has to be careful to not fall into traps that are set by the invisible hand that moves the market.

As an investor traverses the Indian equity markets, he is sure to encounter all kinds of theories and advice as almost everyone is a self-professed expert when it comes to investing in equity markets in India. This phenomenon is compounded by the fact that there is little to no regulation of so called 'advisors' and 'experts' in Indian stock markets akin to the regulation in mature markets in the west.

As such, any newly initiated investor will be bombarded with ideas, tips and information for picking investment worthy stocks as well as trading strategies for short term gains. Furthermore, there is an overload of information and news which one encounters over the internet, newspapers, research reports and news channels alike.

It thus emerges that it is more important to know what to avoid than to know what to rely upon.

Some of the factors that may be encountered on a regular basis and thus may appear very pertinent to a particular stock's performance, but should in fact not be relied upon as the sole basis of decision making are discussed below.

1. REGULATORY EVENTS

There are plenty of rumours and news that makes rounds on a daily basis about regulatory changes and events. Market experts analyse such news and extrapolate which stocks would be benefitted and which stocks would be adversely affected. The Indian markets, especially, witness a characteristically volatile reaction to such regulatory developments as soon as such events take place. It thus becomes even more tempting for an investor to delve into a stock or to go short on a stock on the hearing of such regulatory developments taking place.

Some instances of such developments include:

a. Judicial rulings

News or rumours of judicial rulings being pronounced which have a positive or adverse impact on the business of certain companies is a development that inevitably invites a wild reaction on the stock price of the affected company. Such news is thus, often relied upon by traders or investors to initiate a position in stocks without even delving into the finer aspects of the judicial ruling or reading the judgement in the first place.

For instance, consider the news of a judgement of Supreme Court passing an order cancelling coal block allocations under the auction by the Government of India in favour of power generation companies or in favour of steel manufacturers. The prima facie view formed with such a development is that the companies whose blocks have been cancelled stand to lose and as such the market also shows a knee jerk reaction in driving the prices of such stocks down.

b. Regulator's action

Action by any regulatory body governing a particular sector, has a bearing on the business of the companies operating in such a sector. For example, news of order passed by the power regulatory authorities to allow power generation companies to pass through and recover the higher coal fuel cost from state electricity boards thereby improving the price realization per unit of power by such companies would prima facie augur well for the power generation companies and would lead to the market players going on a buying spree with respect to the stocks of such companies.

In both the above instances, it would not be a good idea to sell or buy the stock in question purely on the news flow of the regulatory event. The business outlook of the company has to be seen in a holistic sense and decision to enter or exit a stock cannot be based solely on a solitary regulatory event, which even if material, may not persevere and may even be overturned by subsequent court order or legislative action.

It is very tempting to take a quick dive into the stock in case of such regulatory developments especially where the speculation instinct takes over or the greed quotient for a seemingly obvious quick buck dominates.

However the investor needs to understand that any such legal changes or developments may be material or transient insofar as its impact on the business prospects of the companies is concerned. Furthermore the exact nature and extent of the impact, favourable or otherwise would depend on the intricacies of the regulatory development and the sensitivity of the business model of the company to the exact regulatory development.

For instance, the judgement of the Supreme Court cancelling the coal block allocation may at first glance appear as an adverse development for a power generation company. However on closer inspection it may turn out that the company in question is in any case not operating the coal mine owing to pending environmental approvals or high recovery costs or other reasons. Instead, it is relying on imported thermal coal which is working out cheaper, in which case there would really be no impact of the judgement of the court on this company.

To take a real life example, in September 2014 the Supreme Court of India came out with a ruling cancelling the coal block allocations made by the Government since 1993 to various companies. One of the companies in the

Equity:In

affected lot was JSW Steel. The stock of the company took a nosedive on the announcement of the judicial ruling. Any person relying on this ruling would have either shorted the stock or being long on the stock, would have exited his long position. However if you see the chart of the stock of JSW Steel given below, you would see that the price of the stock reacted to the news adversely however thereafter recovered to its previous levels thus demonstrating the fact that the knee jerk reaction of the market to drive down the stock was uncalled for and the fundamentals of the company remaining intact, the stock price recovered to the previous levels. Thus an investor who may have been long on such a stock and would have decided to exit his position solely on the basis of the said judicial ruling would have found himself to have made a mistake as the judicial ruling quite obviously did not affect the underlying business prospects of the company in a material way.

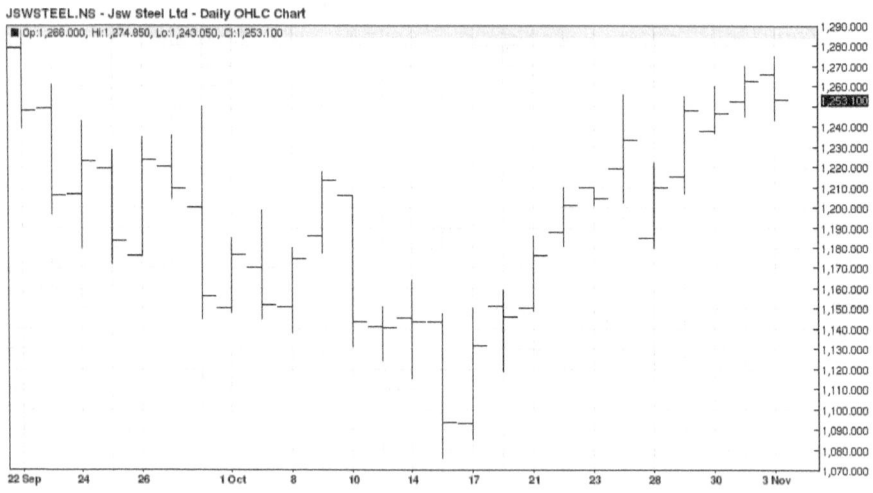

Similarly the regulatory authority's order to allow power companies to pass on higher fuel costs to state electricity boards may at first glance appear to be lucrative for a particular power generation company. However, on a finer inspection, it may turn out that in case of such a company the order may be redundant since the power tariff built into its long term power purchase agreement with the SEB may already be factoring in higher fuel costs and thus there may not be any pass through incremental revenues to the company owing to the order. Alternatively it may be seen that the order of the authority does not have the perceived benefit given that the order is thereafter appealed by the SEBs to the higher level and the operation of such order is stayed by the appellate body.

In April 2013, in the case of Adani Power, the CERC made a ruling whereby it directed the SEBs to compensate Adani Power for higher fuel costs incurred owing to the higher cost of imported coal used by the power generation company as opposed to local coal. However as would be seen from the stock price chart of Adani Power during that period, the stock, while it did initially react favourably to the news, did not persevere with the uptick given that the full effect of the order, on the business prospects of the company did not play out as expected. Thus, initially the stock moved up from INR 45 levels in April 2013 to INR 60 levels by June 2013, however, thereafter the stock started floating downwards and broke below the INR 45 levels by August 2013 to touch lows of INR 32. Thus, anyone who may have bought the stock solely on the basis of the regulatory development, being the CERC order, would have seen his investment in result a loss contrary to the expectation.

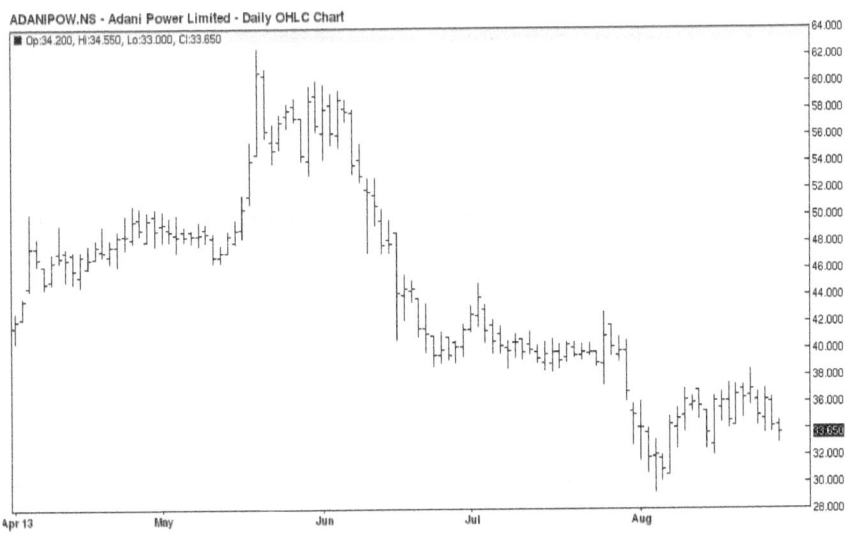

As such regulatory events on a stand-alone basis should not be made the basis of entering or exiting positions in stocks.

2. TECHNICAL CHARTS

Anyone who has been exposed to business news channels in India would have witnessed the parade of the technical chartists and experts on the news channels on dishing out advice on how to trade stocks on a daily basis and make a quick buck on the Indian markets. Not only is there a plethora of such technical experts, they have a never ending set of stock trading recommendations in the media, so much so that it becomes difficult to resist for any newly initiated investor to try out their recommendations in the hope of some quick gains.

Sooner or later one would realize that there does exist a typical pattern in the views and recommendations doled out by the said experts.

The views of a technical chartist typically go like this:

"The Reliance Industries stock which currently trades at INR 850 may go up to INR 865 if it crosses INR 855 but will fall to INR 840 if it breaks INR 850."

It would take a genius to figure out how to trade on the basis of such information or expert advice. You buy the stock at INR 850 only to see it break and go to INR 840? Or you wait for it to cross INR 855 and then buy it only to see it recede back to INR 850 levels?

Even if you were to find yourself relying on the advice and being able to unscramble the highly conditional trading advice, there is not a lot of money to be made in stocks, relying on technical charts. More so in India where the stock price, regardless of what the chart says, may gyrate significantly if any supervening events come into play. These may be in the form of a regulatory announcement illustrated above, or a sudden large sell or buy order by a large stake holder such as a Foreign Institutional Investor (FII) or a Domestic Institutional Investor (DII) which totally disrupts the volume and price chart of the stock in question.

For instance, below is the chart of Mahindra & Mahindra for the months of November 2015 to January 2016. One would note that as per technical patterns, the stock was appearing to be in an uptrend from November and may have been recommended by the technical chartists for a buy strategy. However anyone who would have taken a long bet based on the advice of technical chartists may have suddenly found themselves on the wrong end of the gun when, out of the blue, the Supreme Court made a ruling, in December, banning sales of diesel vehicles in Delhi, one of the major markets for such vehicles in India. As a result the stock of M&M took a huge knock in December 2015 and January 2016 thereby belying all semblance of order and predictability at the back of technical charts.

A more detailed discussion on technical charts and trading is covered in a subsequent chapter of this book. Suffice it to say that trading on the basis of the technical charts is not a recommended course to follow when it comes to Indian equity markets.

3. ENTRY OR EXIT OF MAJOR INVESTOR

Some of the major players in the stock market become darlings of the media and their moves into and out of a counter are tracked closely. Bulk deal reports are analysed closely to decipher what moves these investors are making and tendency remains to follow these investors blindly.

Whether it be Warren Buffett in US or investors such as Rakesh Jhunjhunwala or Nimesh Shah in India, the equity market players love to place them on a pedestal and chase their every move. Talk of the investment moves of such 'legendary' investors becomes folk lore and is sought to be replicated by the ordinary folks in the markets.

The question thus inevitably arises, as to why one should expend intellectual energies in cherry picking stocks by analysing companies when you could simply follow the lead of ace investors and replicate their stock picks. More so, given the fact that there is no illegality or restriction in doing so and the information regarding stock positions of the prominent investors are available with relative ease on the public domain.

The major stock holdings of Rakesh Jhunjhunwala in listed Indian companies as on December 2015 is provided below as a sample of the portfolio that one may wish to emulate.

Company	%Holding	No of Shares (in Lakhs)	Rs Crore
Titan Company	9.05	804.66	1,799
Lupin	1.76	78.83	737
CRISIL	5.67	40	444
Rallis India	10.03	195.08	349
Delta Corp	6.84	155	182
Aptech	41.57	170.56	124
Geometric	19.35	122.51	122
NCC	11.54	296.08	89
Praj Industries	8.45	150.02	70
Firstsource Solutions	3.8	250	61
Escorts	4.08	50	60
TV18 Broadcast	1.34	229.4	56
Kesoram Industries	6.83	75	55
Pipavav Defence and Offshore	1.43	105	48
Prime Focus	6.14	113.95	38
Geojit BNP Paribas Financial	7.88	180	36
Anant Raj	2.12	62.5	35
Sterling Holiday Resorts	3.67	25.05	20
SpiceJet	1.92	100	19
A2Z Maintenance and Engineering	16.7	123.88	16

However, it is not recommended for anyone to blindly invest in a stock based solely on the fact that any of the prominent investors have taken a position in such a stock. The fact remains that every investor makes mistakes. No one is invincible. History would show many instances of well-known investors and traders committing mistakes in terms of wrong stock picks and some even going bust altogether despite their legendary status and acumen.

Of course there are also major punters in the market who disguise their activities as 'value investing' but are in fact front running stocks on the news and inside information. Either way the fact remains that you cannot base your decision to invest in a stock purely based on anyone else's decision to do so.

It is better to make your own mistakes and efforts and learn from these. In the process the investor would tend to develop a much deeper and sustainable understanding not only of the stock prices of various companies but also the intricacies of the businesses of the companies he analyses. Such learning would be a valuable aid not only in his investing in the Indian markets but would also find supplemental applications such as investing in foreign markets, understanding and developing one's own business and also coming up with newer investment strategies adapted to the investment objectives and risk appetite of the investor in question.

When it is your capital on the line, it is you and only you who should have the pleasure or pain of augmenting or diminishing such capital by way of exercise and application of your judgement and analyses.

4. NOVEL IDEAS

Time and again you will come across people who will give you novel ideas and reasoning on why a company's stock should be bought.

The fact that such conversations are sure to be encountered as casual dinner party conversations in the Indian social as well as the corporate circuit, is yet another distinctive attribute of India. It is ingrained amongst the Indian populace to exhibit their intellect and expertise to all and sundry by showering any willing listener or casual bystander with ideas on where to invest. Most of the time such 'advice' is unsolicited.

A novel idea typically signifies a totally different way to look at a stock than it has been traditionally looked upon and makes a case for the re-rating of the stock to entirely new levels of price.

For instance, in and around 2007, there emerged like wildfire, a novel idea, on how the sugar companies which have traditionally been viewed as being engaged in a cyclical commodity business would see a re-rating on account of the benefit from the mandatory blending of ethanol in petrol to curb emissions in fuels and curtail the burden of the rising crude prices which were north of USD 100 per barrel at that time.

Ethanol, produced from molasses in sugar mills thus presented the prospect of generation of additional revenues for the sugar companies, at the back of huge potential demand, and called for a re-classification of the sugar companies with a flavour of oil and gas.

As such there was a spike in the stock prices of sugar companies. However as history would bear witness, the sugar companies as an investment in the last five to seven years have generated poor returns for the investors. This has happened on account of a number of reasons. Firstly the fact that sugar prices themselves have declined from pre-2010 levels of USD 0.65/kg to USD 0.40/kg in 2015. Secondly, crude oil price itself has descended to mid USD 50 per barrel levels by 2015 and trended to USD 30 per barrel by 2016.

Consequently, the stock prices of sugar companies have largely underperformed and the companies themselves have seen poor financial performance on account of the above mentioned factors. Stock prices of sugar companies have thus spiralled downwards to levels much below those that were prevailing in 2007.

Company	Price as on 31st March, 2007	Price as on 31st March, 2015
Balrampur Chini	66	49.5
Bajaj Hind	165	14.5
Shree Renuka	23.5	13
Dhampur Sugar	74.5	36
Triveni Engg	54	51

A novel idea should thus not be made the sole basis of hurrying into a position in a stock. If the idea is meritorious, it will play itself out and there will be plenty of opportunities to invest in the businesses benefitting from the paradigm shift it brings. Thus the investor should focus on the underlying business prospects of the company as a whole and not just the novel idea on a stand-alone basis for his investment decision.

5. PROMOTER RELATED NEWS

Yet another peculiar tendency of the Indian investors and other market players, is to place promoters of Indian companies on a pedestal. Many times certain promoters of Indian companies are tracked and worshipped for their actions and are considered invincible in all their pursuits and strategies.

However, as we have often come to see, like anything or anyone on a pedestal, the fall, when it takes place from the pedestal is more pronounced and eye catching. Many a promoters have risen and fallen in the context of the Indian equity markets. When they have fallen from grace their stocks have plummeted. Conversely when they have been perceived to be on a winning streak their stocks have also sky rocketed. Such exaggerated movements in the stock prices have typically taken place regardless of any significant change in the underlying business prospects of the company in question.

For instance, till 2008, Satyam Computers was counted amongst the top five software companies in India and rubbed shoulders with Infosys, TCS, HCL Technologies and Wipro.

The promoter of Satyam, Ramalinga Raju was considered to be one of the emulated promoters in the Indian IT space, someone who could do no wrong. However in mid-2008 when the Satyam scam broke out, it came to the fore that the promoters of Satyam had in fact been party to one of the largest corporate scandals involving overstatement of assets to the tune of thousands of crores by fudging of accounts and forging of documents. The moment the scandal broke out, the Raju promoter group fell from grace and so did the stock price of Satyam,

Equity: In

which came crashing from INR 400 levels to sub-INR 100 levels. A chart showing the performance of Satyam's stock during the period is provided below.

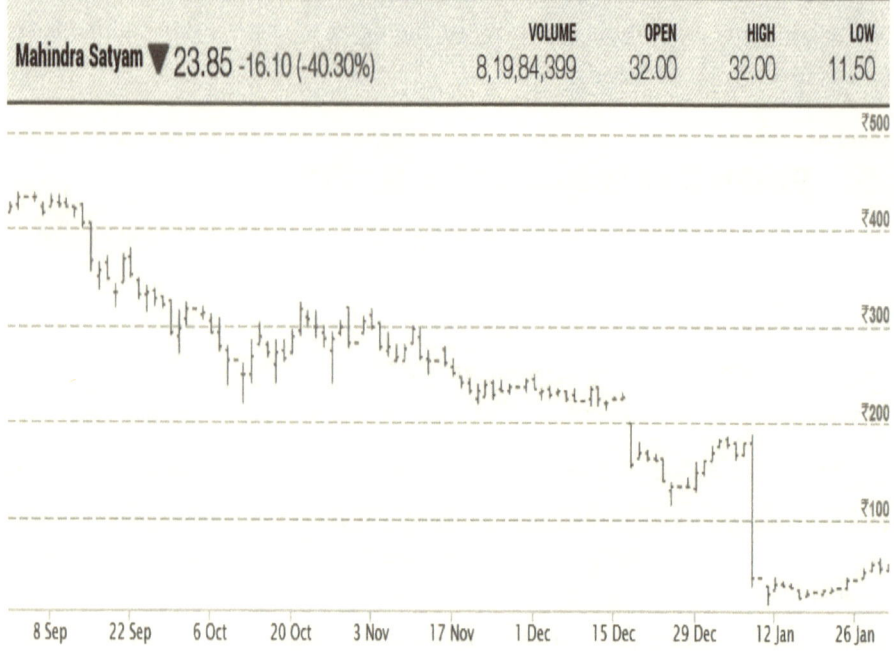

Should this news regarding the promoters of Satyam have been made the basis of going short on the Satyam stock? Or should the sharp fall in the stock at the back of such news be a trigger to buy the stock?

In 2014 when the Narendra Modi Government was elected, the stocks of certain companies whose promoters were perceived to be close to Mr. Modi sky rocketed. Prominent amongst these were the Adani group stocks. The surge in the stock prices was not only disproportionate to any rational business advantage Mr. Modi could bestow on such companies but the sudden nature of the spike was prominently irrational in terms of its pace and quantum.

The chart of Adani Power in 2014 is provided below.

As would be seen from the above chart, the spike that was seen at the back of the perceived promoter related events soon unravelled itself and the stock price of Adani Power found itself at the previous levels owing to there being no change in the intrinsic business prospects of the company.

Similarly when Mr. Jignesh Shah came into the eye of the commodities scam in 2013, MCX Limited – the commodities exchange promoted by Mr. Shah saw its stock price fall by over 70% in a matter of days. The promoter related news was considered as a nail in the coffin for MCX and caused many to exit their positions in MCX. Up till this point MCX was the dominant commodity exchange in the country and the controversy with the promoter notwithstanding, the earnings and business prospects of the company were not affected. However as would be seen from the stock price chart of the company below, the stock recovered from its fall and was able to see levels preceding the June 2013 levels at the back of business performance and the subsequent change of promoters from Jignesh Shah to the Kotak group, while the travails of Mr. Shah continued long thereafter.

Equity:In

The above and many other such instances in the Indian corporate history demonstrate that the plight of the promoters or news about the promoters of a company should not be made the sole basis of investing in or selling a particular stock.

6. CORPORATE EVENT

Corporate events such as dividend declaration, bonus issues, divestment by the Government, or better than expected quarterly results often sees run up in the prices of the concerned stocks and pose a tempting factor for the investors and traders to build a position in a stock. Should these factors be considered as a basis for taking a position in a stock?

For instance, an investor would often encounter news or information that a company is rumoured to be announcing results for a quarter that will be outperforming street estimates in terms of revenue growth or PAT margin. Typically it would be seen that there has been a run-up in the stock price of such a company leading to the results announcement. However as would be seen more often than not, the stock price of the company also takes a nose dive immediately following such an announcement. Thus contrarily, a company that announces superlative quarterly results sees its stock price dip post the announcement. This is owing to the typical tendency in the Indian equity markets for the speculators to front-run the stocks on inside information and rumours whereby the stock sees a run up leading to the corporate event and post the event coming to pass the speculators book profits and exit their position in the stock thereby leading to a fall in the stock price.

In January 2016, Jet Airways, on the back of lower crude prices leading to lower aviation fuel costs, was expected to announce superior quarterly results for the quarter ended December 2015. The aviation fuel cost being one of the major cost components for the airlines had come down substantially owing to the crude oil price falling from USD 50 per barrel to USD 30 per barrel in the last quarter of 2015. Further the airlines occupancy factor being at an all-time high, it was expected that all airlines would benefit and report stellar quarterly results. And so it followed that in February 2016, Jet Airways did, in fact, report its highest ever quarterly profit of INR 400+ crores which translated to INR 40+ per share of profit for the quarter. This by itself should have been seen as a compelling argument to build a position in the stock. However, the behaviour of the stock price conveyed a different story. The stock price of Jet Airways ran up from INR 300 levels in October 2015 to INR 700+ levels by January 2016. However, post the announcement of the stellar quarterly results we saw the stock price of Jet correct to INR 500 levels within February 2016 itself. Thus, any lay investor who may have been enthralled by the quarterly results announced by Jet and rushed into a position in the stock in February 2016 would have found himself on the wrong side of the fence staring at a sudden depletion in this stock's worth despite the company having performed well for the quarter.

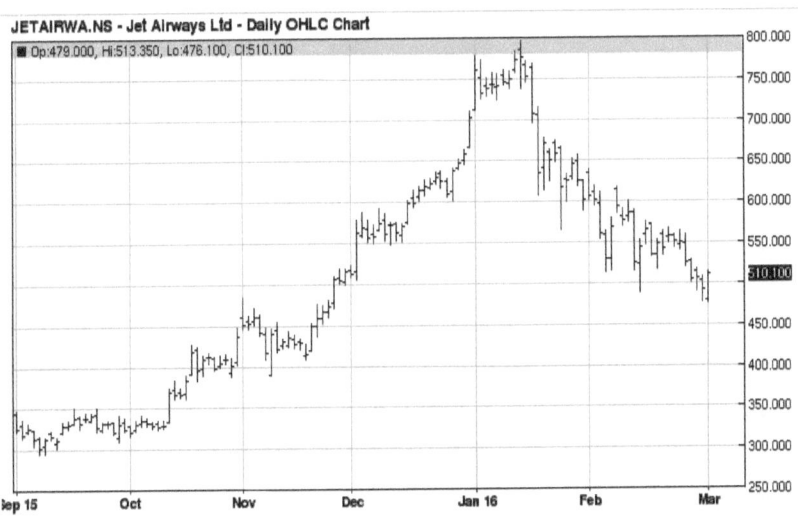

Keeping the above behaviour of the stock price in the Indian market in mind, it is not a recommended course of action for an investor to build a position in a stock purely on the basis of the news or information of a corporate event. Such corporate events should only be considered as a plotting point in analysing the overall prospects of the company and its business, and have been discussed in detail in subsequent chapters of the book.

7. MERGERS & ACQUISITIONS

Mergers & acquisitions (M&A) are the Indian market's favourite triggers for investment and speculation in stocks. It is the most sensational factor and attracts the maximum attention to any company's stock as opposed to any other factor, even more than fundamentals of a company in terms of its business or financials.

The attraction to punt in a stock based on imminent occurrence of a takeover or other such corporate mega event is probably rooted in a combination of the attraction of the folk lore status of such trades and the high returns supposed to be made by arbitraging the differential between stock price and the supposed transaction price under the M&A event.

Similarly any major change in control or substantial shareholding of a company attracts a mandatory open offer under the Takeover Code of SEBI thereby providing the 'minority' investors to play for the quick gain of buying the stock in the market and tendering it in the open offer at a higher price.

Again, a delisting offer for a company in India requires the promoters to go through a price discovery process by way of reverse book building i.e. a reverse auction in which the minority shareholders tender their shares at the desired price and the most favoured price is discovered as the delisting price. As such the persons in the 'know' of an impending delisting offer tend to speculate in a stock by building a position in it and then bidding their holding at a much higher delisting price under the reverse auction.

As such any rumours or news of any of the foregoing corporate events taking place with respect to a company sets a fire under the stock with persons building a position in the stock regardless of the fundamentals of the company in question.

However it would be seen, especially in the context of the Indian markets, that most of the time, if not always, the stock price sees a run up to or beyond the price at which the corporate action is taking place, even before the corporate event becomes official and thereafter the stock price corrects on the announcement of the particular corporate action. This behaviour of stocks is typical to Indian markets given the high propensity on the part of the market players to rely on rumours and information and front-run the stocks in question. The result most commonly is that any investor who entered the stock hoping to benefit from the corporate transaction, sees himself facing a loss or mark down on the value of his holding on the corporate transaction being announced.

For instance, in March 2015 when Anil Ambani group controlled Reliance Infrastructure agreed to buy out Pipavav Defence at INR 63 per share the stock price had already run up to INR 85 per share at the back of the market speculation of the take-over. Subsequent to the announcement the stock price corrected to the INR 60 levels that discounted the open offer price by Anil Ambani group and thereafter the stock price continued to languish at similar levels for the next year or so. Any one banking on the take-over to make a profit on the Pipavav Defence stock would have seen their investment call play out contrary to their expectations.

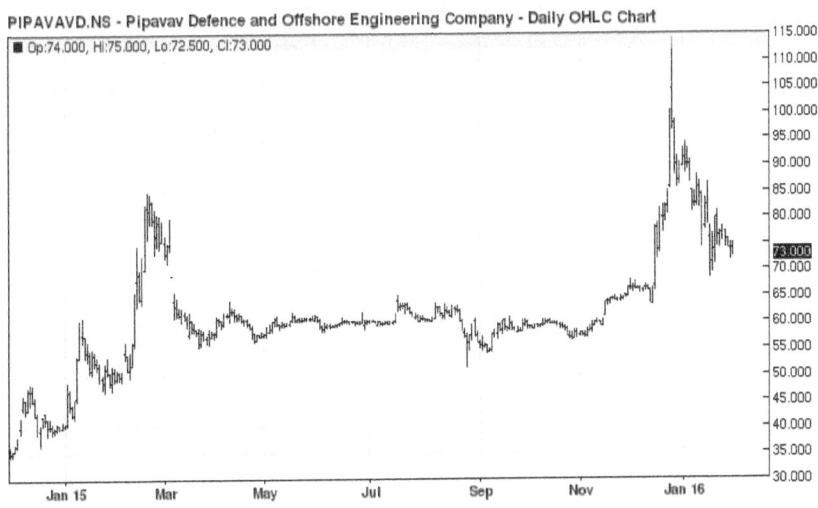

Equity:In

Another interesting example of a take-over story gone wrong is that of Mangalore Chemical and Fertilizers. MCF being a Vijay Mallya group company saw a takeover attempt on it by Deepak Fertilizers in 2014 at the back of the financial turbulence affecting Vijay Mallya and his group companies. The stock price of MCF which quoted at about INR 60 per share in the beginning of 2014 saw a run up in anticipation of open offer by Deepak Fertilizers being triggered due to it garnering a substantial stake in MCF from the open market. To make matters more exciting for the stock market punters, Vijay Mallya got the support of Zuari group to make a counter offer for the shares of MCF as a defence against the hostile bid by Deepak. The resultant effect on the stock price of MCF was a rise to INR 100 levels by September 2014 as the story unfolded. However any investor who may have taken a position in the MCF stock in the excitement of the takeover activity would have found his fingers burnt as the stock soon took a nose dive and one year later was languishing at INR 40 per share given the weak underlying fundamentals of the company. Below is the chart of MCF for the above period.

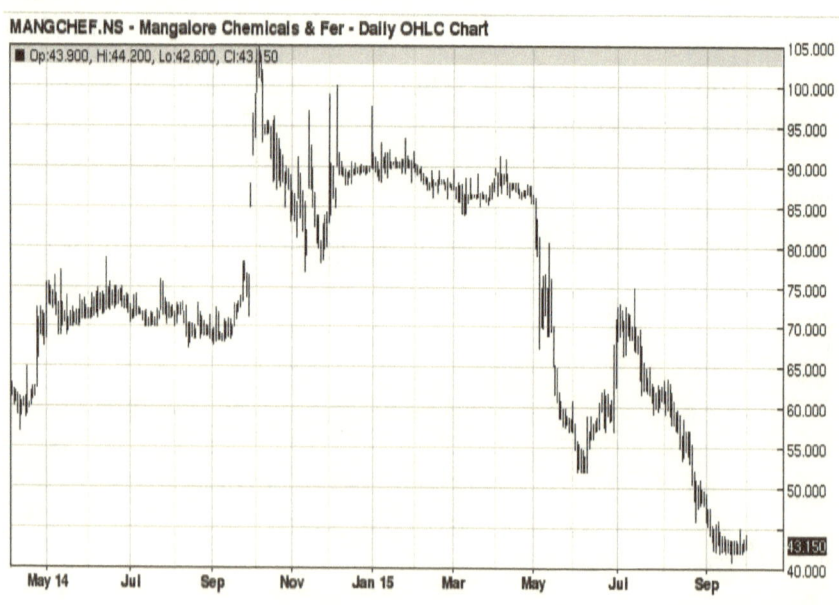

The above, as well as the plethora of other examples clearly illustrate that there is not much merit in taking a position in a stock based solely on market information or rumours of an impending merger or acquisition. The information of such corporate action need only be considered to evaluate the overall prospects of the business of the company and should not be made the sole basis of investment in a stock.

If not all of the above, then what is to be considered in making an investment decision with respect to a stock - especially in the context of the Indian equity markets where not everything works in the same fashion as it may work in the mature western markets?

The answer lies in a simple approach recommended by this book, to be adopted by anyone using common sense and not getting befuddled by the plethora of news flow, ideas and distractions that may cross one's path.

There are three main factors which need to be evaluated and understood by an investor while making an investment decision and configuring a portfolio comprising of meaningful and fundamentally strong stocks in the Indian markets. These are:

    A. PROMOTER GROUP PROFILE
    B. BUSINESS PROSPECTS OF THE COMPANY
    C. VALUATION OF THE COMPANY

In addition to these main factors, there are also certain secondary factors which ought to be evaluated to either reinforce the investment decision in a stock or to reject its inclusion in one's portfolio.

Each of these factors is discussed in detail in the upcoming chapters of the book.

CHAPTER 3

MAIN CRITERION ONE: PROMOTER GROUP PROFILE

> *The worth of a company is no more or less than the quality of the promoters running the company, regardless of its business prospects and financials.*

The Indian corporate diaspora is beset with a variety of promoter categories.

When a stock picker is evaluating an investment, he needs to carefully study the category of the promoter of the company and the profile of such promoter. Even before picking a stock, or before analysing the business of a company, or even before opening the annual report and financials of the company, this factor needs to be evaluated.

It is an important enough factor that takes precedence over other factors. I cannot emphasize this enough.

Especially in the Indian context, this is more often than not a more relevant factor to consider than most other factors in question. Why so?

The nature and conduct of a promoter determines the destiny of a company and thereby directly influences the performance of the stock price. The influence of the promoter on the company is not only with respect to the method of operation and success of the business, as would be the case for all companies, anywhere in the world. In India, the influence of the promoter spreads way beyond that.

A company which otherwise has a sound business presence and favourable prospects may still see its financials depleted at the hands of the promoter group in numerous ways. Similarly, a company that may have promising business prospects may still see its stock underperform owing to the governance practices or reputation of the promoter group.

The ways in which the practices of the promoter group can affect the company and its stock, range from questionable corporate governance practices to outright stripping of funds from the company for the personal benefit of the promoters. To better understand the implications and evaluation of this factor, we should first sight the categories of Indian promoter groups.

Broadly the prominent categories of the promoters in India are as follows:

1. BUSINESS FAMILIES

One of the dominant promoter categories in India is the business families that own business houses active in diverse business verticals.

Ranging from the Birlas to the Tatas to Ambanis, Godrej, Jindals and Adanis. While some of the business families have been around for multiple generations namely Tatas and Birlas, the others are first generation business houses such as Dilip Shanghvi, Adanis, and Azim Premji.

In fact if you browse through the Forbes India's richest Indians list, you would find the presence of heads of the Indian family business houses a regular occurrence in the list.

The 2014 list of Forbes richest Indians had its top ten dominated by Indian business family heads such as Pallonji Mistry (SP Group), Mukesh Ambani (Reliance), Kumaramanglam Birla (Birlas), Hinduja Brothers and Dilip Shanghvi (Sun Pharma).

Some of the families that have been around for multiple generations have gone through splits and have divided their business empires between the numerous family members that have emerged in the third or fourth generation, such as the Birlas and the Jindals. This has led to a large number of companies owned by the same business family albeit a different branch thereof. The result is a maze of companies all named after the business family in question, engaged in multitude of businesses with it becoming extremely difficult for a lay investor to decipher which business is run by which branch of the promoter group or who is actually at the helm of the affairs.

Another salient aspect of the Indian family owned businesses is that far from separating the ownership of the company from its management, most of the families are actively engaged in the affairs of the business of the company in question. Moreover the management baton of the company is passed from one generation to another in a dynastical fashion regardless of the professional competence of the family members or the best interest of the company.

While per se it is logical and commonplace for the family members to be actively engaged in the management of the companies they own and control and have built up from scratch, it is often times, in the Indian context that the profile of the promoter family assumes importance in determining the investment worthiness of the company's stock. This is more in the case of certain negative aspects of the promoter family group affecting the financials of the company and the performance of the stock than being a case of the positives.

In India, it has been seen that many of the family promoter groups have a tendency to treat the companies as their personal fiefdom, throwing all semblance of good corporate governance to the wind. Such promoter families do not distinguish between the funds of the company and their personal assets. Nor do they regard the public minority shareholders as partners in their business. Given such a mindset there have been numerous occasions in the past where infirmities in the management of the company have come to light on the part of the promoter group. As a consequence the stock price of the company has languished or even under-performed.

Some of the practices which have been known to be followed by some of the promoter family groups include:

a. Remuneration

Drawing excess amount of remuneration and perquisites from the listed company. While the Companies Act provides for limits with respect to the managerial remuneration that may be drawn, it does not prescribe any method for measuring the justifiability of remuneration paid, being within the statutory limits, and commensurate to the contribution by such personnel towards the management of the business of the listed companies. Moreover there are many loopholes whereby the statutory limits on remuneration may be bypassed by the promoters where they so wish.

There are instances when promoters draw salaries not only for themselves but also their spouses and other relatives who are not actively involved in the management of the business. Similarly there are instances when personal travel and other expenses are paid for by the listed company and passed off as an official expense to the detriment of the minority shareholders. Furthermore, in many instances, substantial perquisites are also availed by some promoters by using the funds of the listed company for the purchase of assets such as residences and cars which, for all practical purposes, are the personal assets of the promoters and used fully for their personal use. As such the funds of the company which may be otherwise deployed to generate returns for the shareholders are instead diverted for the benefit of the promoters thereby totally short-changing the minority shareholder 'partners' in the business.

b. Related Party Transactions

Apart from the route of remuneration and perquisites, another channel often used by dishonest promoter family groups to siphon-off funds from the listed company, is by way of related party transactions. Often times privately held companies are incorporated by the promoter groups in their own name or under benami ownership of third parties. Such companies are given contracts for supply, purchase, distributor rights or infrastructure use by the listed company at concessional rates. As a consequence profit is transferred to these privately held companies at the expense of the minority shareholders of the listed company.

Similarly, in certain cases, some critical assets, such as a pipeline or other infrastructure asset has been parked by the promoter in the name of such a privately held company and the listed company has been made to pay high usage charges for such assets thereby transferring wealth of the listed company to the unlisted privately held company to the detriment of the minority shareholders.

c. Construction Contracts

Another avenue which has been known to be used by the promoter family groups to withdraw funds from the listed companies to their personal kitty is by way of project or construction costs. Listed companies in the infrastructure space have been known to award large projects or capex contracts to trusted construction companies at an inflated price and take back the padded portion of the price in private companies owned by the promoter groups in India or overseas by way of kickbacks. These funds are then used by the promoter family groups for building their personal assets or even routed back to the listed companies to shore up their own shareholding in the company.

In effect the public funds i.e. funds borrowed from banks by these listed companies and minority shareholders' funds are thus being used to pay for project costs and siphoned-off by the promoters and used to shore up their ownership or their personal asset base. What adds insult to injury is that most of the projects in the infrastructure space have a revenue model wherein the Government pays the project company based on its capital expenditure. Thus by shoring up the project costs the promoters are not only benefitting themselves, they are further denting the public exchequer by having the government pay a higher tariff for the project in question.

d. Preferential Allotments

Another area which is ceremonially abused by the unethical promoter family groups is that of 'Preferential allotments.' Preferential allotments of shares are allowed at a discount to the market price of the stock of the company. Promoter family groups readily do preferential allotments wherein the shares are allotted to certain institutions or investors who are in effect fronting for the promoters themselves.

The preferential allotment being at a discount, the promoter is thus able to buy equity in his own company and house it in the name of an institution at a discount to market without triggering the requirement of an open offer under the SEBI regulations. The promoter thereby benefits by way of discount and cheats the minorities to this extent and also to the extent of the circumventing of the takeover requirements. Moreover such preferential issues are brought on by the promoter groups when they have visibility over certain key inside developments in the company and feel that the company's stock would perform well in the ensuing period. The promoter family groups are thus able to 'trade' on inside information without invoking the wrath of the inside trading regulations of SEBI.

e. Delisting

Delisting is another mechanism used by the promoter family groups to benefit themselves to the detriment of the public minority shareholders. Promoter family groups have been known to carry out the initial public offering (IPO) of their company at a high valuation and then drive down the earnings of the company by booking their own personal expenses or higher project costs. Not only do they benefit by withdrawing the funds raised from the IPO to their private kitty but the further consequence is that the stock price slides off the cliff given the dismal earning performance of the company in question.

Once the price has tanked to a mere fraction of the IPO price the promoter family group announces a delisting and buys off the minority shareholders at a fraction of the price they paid in the IPO, using the very funds the promoters have raised from the IPO into the company and siphoned out of the books. The promoter family group thus manages to take the listed company off the exchanges and regain full ownership of the company thereby avoiding any future accountability to minority shareholders and re-establishing their personal fiefdom over the assets and business of the company, and in the process pocketing a substantial chunk of the IPO proceeds to their private kitty.

The above and many more ingenious modes are used by the business family groups to swindle the public, the banks, the government and the minority investors, treating the funds and assets of the listed company as their personal assets and not regarding the public shareholders as their partners.

The above practices have surfaced in the context of Indian companies time and again and have correlated with the underperformance of the stocks of such Indian companies. No minority shareholder has benefited by investing in the stocks of the companies where the promoter family has been engaging in such practices irrespective of the business prospects or financial position of the company in question.

This does not go to say that family owned and promoted businesses should never be considered for investment.

It only goes to drive home the point that the standing of the promoter is of paramount importance and is the very first point that should be considered by any investor when making an investment into a company, especially in the Indian context. The above examples demonstrate the nature and extent of havoc a promoter group can wreak on a perfectly healthy company and the plundering of the assets of the listed company on the hands of such an unethical promoter group.

Do not even bother about opening and studying the balance sheet of a company if the promoter group is of questionable integrity or has a past track record of having indulged in any practices which are anti-minority.

Do not bother looking at the valuation ratios of such a company. If the company trades at a low PE multiple, there is obviously a reason for it.

No matter how rosy and promising be the prospects of the business their company, do not even try to invest in such a company as chances are that the rosy earnings will be mopped up by the promoters to their family's personal kitty while the investor will be left holding a lemon.

The question thus arises, how do you tell which of the promoter family groups are safe to invest in and which ones are to be avoided?

Given that this is the first and most critical question before considering any other factor regarding the stock or the company, due and proper attention needs to be paid to this criterion. At the same time there is no prescribed formula or test to ascertain the answer to this question. An investor needs to assess the promoter family profile by having his ear to the ground and delving into proper research and analysis.

If you are able to distinguish between the promoter groups to back and the ones to avoid, you have more than half the battle won. There are many successful investors who only pick the companies with the right promoters and management and let them do the wealth creation for them rather than racking their brains about the prospects of the company or its valuations or any other factor.

If you consider the promoter family groups in India and eliminate the ones who are to be avoided, you would zero in on the ones who may be backed by process of elimination. Some of the red flags which may be considered in evaluating the promoter families to be avoided include:

a. Personal Wealth

If you see a promoter family group with a lavish lifestyle and personal wealth beyond what is sustainable by the reported personal remuneration drawn from the company by the promoter family members who are engaged in the management and the dividend payout to such promoters, then it is best to avoid such promoter's companies as an investment pick.

If they are having a lavish fleet of personal jets and cars, bungalows in multiple places including a vacation bungalow in Goa and a private yacht in the Mediterranean, you can well enough judge where the funds for such assets have been withdrawn from in a surreptitious manner.

Thus the personal asset base and lifestyle of the promoter family is a good indicator of questionable corporate governance and a red flag to be evaluated. As such any investor looking to invest in a company owned by a promoter family should review the status of the personal wealth and lifestyle of the family in question.

b. Privately Held Companies

A promoter group which resorts to holding some businesses in their private kitty is no different than a partner in your business who also carries on some business outside the ambit of your partnership on the side.

Inevitably such a situation would draw the management commitment of the promoter away from being entirely concentrated on the listed companies and many a times also lead to situations where undue favours are bestowed on such 'privately held' companies at the expense of the listed companies. For instance, a promoter engaged in the business of real estate or infrastructure development in his listed company, may award contracts for construction to his own privately owned EPC company at high value and thus skim the cream from the listed company's profits to the detriment of the minority. Promoter family groups that have their hands in such privately held companies should be avoided and any investor looking to invest in a family promoter group driven company should also research the business interests of the family other than the listed companies in question.

c. Family Representation on Board

A board of directors that wreaks of cronies or is otherwise packed to the gills with family members is a tell-tale sign of the fiefdom form in which the promoter family group intends to run the company. The board, far from being the champion for good corporate governance in these cases, in fact acts as a façade to validate the malpractices of the promoter family group. A perusal of the constitution of the board of directors of a company is a recommended exercise to be undertaken by the investor because such a review would throw insight on whether the board is a fairly constituted professional board with a balance of promoter family representatives and independent professional directors, or it is a puppet board stacked with family members and cronies of the promoter group.

d. Management Team

The constitution of the management team of a company should be seen by an investor as this may also be a tell-tale sign of how the company is managed.

A promoter family driven company in which the mantle of the Chairman, the MD, Joint MD and other key posts is adorned by the family members itself is an instant red flag. While this may not always be a bad sign, especially in cases where the family business is into the 3rd generation and the 2nd generation has actually grown to the position of MD on merits after having worked through the ranks.

But in the vast majority of cases you would find that the position of the MD or board level has been bestowed on the 2nd or 3rd generation members ahead of the more qualified and longer serving senior management. Indian family promoter driven companies with the family members running the company on day to day basis especially family members with little or no prior experience in the sector or business of the company, would be a significant reason to consider the company as an unreliable model for corporate governance and fair business conduct.

e. Past Performance

A promoter family group company which has languished both in terms of earnings and the stock performance over the years needs to be investigated by the investor. There are a plethora of such companies and unsurprisingly the earnings of these have not prospered even when the business environment and cycle has been favourable. This is because in the good times the promoters have been nimble footed to step in and sweep out the lucrative earnings for their personal kitty by creative accounting jugglery and structuring of the sort discussed above.

Such promoter driven companies are a hallmark of apathy towards wealth creation for the minority shareholders and are best kept away from. Thus an investor ought to review the past earning track record and share price performance of a company as a guidepost of the promoter family's attitude towards minority shareholders and wealth creation and accordingly decide on whether or not it is a safe bet to invest in the company in question.

f. Litigation

There are cases of family members of a promoter family group being embroiled in constant litigation with third parties or inter-se each other. Litigation with third parties generally revolves around failed business partnerships and joint ventures. Litigation inter se family members takes place where there a battle for control or share in the family estate emerges. In any of these cases it ought to be recognized that a company owned and controlled by a litigation-prone promoter family group is not the best suited to be backed up for investment. Where the litigation pertains to third parties it may be an indication of dishonest business practices and dealings with partners. Where the litigation pertains to inter se family members, it could inevitably translate into a disruption into the management of the affairs of the company. As such an investor who finds litigation surrounding the family members of the promoter group ought to evaluate such litigation to determine the prospects of backing up the promoter family owned companies.

Given the long list of red flags, it would not be illogical for an investor to be circumspect of investing in an Indian family promoter group driven company at all.

However, not all promoter family group driven companies are having questionable management or corporate governance standards. There are some companies in this category controlled by promoter families that have set the benchmark in good corporate governance coupled with the professionalization of management and shareholder wealth creation.

Some outstanding examples of such Indian promoter family groups are illustrated below.

i. Aditya Birla Group

The Aditya Birla group is a multi-generation family promoter driven conglomerate with presence in a wide range of businesses ranging from cement to textiles to telecom and metals.

The group, whilst functioning under the stewardship of different family members from time to time, with Kumaramanglam Birla at present, has gone from strength to strength in the business performance year on year. While the ownership of the group companies remains under the control of the Birlas, the management has been professionalised with nearly every vertical having a professional 'non-family' CEO and CFO. The companies have been managed transparently and there has seldom been any whiff of mismanagement or misappropriation of funds.

ii. Tata Group

Controlled through the Tata family trust, the group started out as a family group with a Tata family scion on the helm generation after generation. Even recently after the retirement of Ratan Tata, the onset of Cyrus Mistry would not be considered as a departure from the tradition given the marital tie between the Mistrys and Tatas and the fact that Shapoor Pallonji group is now the largest shareholder of Tata Sons (the group companies' holding company). Nevertheless this group has retained its unblemished reputation for strong management and ethics, with group companies such as TCS and Tata Motors performing consistently year on year with transparent earnings and visibility.

iii. Premji

Azim Premji promoted Wipro has been one of the torch bearers of Indian IT services revolution from the later part of the 20th century along with companies such as Infosys, and TCS. It has been a family promoter group driven company with next generation, Rushaad, entering the fray recently. However Wipro has still maintained high standards of professionalism with Mr. Premji stepping back from active management years ago. Even Rushaad has come up through the ranks and has not been bestowed the mantle and the throne merely on account of being the family heir. The company has been a bell weather of the Indian IT space with fair and transparent financial conduct. The promoter family values are reflected not only in their minority friendly way of managing the company but also in the charitable initiatives of Mr. Premji who is one of the biggest philanthropists in the country having committed a chunk of his personal wealth to charitable causes.

In conclusion, the choice of investing in a business family promoter group company needs to be taken very carefully after studying all aspects of the promoter family's disposition and handling of not only the business but also the distance between the family ownership and management as well as the nature of corporate governance practices.

More often than not you would come across such category of promoter families which are best avoided as there exist ample areas where they can fleece the minority shareholders and treat the listed company as their personal fiefdom. However this is not to rule out any and every promoter family driven company in India and once you find the right one you can consider evaluating other factors to decide whether or not to invest in the company.

2. MULTINATIONAL CORPORATIONS

In the post liberalisation era of 1990's, many multinational corporations have stepped into India and promoted their local presence. These MNC groups are found to be present in diverse sectors and operate both via the listed and unlisted company route. Some of the prominent listed examples include Unilever, Procter & Gamble, Gilette, Nestle, ABB, Siemens, Lafarge and Holcim (through ACC and Ambuja Cements).

Prima facie, MNC promoted companies fulfil the first criteria for investment i.e. having a satisfactory promoter group at their helm, so as to warrant an investment into the company.

This is so, as being part of a systems driven MNC corporate culture, such companies offer a viable option for investment insofar as the corporate governance criteria is concerned. MNCs are characterised by professional management, transparent policies and visibility in earnings. Some of the questionable practices outlined in the case of the family promoted companies are generally not present in MNC companies primarily owing to the fact that there is no personally invested family or individual looking to profiteer out of the financials of the MNC. Add to this, the fact that such companies have comprehensive systems of internal control and audit as well as the adoption of best practices under the watchful eyes of world's best consultants and auditors. As such, these companies generally tend to fulfil the first requirement in picking of an investment target.

However, this is not to say that any and every MNC promoted company may be blindly invested in.

There have been instances in the past with certain MNC groups where certain practices of the company have been called into question by the minority shareholders or the regulators. Some prominent examples include:

a. Holcim – ACC, Ambuja Cement

In the second half of 2012, Holcim attempted to hike up the royalty being paid by ACC and Ambuja Cement to their Swiss parent to 2% of the top line of the Indian companies. This led to negative reactions from the minority shareholders as it was not seen just and equitable as a charge given that the MNC parent of ACC and Ambuja was not lending any branding to the Indian companies. Nor was the consideration worth 2% of the revenues reckoned as justifiable, given the nature of the business of these companies being primarily that of a commodity.

The stocks of the companies reacted adversely to the development and ultimately Holcim had to roll back on the proposal, settling for 1% royalty instead. In fact this was one of the prominent cases which dictated the Government of India to bring in legislation to protect minority interest, where by any matters in which the promoter was interested in required the majority approval of the minority shareholders and the promoters would have to abstain from voting in such matters.

b. Vedanta – Cairn

In July 2014, the parent of Cairn, i.e. the UK based Vedanta group, sought to carry out a transaction whereby Cairn, the cash rich oil producer subsidiary company, lent substantial cash sitting in its balance sheet to its debt laden parent company at below market rates of interest with the objective that the parent would use the funds to pay down its debts which carried a higher interest liability. The rationale for the transaction as sounded by the promoter of Cairn was that by advancing its cash to Vedanta, Cairn would earn higher interest than what it was currently earning on it's surplus resources, while Vedanta would be able to save on its interest outgo since the rate of interest it would pay to Cairn would be lower than what it was paying to the banks.

While this may make for sound financial engineering, it was perceived as an adverse move for the minority of Cairn primarily on account of the fact that the expectation of the minority shareholders would have been that Cairn would utilize the funds for earning high equity returns on the same by deploying such cash in growing its oil exploration and production business, rather than below par debt based returns.

As such the stock price of Cairn India took a nose dive from its highs of INR 360 per share in July 2014 to INR 250 by December 2014.

Thereafter the promoter came out with a scheme to merge Cairn India with the parent Vedanta Limited with the view that the loan and the liability be cancelled out and in effect the cash of Cairn India get integrated with the financials of the parent. This move was also not received well by the minority shareholders of Cairn India who felt that the proposed swap ratio for their Cairn India shares versus Vedanta shares was not fairly valuing Cairn India and was skewed in favour of Vedanta.

The cloud of such practices of the promoter parent of Cairn coupled with the tumbling crude oil prices has had the stock price of Cairn India languish since and in 2015 it came down all the way to INR 130 per share.

Equity:In

c. Sharp India

In the case of Sharp India, subsidiary of the Japanese electronics multinational, the company belonged to a reputed MNC promoter group.

However the lineage of the company, in fact, has played out to the disadvantage of the company as the Japanese parent of the company has gone sick amidst mounting losses. Owing to the travails of the parent, the Indian company's operations have suffered from the lack of financial and operational support, to the point that in 2015 the manufacturing operations of Sharp India were shut by the parent pending further clarity on the fate of the parent company.

Thus the stock price of Sharp India fell in 2015 from its highs of INR 70 levels to INR 30 and has since languished at such levels with the financial strength of the company having been depleted. It is only since March 2016 when the news of Sharp Japan being taken over by another MNC, Foxconn, came through, has the share price of Sharp India recovered, albeit its India operations still remain under a cloud of uncertainty.

As such, while the search may be easier for an appropriate investment candidate in the MNC promoted company universe, it is nevertheless recommended to do a basic background check to see in case the MNC group in question has been in the spotlight in the past for any anti-minority practices or is otherwise labouring under financial or other stresses in the international market.

Furthermore it is not a wasteful exercise either for one to look at the general track record of the MNC group not only in India but globally to see whether the MNC in question has been known to build shareholder value, how its stock price has performed over a ten year horizon globally and what kind of dividend paying policy has been practised by the MNC.

Once the investor finds a MNC group which does not yield any red flags in terms of corporate governance, financials or the past track record of shareholder wealth creation, the investor may safely evaluate the MNC as an investment option having regard to the other basic criteria recommended in this book.

3. INDIAN GOVERNMENT COMPANIES

Perhaps as controversial and as unique to India, as the family promoted companies, is the plethora of companies in the Indian listed space which have the Indian government (Centre or State), as their promoter.

The Nehruvian-Congress legacy of the mixed economy with the socialist sentiment to boot has ensured that there is no shortage of such companies and public sector undertakings (PSUs), as these are referred, are found to be engaged in almost all segments of business.

In banking, State Bank of India, Union Bank of India, Punjab National Bank and so on.

In metals and mining, Steel Authority of India Limited (SAIL), National Aluminium Company (NALCO), Neyveli Lignite and Coal India Limited.

In Power, National Thermal Power Corporation (NTPC), Power Trading Corporation (PTC) and Power Grid.

In Oil & Gas, Indian Oil Corporation (IOC), Hindustan Petroleum Corporation Limited (HPCL), Bharat Petroleum Corporation Limited (BPCL) and Oil & Natural Gas Corporation (ONGC).

In fact, ironically, some of the above PSUs were erstwhile MNC companies which were nationalized in the post-independence era of India by the Government of India taking over such companies in the 'national interest' and unceremoniously throwing out the MNC promoter. Shell's Indian Petroleum arm was nationalized and became BPCL.

While the errant family promoter groups exploit the listed companies to fill their private coffers, the scope of the mismanagement of the PSUs by the Government centres on the so called 'public purpose' i.e. the greater good.

It is not an easy task to pick a PSU to invest in, as there are large number of issues that surround the management or operation of such companies by the Government.

Some of these include:

a. Managerial Personnel

The managerial personnel of PSUs are typically appointed through a cumbersome process devised by the Government.

This includes lengthy interview process by the Public Enterprises Selection Board (PESB), followed by multiple clearances and approvals ranging from vigilance, CBI, ministries and the PMO. The entire process is fraught with delays and imperfections, resulting not only in delayed appointments and vacant positions but also many a times the finally selected candidate is not necessarily the most ideally suited to managing the PSU but someone who has the best public relations or lobbying skills. As a consequence the management of PSUs is always a hit or miss regarding the quality of the persons at the helm.

For instance one of the listed companies in the PSU space, Oil India Limited, which is the second largest state owned oil & gas exploration and production company, found the post of its Chairman and Managing Director (CMD) vacated in 2015 by the then CMD Mr. S.K. Srivastava who superannuated.

The Central Government had advertised to conduct interviews to select the successor of Mr. Srivastava well in advance of his retirement as is the prescribed procedure and the PESB had carried out a round of interviews and submitted their recommendation to the Government. However the candidate so recommended was not selected by the Government and a second round of interviews was called for. Again the recommended candidate was not selected and the position remained vacant for many months. The Government ultimately put in one of their bureaucrats as an acting CMD while the search for the CMD continued well into 2016.

The position finally came to be filled by a full time CMD more than one year after the retirement of the previous CMD.

This would surely not be a confidence building situation for any minority shareholder who has invested into the shares of OIL hoping to benefit from the performance of the company and its stock price. A company of such size and scale, operating in a segment which is of national strategic interest, remaining headless for more than a year will inevitably suffer in its business in terms of direction and management, thereby hurting the minority shareholders of the company.

Yet such occurrences are frequent and common place with PSU companies, and the fact that such companies are listed, only makes the pain worse.

b. Earnings

One of the major anomalies of PSU companies has been the lack of visibility of their earning structure and profitability at the hands of the promoter i.e. the Government.

One would expect that a company being owned by the democratically elected Governments would be the trend setter in transparency and corporate governance. However the fact remains that in the Indian context, many PSUs, it not all, have had their business earnings disrupted by the public oriented ad hoc policies of the Government.

For instance, Oil PSUs such as Indian Oil Corporation have had to bear the burden of subsidies on petrol, diesel, LPG and kerosene which have been passed on by the Government to the public at large and recompensed out of the profits of the Oil PSUs. Consequently for years on end, no investor has had any clarity about the nature and quality of earnings of such Oil PSUs even though these companies boast of market capitalization of thousands of crores and even lakh crores such as in the case of Indian Oil Corporation and ONGC.

As a consequence the stocks of such companies have not only underperformed but remain undervalued, not just in comparison to their private sector peers but even lower than the replacement cost of their business undertakings.

What boggles the mind, is the question, that in case it is considered necessary by the Government to run an enterprise which sells its products below the market price, i.e. subsidizes the products in the national or public interest, then why on earth would such an enterprise be allowed to operate as a listed company? Would it not be prudent for the Government to simply delist such a company and run it as a Government department, funding the subsidies and losses of such a company through a budgetary allocation?

c. Dividends

In cases where the Government has had trouble meeting its budgetary revenue targets, it has often resorted to plundering the resources of cash rich PSUs by way of extravagant dividends. This has been done even when paying such dividends may not be in the best interest of the PSU as it may have had more optimal utilization of its cash by way of reinvestment in the business.

Companies such as ONGC and OIL, in the regime of high crude oil prices, where they had benefitted by way of higher sales realization on their oil and gas production, have had to pay huge dividends simply to enable the Government to bridge its revenue deficits. This, of course, has been over and above the subsidy burden imposed on the companies in the first place.

As such, in a high crude oil price regime, where it would have made much more sense for an upstream oil company such as ONGC to ramp up its capital expenditure for exploration as well as development and production activities, especially with the deep offshore oil blocks where the exploration and development are complicated and high cost high risk, it has been seen that the high dividend and subsidy burden on ONGC and OIL in fact crippled the ability of these companies to take the appropriate and aggressive business steps. As a result the share value of the companies suffered given the lack of growth visibility in their production portfolios, compounded by the earnings uncertainty under the subsidy regime.

d. Divestment

Divestment is the antithesis of the public sector's involvement in business activities. In other words, it is the unwinding of the Nehruvian socialist economy legacy. In theory the divestment philosophy appears meritorious insofar as it would lead to lesser ownership of the Government and as a corollary, lesser interference with the management of the PSU in question.

While the divestment agenda of the Government gained momentum in the BJP-NDA government under Atal Behari Vajpayee, the totality of divestment efforts of the Indian Government has been a mixed bag.

The Government of India successfully managed to divest companies such as Bharat Aluminium Company (BALCO), Hindustan Zinc Limited (HZL) and Videsh Sanchar Nigam Limited (VSNL), though each of these divestments has since hit legal and other hurdles.

VSNL being one of the prominent listed Indian companies to be divested has seen lack lustre performance in its stock price even post the divestment in 2002 even though the company was bought over by the reputed promoter group of TATAS.

The chart below shows the stock price of VSNL (now Tata Communications) since the time of its divestment till date.

Equity:In

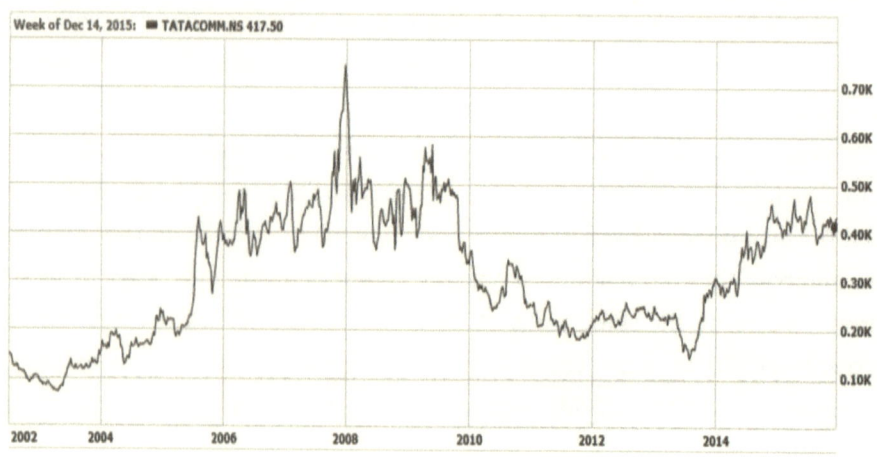

What has further plagued PSU companies in course of the divestment exercise of the Government of India is the fact that many a times the Government has undertaken divestment to raise funds to balance its budget, but finding no takers for the stocks of the PSUs being offered for sale, the Government has used its own PSUs to mop up the shares on offer.

For example when divesting the shares of IOC, the Government called upon the likes of ONGC and LIC to buy IOC shares simply because there was not enough investor interest for IOC shares, for reasons enumerated above.

Thus the balance sheets of the PSUs have been saddled with dead investment which may or may not be accretive to the business interests of such PSUs. This move has compounded the problems of the PSUs as the financial performance of these companies has been handicapped not only by the policies and interference of the Government in their own affairs but also by the poor return on investment these PSUs generate on their investment in other underperforming PSUs, which investments have been made purely at the behest of the Government.

This sub-optimal utilization of the available cash of the PSUs has thus been another bane of the PSUs at the instance of the Government's 'divestment' initiatives.

e. Diplomacy

In several cases, the PSUs have also been used by the Government as its personal business arm to make commitments and investments in foreign countries with a view to generate political capital for the Government.

It has often transpired that the Government officials while on a diplomatic engagement with another country have committed to the PSU company undertaking investments in such other country or acquiring assets/companies operating in such other country.

An oil company being compelled to buy a major oil company in a foreign country, or a steel company being compelled to invest in iron ore mining in a foreign country have been instances that have been seen to occur in the annals of PSU history even though on a stand-alone commercial basis the investment or acquisition may not be the most optimal option for the PSU keeping in mind its business operations and prospects. This has been a governmental version of treating the PSU as its personal fiefdom and utilizing the resources of the PSU indiscriminately.

f. Expenditures

Many a times PSUs have been known to incur unnecessary expenditures at the behest of the government. From issuing sponsorships for governmental events to hosting government officials on their tours to the various parts of the country where the PSUs have their offices and guest houses. It is commonplace in India for cars, guest houses and staff of the PSU to be used by the Government officials to ferry their families and associates and host parties and events for such officials as and when they visit the regional offices of such PSUs. The PSUs have often been asked to allocate extra expenditure in the constituencies of the MPs of the ruling government so as to prop up the campaign prospects of such MPs. All in all the Governments in India have been known to abuse their position as the promoter of the PSUs to the detriment of the PSUs and the minority shareholders.

Each of the above instances demonstrates that there are many ways that the PSUs are compromised by the Government in the name of the so called public interest, even though such PSUs are listed companies, little or no regard is had to the interest of the minority shareholders who sit on the sidelines while the PSUs are run as governmental departments or extensions.

This only begs the question as to why the Government insists on continuing these PSUs as listed entities and does not go ahead and delist the companies' shares and convert them into a Government department where it can have free hand to run their affairs any way it deems fit without any inhibitions or accountability to minority shareholders. More so, given the fact that precedents regarding the divestment of PSU undertakings have shown that there are not many ready takers for the shares of PSU companies and even where the divestment has taken place, the PSU has continued to be tangled in post divestment issues which have led to massive underperformance of the stock prices of such PSUs.

It is as such a difficult proposition to pick a PSU to invest in *de hors* the governmental interference factor. Nevertheless there are some jewels of companies in the Governmental portfolio which merit a look for investment given their domineering business presence in their respective sector, superlative valuations and business prospects. An investor could thus tread cautiously and look to invest in the shares of a PSU only where he is convinced of the minimal level of governmental interference in the PSU, transparency in the earning structure of the PSU, compelling business prospects and valuation.

4. NON-PROMOTER COMPANIES

There do also exist a category of companies in the Indian listed company space which do not have a defined promoter group.

In fact these are a unique set of companies which are akin to companies in the global capital markets, which have been in existence for a long period of time, are in the forefront of their business segment and have undergone numerous changes in ownership over the stretch of their existence. As a consequence, the original promoters of the company have been diluted out of their promoter position or they have exited and their shareholding has been taken over by institutions or management itself. These companies are thus controlled and run by a strong management hierarchy and exist as autonomous corporations, not susceptible to typical promoter interferences as we have observed above.

Some of the examples of companies in this space in India include Larsen & Toubro, ITC, HDFC Limited, and HDFC Bank.

Given the absence of a strong promoter influence, these companies do present a default green signal on the first criteria for shortlisting as an investment target. However due regard must be had to the overall profile of the company and the major shareholders to ascertain whether there is a strong shareholder group that nevertheless controls the company and has a substantial say in the running of its affairs.

Furthermore, in case of such companies, the absence of the promoter group, in turn, necessitates an evaluation of the management team of the company in lieu of the promoter group. A strong and competent management team with a demonstrated track record of business performance and value creation shines through and fulfils the first criteria for investment. On the other hand, companies without promoters, having a management team with a wishy-washy track record or one which is embroiled in in-fighting or comprised of individuals not befitting the positions they hold, would be avoidable as investment picks.

APPLICATION OF PROMOTER CRITERIA

Now that we have seen the broad categories of the promoter groups that exist with respect to Indian listed companies, the question arises as to how to apply this first criterion for short listing the investible companies.

As was mentioned above, the quality of the promoter group as the first threshold to cross cannot be over emphasized. There may be companies which are in the most lucrative business and have the most promising business prospects, yet these companies would not make a good investment proposition owing to the simple fact that the promoter group would run the company as their personal fiefdom and siphon off the super profits from the company's books for their personal gain or otherwise not be able to capitalize on the competitive advantage of the company owing to their lack of competence. This would leave the entire exercise of evaluating the prospects of the business of the company as an academic one since these prospects would only be enjoyed by the promoter group and not the minority shareholders or these prospects may not translate to superlative earnings for the company owing to the lack of management calibre of the promoter group.

Similarly, there may be a company with a superior market position and dominance yet it may not translate to wealth creation for the minority shareholders since it may be controlled by a Government that imposes policy measures on the company whereby the bulk of its profits are diverted towards the public exchequer or public objectives.

As such, when you decide to invest in a company, take a look at the promoter profile even before you take a deep dive into its business prospects or financials. Ascertain whether the promoter group is competent, investor friendly and runs the company in a fair and transparent manner so as to create wealth for all shareholders uniformly or whether there are ad hoc policies or measures imposed by them which are anti-minority.

Some of the high level factors that give an indication of the quality of the promoter group and may be evaluated are:

1. EARNINGS PERFORMANCE

If the earnings of the company have shown stagnation over the past several years despite the company being in a growing business/sector it is a sign that the promoter group is not able to create shareholder wealth, or that such a promoter group is concertedly drawing out the profits of the company to their personal kitty. Conversely a company whose earnings have grown consistently quarter over quarter indicates a promoter group that is not only competent to deliver on the business prospects of the company but also conscientious to not skim from the profits of the company for their personal gain.

2. SHARE PRICE PERFORMANCE

If the share price of the company has stagnated over a period of five years or more despite the broader markets performing well and the peer group of the company also doing well, it is a sign that the company may be avoided as such underperformance in the stock price of the company is a symptom of promoter related intrinsic issues with the company which may continue to dog the company's stock price into the future.

3. OTHER GROUP COMPANIES

Other companies of the same promoter group may be seen for their performance as well to get a sense of the quality of the promoter group and their track record for shareholder wealth creation.

4. COMPOSITION OF THE BOARD & MANAGEMENT

The composition of the board of directors of the company and its management team is also a key indicator of the promoter mindset and corporate governance practices. As mentioned previously, a board dominated by the promoter family members and their yes-men would be a tell-tale sign of the intention of the promoters to run the company as their personal fiefdom. Similarly a management team of the company comprising primarily of family members would also be a cause of concern regarding the quality of management of affairs.

5. GENERAL BACKGROUND

The background and credentials of the promoter group are the other helpful indicators. Whether they have been in the news for wrong reasons, whether there has been litigation or allegations of wrong doing against them. The graph of their lifestyle versus the graph of the company's earnings, their presence in parallel privately held businesses may also be seen. Regard should also be had to the fact whether there have been any failures of businesses promoted by the group in the past, or the promoters have defaulted in their borrowings from the bank.

All in all, profiling of the promoter group is a fairly common sense oriented process and one would inevitably reach the logical conclusion regarding whether or not to avoid a company based on the promoter profile.

It goes without saying that the working principle to be applied in this case is 'When in doubt, leave it out.'

CHAPTER 4

MAIN CRITERION TWO: BUSINESS PROSPECTS

> *Always understand thoroughly the business of the company you wish to invest in. If you do not understand what a company does, don't buy its shares, regardless of its PE ratio and other financial metrics.*

Once an investor has cleared the first hurdle for selection of a company for investment, i.e. he has found a company which has a promoter group worth backing, the investor should move to the second factor for selection of an investment.

The second factor to be evaluated when deciding to invest in a company is not the financials of the company, rather it is the business prospects of the company. However to understand the business prospects of the company, you have to first understand the business of the company as a starting point.

The uninitiated investors, when they start investing, jump into the exercise of looking at a company's financials and valuation ratios. They get into number crunching and analysis straight off the bat to see the price earning (PE) ratio of the company, it's 52 weeks' high and low price, the moving averages of the share price, the revenues and earnings, the net worth and book value. The more educated the investor, greater the level of analysis of the financial statements of the company. This is generally followed by peer comparison and the company showing cheaper valuation is picked as the investment target.

However, it is redundant and academic to evaluate the financials and valuation of a company without first understanding its business. You have to understand, on a very granular level, what the company does and then evaluate the potential of its business in the macro-economic context. Only after that, the financials of the company come into play and assume relevance.

Just like a company which does not have a credible promoter group, should not be invested in regardless of it appearing cheap in terms of valuation, in the same way, a company which does not have a promising business ought not to be invested in regardless of the cheap valuation of its stock price. After all, by investing in a company's stock, the investor is in effect taking a part ownership in the business of the company and a faltering business would not make for a good ownership prospect, regardless of the cheap price at which it may be available.

It may well come to pass that the business of some of the companies is not comprehensible to an investor given the investor not having a technical understanding of the business in question or not being qualified to understand the intricacies. What should the investor do in such a case?

Simple…avoid such companies.

If you do not understand what the company does, why would you invest in it at all? Would you ever consider starting a business on your own and putting your hard earned money in it, when you do not understand the business? Would you take up a vocation or business that you are not competent to understand or operate?

No.

The same logic applies to stock market investing and thus, this second criterion for picking investible stocks takes precedence over financials and valuations.

Once you have understood the business of the company, you need to evaluate the potential of the business in terms of the future business growth, in the context of the macro environment of the country, the regulatory framework, the economic cycle of the business and the competitive position of the company itself.

Only a business that appears lucrative and promises to grow in the future on a continuous basis, is worth your investment. It is as simple as that. Yet, a simple notion as above gets obfuscated by the complexities of financial metrics, valuation multiples, price averages, peer group comparatives and the market chatter.

What the investor needs to focus on is the business of the company and its growth prospects as the second criterion with a tunnel vision and in-depth analysis.

Let us take some examples to flesh out the application of this very important criterion in conjunction with the first criterion, with case studies of some of the prominent Indian listed companies.

1. INDIAN OIL CORPORATION

If an investor looks to invest in a company such as Indian Oil Corporation (IOC), then before delving into the financials of IOC or its valuation, the investor should understand what IOC as a company does for its business.

IOC is the largest crude oil refiner in the country. It is a fortune 500 company and ranks in the top three by revenues with sales in excess of INR 4 lac crore. It has a refining capacity of more than 50 million tonnes per annum and provides fuel, i.e. petrol, diesel as well as LPG and kerosene, which are the life blood of the country. It is in a dominant position in the Indian domestic market with downstream integration in the form of an extensive retail network of fuel outlets as well as a large cross country pipeline distribution network. IOC also imports and sells natural gas to domestic consumers, such gas being used for transport fuel, running of power plants, fertilizer plants and piped gas for domestic use. IOC is also present in the upstream segment of oil and gas, i.e. it is engaged in the business of exploration and production of oil and gas from oil and gas blocks.

Thus, an understanding of the business of IOC entails understanding the above businesses of IOC as well as the flow of the above products in the Indian economy.

This then needs to be understood in the context of the competitive landscape, with companies such as Reliance and Essar giving IOC competition in the refining space, while companies such as Bharat Petroleum Corporation Limited (BPCL) and Hindustan Petroleum Corporation Limited (HPCL) competing with IOC in the downstream oil marketing space and companies such as ONGC, OIL and Cairn competing with IOC in the upstream space.

Once an investor grasps an understanding of the business of IOC, he needs to evaluate the future prospects of such a business. This entails an understanding of the prospects and demand growth for IOC's products and services.

As would be borne out by a study of the macro-economic data as well as projections forming part of the five year plans and the planning commission, with the economy set to grow over the next decade, the demand for oil based fuels is slated to grow year on year, so is the demand for natural gas. An in-depth study of such growth projections would yield a finding on the quantum of growth and how IOC is poised to capitalize on such growth on the back of its expanding refining capacity, marketing network and other business development initiatives.

Thus on first glance, IOC is a company which has superlative business prospects and is well placed as a company to take advantage of these prospects at the back of the Indian economic growth story.

However to be able to apply the criteria for investment in IOC you would need to start at the top, i.e. the promoter group criterion would precede the business prospects criterion.

The promoter for IOC is the Government of India. And much as other PSUs, IOC is also plagued by the fallacies of being driven by the Governmental policies which are not always meritorious or oriented towards the minority shareholders.

The Governmental control on IOC implies that the appointment of the top brass of the company takes place by way of a cumbersome government defined procedure involving the Public Enterprises Selection Board (PESB) which advertises and interviews eligible candidates and recommends the suitable appointee to the Government. Post this recommendation the candidature of the appointee moves through a laborious process of multiple approvals till the level of the Prime Minister headed committee as well as clearances by the vigilance and intelligence agencies. The end result often is that the person appointed through the process may not be the most competent, but one who is senior most, or with the cleanest record or one with the best lobbying skills. In the process, it has often been seen that the management of companies such as IOC has suffered due to unsuitable incumbents in significant positions of the functional directors.

The management of IOC is also hamstrung by multiple procedures and restrictions imposed by the Government of India on it, such as the requirement to comply with the guidelines of the Central Vigilance Commission (CVC) and undertake its projects, purchases, sales and other core operations through tender process whereby often the counterparty chosen may not be the most competent or ideal for the progression of business prospects of IOC.

Further, and even more damaging to the business prospects of IOC, has been the arbitrary subsidy burden imposed by the Government on IOC year in and year out by having IOC sell petrol, diesel, LPG and Kerosene at below market prices. This has been done in the public interest as traditionally the high crude oil prices have led to very high refinery gate prices for the aforesaid products which, if passed on to the consumers, would lead to a spike in inflation across products and thus lead to unsustainably high Consumer Price Index (CPI) and Wholesale Price Index (WPI) which would, in turn, impair the growth of the economy. Thus the Government of India has had no qualms about passing its burden of fiscal management to companies such as IOC by denting their balance sheets with the burden of such fiscal costs such as the petroleum subsidies.

The net result of all of the above and other encroachments by the Government of India into the business prospects of IOC is that the balance sheet of the company has bled for many years with lack lustre performance in its earnings notwithstanding the market leader position and superior business prospects of the company.

Consequently the stock price has languished and the net worth of the stock does not in any way reflect the real business prospects or market position of the company. On a top line of more than 4 lac crores, the company reported a net profit of merely 4000 crores in 2014-15, being less than 1% net profit margin.

If you were to apply typical investment criteria of PE ratios and the like to IOC, without applying the basic criteria discussed above, you would likely come off enchanted by the company as an investment target as the company's stock has been trading at low PE multiples relative to the broader Indian markets.

However the approach to investing in the Indian equity markets cannot conform to a typical approach of application of ratios and determination of valuations based on financials alone.

On application of the promoter profile criterion one would come off most likely rejecting IOC as an investment candidate given the tendency of the Government, as the promoter of IOC to completely obfuscate the financial and business prospects of IOC.

However even if for the sake of argument, for a moment the promoter criterion is treated as fulfilled, one would then need to evaluate the business prospects of IOC even before delving into it's financials or the valuation.

The business prospects of IOC would have to be seen in the context of the overall environment in which it operates. It is well and good to say that the company is the biggest refiner and has the dominant position in terms of market share in the downstream products retail. It is even more promising to consider that the demand for petroleum products as envisaged by the projections is slated to grow through 2025. However, it is of little or no relevance if the company continues to bleed in the situation of selling its products below market price or even below cost in many cases.

While the case has been strong for avoiding IOC as an investment pick till recently, owing to its not fulfilling the first criterion for investment or even having weaker prospects owing to the Governmental interference and policies, this situation has somewhat changed in the recent past.

With the NDA led government taking charge in May 2014 and the benefit of the crude price falling off from USD 100 per barrel levels to

USD 40 per barrel levels, the Government was able to take some rational and radical steps which have gone a long way in providing visibility and transparency in the profitability and operations of IOC and other oil marketing companies.

The pricing for diesel and petrol has been deregulated and made market linked. Thus, IOC is free to price these products at market linked levels as it deems fit and therefore the under-recoveries or losses on these products have ceased.

Additionally the subsidy which is still being paid on products such as LPG and Kerosene, is proposed by the government to be brought under the direct benefit transfer scheme (DBT), with LPG already being brought under the purview of DBT scheme to a substantial extent. The impact of these measures taken by the Government is that IOC would effectively be realizing market prices for its products and any subsidy which is still to be paid to the economically weaker section of the society, whether on LPG or kerosene would be borne by the Government and paid directly to them in their Aadhaar linked accounts. There would thus be no ambiguity or pollutant in the financials of IOC and one would be able to reasonably peg the financial projections of the company to purely economic factors such as demand growth, refining margins and crude price.

The above measures and developments have somewhat mitigated the deterrents to investment in a company such as IOC and brought its true business prospects and financials into focus. Fulfilling the first two criteria for investment, investors, especially the foreign institutions who were till now avoiding such PSU stocks for lack of clarity, are now able to assess the stock of IOC for its true worth and take a decision regarding investing in it. IOC has thus emerged to the point of being compared on a like to like basis with companies such as Reliance and Essar in the private arena.

A chart showing the stock price performance of IOC from 2012 to 2016 is provided below. This shows that after languishing for the large part till 2014, the stock of IOC has been on an uptrend since the time the resolution of the earnings uncertainties has taken place.

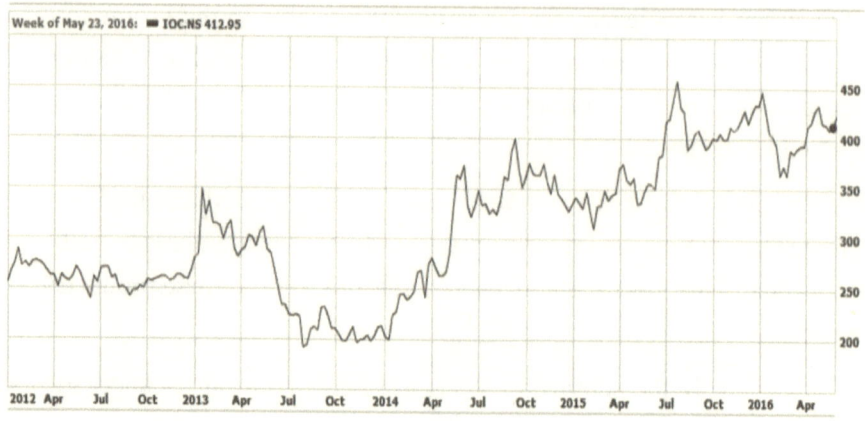

It would thus be seen from an example such as IOC that the promoter criterion trumps business prospects of the company and even where the promoter criterion is fulfilled, then also the business prospects criteria needs to be evaluated based on the ground realities of operations of the company in the context of its management policies, promoter's interference and other relevant aspects rather than looking at the business prospects in a vacuum.

2. NESTLE INDIA

Nestle India is a company that falls in the MNC promoter group category being a part of the multinational Nestle group.

For the large part, it is a company that would easily fulfil the first criterion. The Swiss parent company of Nestle India has been known to be a professionally managed MNC with presence in most of the countries in the developed and developing world. Nestle is known to be a pioneer in its product segments and has been managed with a fair and transparent management culture in Nestle India, replete with professional managers and arms-length dealings.

Except for the one-off incident in 2013 where the hike in the quantum of royalty charged by the Swiss parent from Nestle India, weighed down on the stock and was viewed as an anti-minority measure, the promoter of Nestle has not had any fingers raised on their corporate governance practices. Even in the case of the royalty hike in 2013, the higher percentage was justified based on an extensive arm's length study done by McKinsey.

Given that the first criterion is satisfied by this company, the business prospects merit a careful examination for determining the investment worthiness of the company.

Nestle is a company operating in the FMCG space. It is a focused company with global presence and domination of this space. It focuses on its core products and works to augment the business performance around these products. This is unlike other FMCG behemoths such as Unilever and P&G which are present across the spectrum of products and continuously widen their offerings from food products to toiletries to personal care and hygiene segments, growing organically and inorganically, sometimes even at the expense of losing the benefit of their brand identity.

Nestle, on the other hand, functions primarily in the food products segment and has done so for years. The noticeable aspect of Nestle's business is that it has built and consolidated its position over the years in such a manner that it has come to dominate many of the product segments that it operates in. The dominance in some cases is of such a magnitude that the names of the products offered by Nestle have become synonymous with the product itself.

In India a vast majority of the consumers, if not an overwhelming majority, consume coffee in the form of Nescafe. So much so that Nescafe has almost become a generic name for coffee in India.

Similarly, the instant noodles segment has been dominated by Nestle for many years and Maggi is the only prominent instant noodles brand that is seen across the rural and urban landscape of the country, with the competing brands trailing far behind.

The other segment where the dominance of Nestle is seen is in the baby foods segment where you see mostly all Indian parents supplement their baby's diet with Nan One and Nan Two.

Nestle - a company that churns out quality products that are market leaders and a company that is known for its quality and customer oriented approach.

A company that is known for its innovation and efforts towards constant product development and upgradation.

It thus emerges as a no-brainer that Nestle is in a lucrative business and enjoys a dominant position in it. However having evaluated the business segment of Nestle one also needs to evaluate the business growth prospects. It is not enough that the coffee and instant noodles and the baby food sold by Nestle dominates the market. This fact is more often than not already factored into the stock price of a company such as Nestle in the form of higher stock price and valuation multiples.

What has to be further seen is whether there is a clear and continuing growth path available to Nestle for its sales, profits and the like.

What has to be seen is whether there is consumption growth in products such as coffee and instant noodles and if yes, whether there are competitive threats to Nestle in the form of competing brands such as Top Ramen and Yipee by ITC in Noodles and Bru in coffee.

Moreover whether any emerging trends may be a threat to the sales growth of its products such as the increasing trend towards coffee shop based consumption or the flight of the customers to non-instant coffee brands. Similarly the pricing power of Nestle needs to be evaluated in determining the earnings growth and margin prospects. Whether in the face of increasing costs it would be feasible for the company to increase product prices without hurting sales and improve margins. Whether the products are commoditized and the dominance would continue only so long as they are competitively priced. Whether there is a price war between the competitors and Nestle which would hurt the future earnings prospects. All of the above factors and others need to be seen when determining the future business prospects of a FMCG player such as Nestle before an investment decision can be taken.

Furthermore, as happened in 2015, a FMCG company, especially one such as Nestle, which depends to a large extent on few core products, is susceptible to earnings hit in case any of the core products faces a customer boycott or drop in its sales. In 2015, one of the main products of Nestle, i.e. Maggi instant noodles was called into question by the food regulators on health issues and there was a ban in several Indian states on the sale of Maggi. This resulted in Nestle having to pull Maggi off the shelves and dented Nestle's earnings in 2015. There was also a resultant drop in the stock price of Nestle which fell from highs of INR 7000 in February 2015 to INR 5000 in February 2016 as shown in the chart below. Whether or not the ban on Maggi translates into denting the long term prospects of Nestle as a company or was a one off aberration which the company would rectify in quick time would also be a pertinent factor in the evaluation of the long term business prospects of Nestle and should be considered when determining whether or not Nestle fulfils the second basic criterion for investment. This would in turn clue in the investor on whether or not investing in Nestle at the resultant lower stock levels of INR 5000 is a good idea or not.

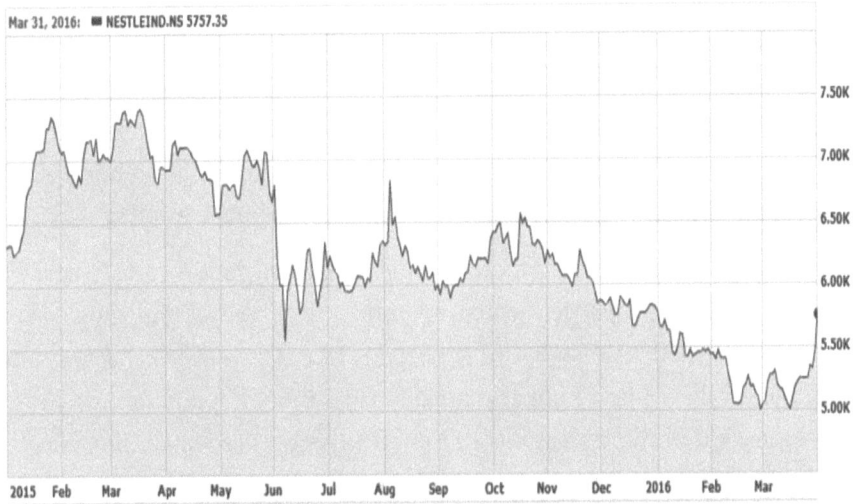

Thus, it emerges that while understanding the nature of business of a company such as Nestle may be relatively easier for a lay investor, the challenge would lie in the investor determining the growth prospects of the said business. In understanding how the growth story in India's consumption patterns translates to a growth in Nestle's revenues. In understanding the competitive landscape of Nestle and its projected market share. The pricing power of Nestle for its products in their respective segments and the trend in its margins. Forming a view regarding these prospects of the business of Nestle will enable an investor to ascertain whether or not it fulfils the second criterion i.e. a business which has favourable growth prospects in the foreseeable future.

3. ITC

ITC is a complex company when it comes to the question of evaluation of its business prospects. This is because the visibility of the business segments in which ITC operates and the relevant weightage of the various segments in ITC's business is not apparent on the face of it to most lay investors.

ITC's business presence is in diverse areas, some of which are highly visible, such as cigarettes, Hotels and FMCG. Others not as visible or consumer centric such as paper boards and the agri business.

At first glance the cigarette business would appear a dampener to any investor given the negative sentiment around tobacco and tobacco products coupled with the ever increasing regulations in the form of higher excise duties and labelling requirements. It appears to be the lawmaker's go to business for augmenting budgetary revenues and for wielding the public interest sword.

The hotel business, on the other hand, is glamourous and ITC is at the forefront with its properties which are not only some of the most prime hotels in cities such as New Delhi (Maurya), Mumbai (ITC Grand Maratha) and Chennai (ITC Chola) but also appear to be money spinners. Add to this ITC's execution of the restaurants in the hotel properties which have become franchises unto themselves such as Bukhara, Dumpukht and Dakshin.

ITC's foray into FMCG is another business that attracts high visibility in the form of products such as Sunfeast biscuits, Candyman candies, Fiama Di Wills toiletries. Similarly, the WILLS lifestyle clothing line is another area that ITC has forayed in and appears to have implemented successfully.

The agri and paper boards business finds visibility in the form of Ashirwad flour and 'Classmate' brand of stationery products respectively.

ITC has also managed to successfully cross leverage its businesses with the FMCG products finding place in the hotels, for example Sunfeast products being placed in hotel rooms and coffee shops, WILLS Lifestyle showrooms in the hotels, and Agri products being used in the kitchens. Similarly some of the signature dishes of its restaurants have been packaged as ready to eat food products and are sold by the FMCG division under the Kitchens of India brand.

However to properly evaluate the business prospects of a company such as ITC, one would need to sift through the noise of the multiple businesses and determine which business or businesses are the key revenue and profitability generators for ITC. As a company that commands a market capitalization in excess of INR two lakh crores and a revenue in excess of INR 50,000 crores, the investor would need to determine which business segment really turns the story for ITC's fortunes.

It is all well and good to say that ITC has great hotels which do well and thus, should be invested in as a company. But when you see that the hotel segment accounts for less than 5% of its Sales and less than 2% of the profitability it becomes quite marginal to evaluate the prospects of the hotel industry in the context of ITC.

Similarly, to consider the agri business as a new horizon segment playing on India's rural story and getting all excited about it may be futile when one considers that the said segment also accounts for less than 10% of ITC's overall profitability.

Thus to evaluate the true business prospects of a complex giant such as ITC one has to cull out the main drivers for the company which on a close study would reveal itself to be the cigarettes business which accounts for over 60% of its revenues and over 90% of its profits.

To decide whether or not to invest in ITC, the investor would thus need to evaluate the future prospects of cigarette business in India and determine whether this business promises increasing profitability and sales in the foreseeable future more so in the face of increased taxation pressures and regulatory clamp down, as well as taking into account the market share and competitive position of a company such as ITC in this business segment.

ITC is thus a good case of application of the second criterion of business prospects where the correct application of the criterion requires an intelligible approach to first decipher the real business of the company rather than blindly delving into the company judging it on the more visible flamboyant aspects of its business operations. Thereafter, an analysis of the prospects of the main revenue contributing segments of the business provides a cue into the investment outlook of the company.

4. JET AIRWAYS

Jet Airways is one of the premiere private airlines of the country. A country which has for the large part of its independent era seen the airline space being monopolized by the state-run air carrier, Air India, has in the past two decades seen the proliferation of multiple private carriers.

While some of them have gone out of operation owing to bankruptcy (Kingfisher, Paramount Airways), the others have seen multiple rounds of ownership changes in attempts for bailout and turnaround (Spicejet).

As such, the evaluation of the business prospects of an airline as a business has been one of the more intriguing exercises in the Indian landscape. Airline business, ever since its liberalization, has been a glamourous attraction for high flying Indians such as Subrata Roy Sahara and Vijay Mallya to big corporates such as Tata Group, Sun Group and Wadias.

Jet Airways has been one of the original private airlines that has managed to sustain its operations and is one of the few listed players in this space in India, with Spicejet and Indigo being the other two.

Before evaluating the financials and valuation metrics of a company such as Jet Airways, an investor ought to evaluate the business prospects of a company such as Jet Airways. To do so, one needs to understand the operating metrics of an airline business.

The airline business has transformed into a highly competitive business with most of the countries seeing multiple private players operating across segments, whether it be budget or luxury travel. This has led to extreme under cutting and pricing pressures on the air fares with every airline trying to woo customers by offering lower rates and discount schemes.

The operating costs of the airline are majorly in the form of fuel costs i.e. aviation turbine fuel (ATF) which constitutes over 30% of the operating costs. Moreover till the recent deregulation of petrol and diesel pricing, ATF was one of the only fuels that the oil refiners were allowed to price freely and this led to the ATF prices being pegged to international crude oil prices. In the era of 100 dollar plus crude prices the ATF prices have been a drag on airlines. Additionally the manpower costs have also sky rocketed with multitude of airlines poaching the relatively scarce skilled manpower in the form of pilots and in-flight staff. In an attempt to augment the skilled manpower base, there has been an influx of expatriate pilots which has also contributed to the higher salary levels.

The combination of high manpower costs and fuel costs along with the declining air fares has been a killer for airlines and has driven many, if not all the airlines into losses on a consistent basis, with airlines such as Kingfisher and Paramount airways going under and airlines such as Spice Jet being bailed out on multiple occasions.

With the crude oil prices tapering off since 2015, and settling at USD 40 per barrel levels in 2016, the pressure of ATF pricing has eased. This is however negated somewhat with greater competition entering the fray for a company such as Jet Airways in the form of Vistara airlines, and airlines such as Indigo having captured a higher market share at the back of efficient and time bound services attracting the business travellers. Thus the segment in which Jet operates finds itself once again crowded and hampers the pricing power of Jet.

On the other hand, the international segment of Jet has collaborated with Etihad airlines and also sold a strategic stake to Etihad against which it expects to benefit from Etihad's international rights such as gates, lounges and code share flights.

Before investing in an airline such as Jet purely on account of its low multiples or purely on account of the lure of a glamourous business such as this one, an investor would be well advised to apply his mind to the prospects of the private airline business going forward in the midst of cut throat competition, benign or challenging crude oil regime and the operations and competitive position of Jet airways against its peers.

A company such as Jet Airways, in the present Indian context has shown good traction in business, especially after the exit of its main rival in the premium travel segment, Kingfisher. While other airlines such as Vistara have entered the same space, Jet has largely managed to hold on to its market share. A chart showing the market share of various airlines in the Indian air space is provided below.

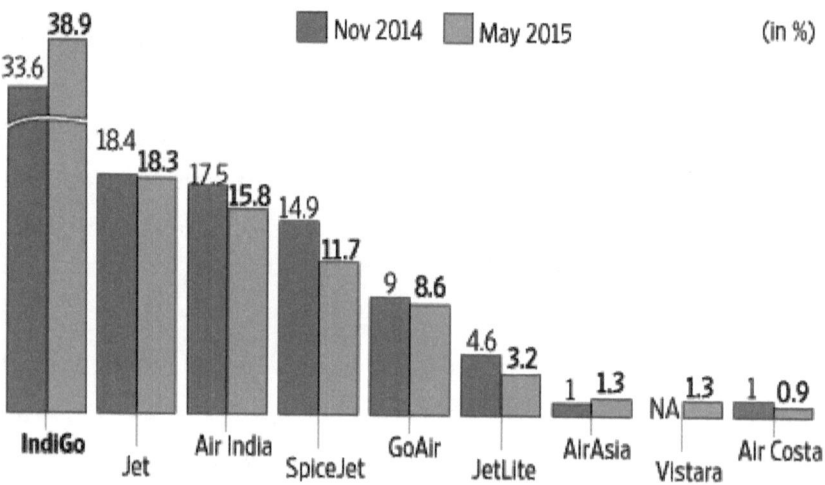

While retaining the market share, Jet Airways has also managed to continue its strong performance in the international space and this has been aided by its strategic partnership with Etihad which has provided a greater flight network and options to travellers via the Jet code share flights.

The positive impact of the business prospects from the above developments has started to make itself evident in the case of the earnings of Jet Airways in the December 2015 quarter where Jet reported a PAT of INR 467 crores against a corresponding loss of INR 1700 crores in December 2014. With the expectation of the positive turnaround of Jet and the positive business prospects in the future, the stock price of the company has since performed well and has moved from levels of INR 400 in November 2015 to INR 600 in April 2016.

However with the first quarter of FY 2016-17, the pricing pressures on the fares in the face of cut throat competition have started to show through and the revenue and earnings of Jet have shown a decline to INR 100 crores in the June quarter.

The investor would thus need to evaluate the business prospects of Jet Airways in the face of the increasing competition, pressures on fares, view regarding the crude price as well as the expected market share and profit margins of the company.

Thus a meaningful and in depth study of the business prospects of a company is key to determining whether or not the company should be bought into, since the prospects determine the future earnings of the company and in turn determine the stock price movement.

5. INFOSYS

The Indian technological revolution started in the 1980's with a group of 'startups' in this space, Infosys being one of the torch bearers. Anyone who invested in this company has been a winner insofar as the multiplier returns this stock has generated. It has been a stock which has made millionaires, if not billionaires out of many.

It is a ritual for the earnings season every quarter to commence with an Infosys press conference and it has been admirable how the management of the company has been run professionally and been transparent not only in terms of its management practices but also the earnings 'guidance' shared quarter after quarter.

Infosys as a company, perhaps easily passes the first investment criterion of promoter group as the promoter founders who were themselves hard core professionals have all stepped down with time and passed the baton to the professional managers rather than trying their hand at dynasty-like succession which has been seen in some of its other peers.

In 2016, the promoters of the company brought in Vishal Sikka as the CEO of the company, someone who is not only a professional but came with the endorsement of being amongst the top management of a global IT powerhouse namely SAP. Moreover, the company has been known for fair corporate governance practices and has been a darling of the investor community when it has come to transparency in earnings and consistent approach of the promoters towards shareholder wealth creation.

Would it then not make this company a no-brainer to invest in? Would you not follow the market wisdom and allocate the mandatory weightage in your portfolio to technology companies and more specifically the bellwether stock of Indian technology space i.e. Infosys?

The answer to these questions is that no matter how obvious a stock may be in terms of its choice as an investment target, for the reasons mentioned above, it still does not allow for an investor to forego the mandatory steps for evaluation of the investment, i.e. the three basic criteria for investment.

The first criterion, i.e. the promoter group, having been fulfilled, the investor has to address the second criterion i.e. the business prospects of Infosys. As we have seen in the previous case studies, to ascertain the business prospects of any company one must first understand what business the company is transacting.

So, what is the business of Infosys? Specifically what are the services it offers? We all know that it is in the IT services space, however most of us, including most of the people invested in the company would not be able to satisfactorily answer this question about Infosys's business activities. It is easy to reckon the goods and services offered by companies such as IOC or Jet Airways, since most of us get to experience such tangible goods and services first hand as consumers too. However, in the case of a company such as Infosys, which is mostly in the B2B (business to business) segment and is providing intangible services, it would be difficult for a lay investor to ascertain the exact nature and scope of its services.

It is all well and good to say that it is engaged in IT, but what exactly does a company such as Infosys do? Does it provide low-end technology driven services to clients such as back office data feeding and management? Or lower end hardware related repair and management services? Or software coding services? Or high-end software development services? What exactly does it do?

If you seriously wish to invest in a company such as Infosys, the second criterion i.e. the business prospects assumes paramount importance in the process of evaluation. And to properly evaluate the prospects of its business, we would first need to wrap our heads around the exact nature of its business. Once you understand the particular segment or segments of technology services that Infosys is present in, you would then need to compare its presence and competitive advantage with those of its peers. You would need to evaluate the prospects in light of its client profile and geographical exposure to be able to take a view on how the earnings appear in the future and key risks to the same.

Failing a proper understanding of the above, merely relying on the projected earnings per share (EPS) and price earning (PE) multiples would make for an unwise move to invest in a company such as Infosys.

In fact, in the first quarter of FY 2016-17, there has been considerable overhang on the business prospects of Infosys at the back of the Brexit developments. Now an investor who does not understand the nature of business of Infosys, let alone its dependence on the European or British markets, would not be in a position to evaluate the impact of developments such as Brexit on the business and earnings of Infosys and would thus be flying blind in case he holds a position in Infosys.

Thus Infosys is a good case in point for a company where deciphering the nature of the business and then determining the prospects is not only challenging but, in case of most investors, failing to do so translates to foregoing a position in the stock of the company notwithstanding the conventional investing wisdom or market trends.

The above case studies illustrate the importance of understanding the business of a company before investing in it. Only when you understand the business activities of a company thoroughly would you be equipped to evaluate the future prospects of such a business in the context of the changes in the macro-economic environment in which the company operates as well as the regulatory environment and competitive landscape. Without understanding the true and proper nature of the business of a company, investing in it solely based on the financial ratios or market trends is as good as giving your money away to a smooth talking salesman who promises a winner of an investment.

And it is reasonable that you may not understand the business of all the companies that you look at. There is nothing unusual in that nor is it shameful to admit. For that matter, no one can understand the business prospects of all the companies that are present, more so in the swiftly evolving technology driven businesses that are emerging on the horizon. The simple answer to such a situation is to avoid investing in what you cannot understand and focus energies and funds in the companies whose business you do understand.

If you cannot fully understand the business of a company such as Google in terms of their cost and revenue model, best to avoid it and look at another company such as Apple.

There is no shame in giving a pass to some companies for this reason. It is better to have missed a few winners because you did not understand their business model than to be stuck in loss-making investments of companies where you do not understand the business and have no way to tell whether the investment will turn around to show a profit or not.

Once you have understood the business of the company in question, it is a loaded exercise to go through the prospects. In doing so you would evaluate number of factors having a bearing on the prospects of the business, these include:

1. BUSINESS CYCLE

If the company is in a commodity business it would be relevant to evaluate the price cycle to evaluate how the earnings of the company are likely to swing in the next few years. For example a person looking to invest in Tata Steel would need to study the steel price cycle in the recent years and the expected trajectory of steel prices to determine the future growth prospects of its business.

2. TECHNOLOGICAL INNOVATIONS

If the company is in a business that is getting disrupted by technological advancements, it would be relevant to evaluate the impact of such innovations on the company's prospects and to see whether and how fast the company is innovating its business model to tackle the disruptions and emerge ahead of these. For example, a company offering photography printing solutions in a world which is moving to digital storage and consumption of content, would struggle in terms of its business prospects and the investor would need to evaluate how the company is adapting to the changing technological landscape in terms of product innovations and diversification.

3. REGULATORY ENVIRONMENT

If a company is in a business which is facing increasing regulatory headwinds, the investor would need to evaluate the impact of such regulatory changes in understanding future earnings trajectory of the company. For example a person looking to invest in Godfrey Philips which is primarily in the tobacco business would need to evaluate its expected revenues and margins in the face of increasing regulatory restrictions as well as incrementally higher tax regime.

4. GEOGRAPHICAL EXPOSURE

If a company is highly exposed to markets and customers which are showing weakness, the extent and nature of weakness ought to be considered and evaluated to decide upon the future business of the company. For example, a person looking to invest in Tech Mahindra, which is a technology company with clients in foreign countries, including clients in Britain and US, would need to evaluate the impact of Brexit and US clamp down on H1B visas on the business prospects of Tech Mahindra.

5. COMPETITIVE LANDSCAPE

The market share of the company, the position vis-à-vis its competitors, the competitive advantage of its products and services, the pricing power of the company and the swiftness with which it acts to maintain its position would be material in evaluating its business prospects. For example an investor looking to invest in Spicejet would need to evaluate its standing in the competitive landscape of the aviation industry, its ability to face pressures on fare pricing and maintain its market share and thus determine the business prospects of the company in the foreseeable future.

6. PRODUCT DIVERSIFICATION OR EXPANSION

In case the company is in the process of diversifying its business or product mix or going in for backward or forward integration, the expected effect of such initiatives on the revenues and earnings of the company in the near future would need to be evaluated. For example a person looking to invest in Reliance Industries which has undertaken a major capex exposure in the telecom initiative i.e. Reliance Jio, which is totally divergent from its conventionally core business, would need to evaluate how this diversification is going to impact the future earnings and revenues of Reliance and then decide on investment into Reliance.

7. INORGANIC GROWTH INITIATIVES

In case the company is in the process of acquiring or merging with other companies, the expected effect of such inorganic initiatives on the growth prospects of the company would be relevant. For instance the announcement of merger of Aditya Birla group companies, AB Nuvo with Grasim, leading to Grasim, also getting exposed to businesses such as telecom (IDEA) and financial services would need to be evaluated by the investor when determining the second criterion in case of Grasim.

The above and all other material factors should be taken into account and only when one reaches a conclusion that the business of the company is sound and it is poised to grow in the near future with a positive trajectory in the revenue and earnings, should one go ahead to the next criterion for evaluating the investment in the company, i.e. the valuation.

CHAPTER 5

MAIN CRITERION THREE: VALUATION

> *A company, valued cheaply, is of itself not a good investment pick. A company valued cheaply and fulfilling the first two investment criteria is a good investment pick.*

Valuation of the company is no doubt an important factor to be considered in deciding whether or not to invest in the shares of the company. It just isn't the first and foremost.

It is a natural tendency of any new investor entering the market, or even an existing investor when scouting for new investment plays, to glance through the PE ratios of various companies and take an investment call regarding which company to invest in, based on such financial ratios and parameters.

A typical approach involves an investor lapping up shares of a company that quote at a low P/E multiple or a low Price to Book value or other such valuation parameters as compared to their peers or the broader market.

For example, a typical investor looking to invest in the oil and gas space may choose to pick up the shares of a company such as HPCL as compared to, say, Reliance Industries on the premise that HPCL shares quote at a lower PE multiple as compared to Reliance Industries and thus present a greater upside for the investor. However, such a simplistic approach ignores matters critical to the companies in question. If a company such as HPCL quotes at a lower PE multiple, perhaps it is owing to the profile of the promoter of the company, i.e. the Government of India and its ways of interfering with the autonomous functioning of HPCL or its policies which tend to dent the earnings and operations of HPCL. Furthermore, a company such as Reliance may be quoting at a higher PE ratio because it has better earnings prospects in the future than HPCL.

A company may be quoting at a lower valuation because it has historically exhibited stagnating earnings or because of questionable practices adopted by its promoter group or even because the poor management of the company casts a cloud on its competitive position.

Thus, it cannot be emphasized enough that before delving into the financial parameters of the companies, it is more relevant to assess the investment worthiness of a company by considering the profile of the promoter group and the business prospects of the company as discussed in the previous chapters.

Only once a company is seen to be from a promoter group that is known for fair and transparent management practices and only when the company appears to be in a business that is not only understood by the investor but shows promise in terms of future earnings trajectory, should an investor move to the financial analysis of the company in question.

When it does come to financial analysis, most investors, not being financial wizards or trained in understanding and interpreting financial statements find themselves lost. This is not unreasonable or uncommon. In fact with the increasing level of complexity in financial reporting being introduced with newer accounting standards, compliance with International Financial Reporting Standards and a greater number of disclosures being demanded by stock exchanges, the financial statements of the companies have become a maze for many readers.

The question thus arises how to ascertain the true value of the company in question? More importantly how to ascertain whether or not the value of the company prompts investment into the company's stock?

There are a number of valuation metrics and approaches, ranging from simple ones to more complex ones. Some of these are discussed below.

1. PRICE EARNING (PE) RATIO

This is one of the most straightforward approaches in determining the relative value or standing of the company. The price-earning ratio considers the annual profit after tax earned by the company and divides that by the number of equity shares in issue to arrive at the earning per share of the company (EPS). The market price of the stock of the company is then divided by the EPS to arrive at the PE ratio. In other words:

PE Ratio = Market Price of the Equity Share / EPS

In arriving at the EPS the Profit after tax (PAT) considered may vary in different approaches. While some investors may consider the PAT for the most recent completed financial year of the company, others may consider the trailing twelve months (TTM) PAT.

Once the PE ratio is determined, it is then compared with that of the other companies in similar segment and the PE ratio of the market as a whole.

In conventional wisdom a company with a lower PE ratio than the market and its peers is considered to be cheaply valued and worth investing in while a company with a PE ratio that is higher than that of the peers or the broader market is considered to be overvalued.

However, this may not always be a correct approach to follow.

Consider that you are evaluating companies in the IT space. You shortlist a company that is not a bellwether such as Infosys or TCS but a lesser followed company with a lower market capitalization. The PE ratio of the company is found to be lower than that of Infosys or TCS which typically quote in high teens. Say the PE ratio of this company is even in single digits, an 8 or a 9 against the PE ratio of Infosys which may be 17 or 18 at the time. This may lead to the natural assumption that the company in question is cheaply valued and ought to be invested in. However, this may not always hold good. On the contrary, the company may be cheaply valued because of some inherent problems in its business prospects or other issues surrounding the company such as poor product offering or poor management team or lack of qualitative client base.

Thus, blindly following the PE ratio of the company to make an investment decision may not be a sound approach. The PE ratio of the company has to be seen in the context of all the surrounding factors, more specifically, the first two criteria discussed above.

Similarly the reverse may be seen with another example. In the automotive space a company such as Eicher Motors commands a very high PE ratio of more than 20 as compared to the peers such as Maruti Suzuki, Tata Motors and Mahindra & Mahindra which are typically quoting at PE ratios in the teens. This in itself does not imply that the stock of Eicher Motors is expensive and ought to be avoided. In fact a high PE ratio of such a company may indicate that the growth trajectory of the earnings of the company is much higher and aggressive than that of the other companies, especially owing to factors such as the company being a smaller player which is able to show a higher growth rate in sales, profit etc given the lower base or owing to the fact that the company has entered certain new product segments which are showing exponential growth. This would thus imply that the company is worthy of investment in spite of, or even due to the high PE ratio.

The PE ratio thus of its own footing, seen in a vacuum, should not be the sole basis of the investment decision in a stock.

2. PRICE TO BOOK (P/B) RATIO

This method of valuation relies on the book value of the shares in question and compares the market price with the book value.

Price/Book Ratio = Market Price per share / Book Value per share

Here the Book Value per share is computed by considering the paid up share capital and free accumulated reserves of the company and reducing any accumulated losses in its latest financial statements and dividing this by the number of equity shares in issue. The resulting number is the book value per share which in other words represents the net worth of the assets in the books of the company which each equity share is entitled to.

This method is more relevant in the case of companies such as those operating in the financial lending space or for banks. The book value per share in case of banks represents the net own funds of the bank which each equity share is entitled to in the balance sheet of the bank in question.

A company whose market capitalization or market price per share is higher than the book value per share indicates that the market ascribes a premium to the share over and above what each share is entitled to in the net worth of the company in question. Does this make the company cheaply valued or expensive?

Logically a lower Price to Book ratio would indicate that the company is cheaply valued and ought to be invested in. Conversely, a high price to book ratio would indicate that the market values each share at a much higher multiple of the actual assets that exist in the financials of the company with respect to each share.

However, as we saw in the case of PE Ratio, a lower or higher P/B ratio is not in itself a clinching factor regarding investing in or avoiding a company. The P/B ratio also has to be seen in the context of the growth prospects and quality of earnings of the company in question, in other words, the business prospects as well as the promoter group of the company.

In the Indian markets traditionally, the public sector banks (PSBs) have traded at low P/B ratios while the private banks have traded at high P/B ratios. This, in itself, does not dictate that investing in banks should be done only via the public sector banks. On the contrary the public sector banks have been dogged by issues of corporate governance owing to the Government being their promoter. Furthermore the public sector banks' business prospects have always been tainted owing to the lack of professional management and their being forced to act in public interest and open branches in nooks and corners of the country to serve the rural population in the spirit of financial inclusion even though such branches may not be viable or profitable on stand-alone basis. The quality of the assets of the PSBs have also been suspect, as the banks have often times been compelled to fund sub-optimal public interest infrastructure projects and on other occasions the management of the PSBs has sought to

Equity:In

lend to suspect borrowers owing to vested interests or lobbying. Moreover the quantum of provisioning for non-performing assets (NPAs) has also been a big question mark and thus the book value per share as per the balance sheet of the company is not necessarily reflective of the true worth of the assets of the bank.

In fact, in the last quarter of 2015/early part of 2016, when the Reserve Bank of India came out with guidelines for Asset Quality Review (AQR) by the banks on the back of concerns about the undisclosed NPAs sitting in the system, it was the public sector bank stocks which took a much bigger hit than the private sector banks.

A comparative chart showing the movement of stock prices of State Bank of India and HDFC Bank from October 2015 to March 2016 are provided below.

A perusal of the charts of SBI and HDFC Bank would show that on the AQR overhang, the stock price of SBI fell from levels of Rupees 250 per share in October 2015 to Rupees 150 per share in February 2016, shaving off as much as 40% off its market capitalization, which for a company with a market capitalization upwards of INR 1,00,000 crores is considerable. On the other hand, HDFC bank fell from levels of Rupees 1080 per share in October 2015 to Rupees 980 per share in February 2016, a mere 10% in comparison.

The above illustrates well enough that a lower P/B ratio does not necessarily imply a value buy and as is the case with PSBs, their inherent limitations have been factored into the market price of the PSB shares and thus the P/B ratio of the PSBs has been lower than that of private sector banks. Conversely, in case of the private sector banks, the better asset quality and the higher expected earnings growth coupled with the better management at the helm attributes the premium to the value in the form of the higher P/B ratio.

Thus, applying P/B ratio as a valuation guidepost has to be done in the appropriate context with due and proper weightage to the other relevant factors.

3. DISCOUNTED CASH FLOW

Discounted cash flow method of valuing an enterprise is one of the most comprehensive methods and is routinely used by the expert analysts working in big brokerage houses and financial service industry.

This method is considered as the favoured method of valuation as it requires a deep dive into the business prospects of the company and projecting the earnings of the company for the future.

Under the DCF method of valuation, the analyst considers the present earnings of the company and the prevailing factors as well as the growth plans of the company. Keeping all factors in mind, the analyst projects the revenue, expenses and the cash flow that would be generated by the company over the next few years. Further, a terminal value is assigned to the undertaking of the company based on the projected assets and liabilities, or the terminal growth of the earnings at the end of the projection period.

The projected cash flow, as well as the terminal value, is then discounted using the cost of capital to arrive at the enterprise value of the company. From the enterprise value the long term debt is deducted and free cash and investments added to arrive at the equity value of the company. The said equity value is then divided by the number of equity shares in issue to arrive at the per share value of the company.

Thus, under the DCF methodology, the per-share value of the company is computed as per the following formula:

Equity Value per share = (Discounted Cash Flow + Discounted Terminal Value − Debt + Free Cash & Investments)/Number of Equity shares in Issue

The DCF method being a comprehensive method involving normative assumptions, has number of variations which have evolved over a period of time. These variations are applied in different industries and by different experts. Since the scope of this book is not to provide a thorough guidance on the application of DCF or other valuation methodologies, the reader would be well advised to refer to financial management texts in case they seek to study the DCF methodology in detail.

The value arrived at under the DCF method is compared with that of the current market price of the equity shares of the company to determine whether the share of the company would have any upside and be worth investing in.

While the DCF Method is the most comprehensive and in depth method for valuation of the companies, it requires a significant level of financial expertise and time to develop a detailed DCF model around the earnings and financials of a company. Moreover a lay investor may apply and develop a DCF model for valuation of one odd company but it may not always be feasible for the investor to develop such a model for many companies at a time to determine which companies to invest in. Even if developed, such models require constant updating and validation with quarterly earnings and changes in the business operating environment of the company. Such frequent updating and modifications may not be feasible for a lay investor.

Thus, while in theory DCF method is the best method to adopt for valuation, it may not be feasible for everyone to implement and follow.

4. SUM OF THE PARTS

Sum of the parts method is adopted for valuation of a company that has multiple businesses under its fold. Under this method of valuation, the various businesses of the company are valued on an individual basis using an appropriate method, usually DCF.

Once the value of the individual businesses has been determined, these are added, i.e. the sum of the parts is computed and divided by the number of shares of the company to arrive at the per share value of the company.

Equity Value per share = (Sum of Discounted Cash Flow Value of each business of the Company - Debt + Free Cash & Investments)/ Number of Equity shares in Issue

A company having many verticals of business is a complex proposition to understand, value and invest in. The sum of the parts method using DCF for each part, while ideal in theory, would be cumbersome to implement, and update on an ongoing basis.

As a way around, in cases where certain verticals account for a fraction of the revenue and profitability of the company, such verticals may be ignored for the valuation and other valuation methods may be applied for the valuation of the single prominent business vertical of the company.

Alternatively, where two or more verticals of the company are prominent contributors to the earnings and revenues of the company, the investor may consider adopting simpler methods of valuation to value the verticals on an individual basis and then add up the values to determine the enterprise value of the company as a whole and thereon, derive the per share equity value of the company as sum of the parts.

5. EV/EBIDTA MULTIPLE

EV/EBIDTA multiple considers the enterprise of the company as a whole and determines the earnings multiple at which business of the company is valued.

The EBIDTA of the company is the Earnings before Interest, Depreciation, taxes and amortizations. It is the money earned by the company to service its fixed undertaking comprising of the capital stock of the company.

The Enterprise value, on the other hand, is arrived at by considering the market value of the shares of the company and multiplying this by the number of shares in issue to arrive at the market capitalization of the equity of the company. To this market capitalization, we add the long term debt of the company and reduce the free cash and current investments of the company to arrive at the enterprise value of the company (EV).

EV/EBIDTA multiple = EV/EBIDTA

Where, EV = Market Capitalization (no. of shares X CMP) + Long Term Debt − Free cash and Current Investments.

EBIDTA = Earnings before Interest, Depreciation, Taxes and Amortizations

The EV/EBIDTA multiple so computed for the company in question is to be compared with the industry and market wide multiple. A company having a higher than average multiple is typically considered overvalued while one having a lower than average multiple is considered undervalued.

However, as we saw in the case of PE ratio, merely having a low multiple is not a case for the company to be invested in. A company may have a lower multiple as opposed to its peers as it is plagued by certain intrinsic issues in its business which do not affect the peer companies.

For example, in the pharmaceutical sector, one may notice that the companies such as Elder Pharma may be quoting at a lower EV/EBIDTA multiple than a rival such as Sun Pharma. This does not by itself mandate an investment in Elder Pharma since such a lower multiple may be symptomatic of the fact that the management of Elder Pharma has been subject to dispute amongst the warring factions of the promoter family. Moreover, a company such as Sun Pharma may be enjoying higher EV/EBIDTA multiples owing to the demonstrated track record of superior earnings growth year on year coupled with a superior portfolio of products in the pipeline which lend themselves to a steep growth trajectory in the earnings of Sun Pharma in the future.

As such, the EV/EBIDTA multiple method must be used in conjunction with the study of the business prospects of the company in question and only where the low EV/EBIDTA multiple is accompanied by growth in the earnings on the back of the lucrative business prospects of the company, should it be considered as a case for investment in the company.

6. UNIT RELATED VALUATION METHODS

Companies in specific industries are often valued on the basis of the unitary metrics specific to such industry. Such a valuation methodology is used as a standard across the globe and is typically handy for acquisitions within the country or across borders.

For instance in the cement industry, companies are often valued on the basis of the EV/tonne of capacity. In other words, for a cement company such as ACC, listed in India, its current market capitalization would be taken and the long term debt added to it, with free cash and investments being subtracted to arrive at the Enterprise value. The EV so arrived at would be divided by the installed capacity of cement manufacturing in ACC to arrive at an EV/tonne valuation. In case the EV/tonne is lower than the global benchmark, then ACC would be considered as a lucrative acquisition target while such value being higher than the global norm would make it a less attractive acquisition target.

Similarly unitary valuation methods are used in other industries, such as:

a. Oil & gas refining – Valuing companies at Enterprise Value per million metric tonnes of installed refining capacity.

b. Oil & Gas upstream – Valuing companies at Enterprise Value per barrel of oil reserves held by the company.

c. Steel – Enterprise value per installed capacity of steel manufacturing.

d. Telecom – Enterprise value per user in the subscriber base of the company.

For a typical lay investor unitary method of valuation is a good benchmark to ascertain whether the company he is looking to invest in, is cheaply valued or expensive. However, the method of unitary valuation cannot be used in isolation and has to be used in conjunction with the other factors i.e. promoter group profile and business prospects of the company. For instance an upstream company such as ONGC may appear to be cheaply valued when its value is considered in terms of Enterprise value per barrel of oil reserve held by ONGC as compared to the global peers. However this discounted value may be occurring in case of ONGC due to its government promoter or due to the lack of visibility in its earnings arising due to ad hoc subsidy sharing policies adopted by the government.

Thus the unitary method of valuation is a guidepost to ascertain the relative value of a company though it may not necessarily be an appropriate method for use on a stand-alone basis.

SUGGESTED APPROACH FOR VALUATION

We have seen some of the methods for valuation of a company above. Apart from these, there are numerous other methods which are also used by experts or recommended in texts. The question thus arises, what is the best method or approach to be adopted for valuation of a listed company.

The fact remains that there is no single method of valuation that can be considered as the best or most feasible. All methods have their own pros and cons and suitability to different users.

While methods of valuation such as DCF are comprehensive and possibly the most appropriate to be adopted in all cases, it may not be feasible for every investor to develop DCF models, more so, for each and every company that such an investor may wish to evaluate for investment. Furthermore, DCF models need constant updating, which in itself is a time-consuming task, which may not be feasible for an investor to carry on with respect to all the companies in his or her portfolio.

Again, other methods may or may not be suitable to be applied to each and every company that an investor may look to evaluate. Moreover most methods may not be appropriate to be used on a stand-alone basis.

The important thing to be understood, which is the thrust of the recommendation of this book, when it comes to the third criterion for investment, i.e. valuation, is that in the exercise of valuation, the investor does not have to arrive at a precise value for the stock in question.

He has to arrive at a conclusion as to the relative under or over valuation of the stock when the price of the stock is compared to its perceived intrinsic value. This perceived intrinsic value is not to be pinpointed in exact rupees and paise, but a range or directional indication would suffice to arrive at a conclusion about the third criterion for evaluation of investments.

In the above context, and keeping in mind the various pros and cons of the various methods of valuation, the approach given below has been found to be an appropriate balance of simplicity and comprehensiveness.

The suggested approach of valuation as recommended here attempts to imbibe the understanding of the business metrics and basic financial metrics to the forward looking prospects of the company without overly complicating the exercise for the lay investor. It is an approach that permits regular updating and at the same time is not deficient in the sense that it may yield erroneous conclusions on a stand-alone basis.

The approach involves the investor understanding the business of the company, analysing the environment in which the company operates, determining the future business prospects of the company and how the earnings of the company are likely to move in the future years in view of all of the foregoing.

Before we proceed to discuss the approach in detail, a word about the sourcing of information by the investor for purposes of his analysis.

The investor should undertake the study of the company, including its business and financials primarily from the annual report of the company as this is the original source of information insofar as the financials of the company are concerned.

Information about the business environment of the company and regulatory and macro-economic aspects can be obtained from industry publications and macro-economic reports such as the annual economic survey.

In addition to the foregoing, the investor may also read through available analyst research reports on the sector in which the company operates as well as reports on the company in particular. Media articles, research reports and other third party publications should, however, be taken with a pinch of salt as these may sometimes be skewed insofar as the perspective conveyed on any issue. As far as possible, the investor ought to go to the original information source for each issue he wishes to investigate, whether it be the financials of the company (annual reports and result announcements on stock exchange websites), price movement of the company's stock (stock exchange websites), developments regarding regulatory environment (relevant judgements, circulars, notifications and acts), developments regarding macro-economic outlook (industry reports, economic surveys). News channels, magazines and newspapers should not be relied upon as the source of information as these are often times carrying biased reports and on other occasions the information provided is inaccurate without there being any accountability on the part of the publishers for misstatements.

Of course, in some cases even the annual reports or audited financials of the companies have also been found to contain major lacunae. While there is no surety about the authenticity of any information beyond a point, the investor has to make use of his nose or instinct when perusing different sources of information in relation to a company to see whether the information reconciles or yields suspicious contradictions. In case of even the slightest of doubts it is best to avoid the company, since suspect annual reports go to the root of the matter and vitiate the very first criterion for investment i.e. satisfactory Promoter Group.

We now proceed to discuss the steps of the recommended valuation approach below.

1. STEP 1 – UNDERSTAND THE BUSINESS

As we have discussed in detail in the preceding chapter, a basic approach for understanding the intrinsic value of the company nevertheless starts out with a deeper understanding of the business of the company. In case the company operates in multiple business segments, then the investor would need to gain an understanding of each segment of business as well as the macro-economic factors surrounding such business including the regulatory framework.

As we have emphasized before, not even the most seasoned analyst, let alone a lay investor, can properly value the stock price of a company whose business is not understood. Valuation is not an exercise done in a vacuum with numbers and ratios alone. It has to be done in the context of the real business of a company with a feel for its real earnings and financial position. In the preceding chapter, we have already discussed certain case studies illustrating the process of understanding of the business of certain companies.

After having understood the business in depth, one should delve into the financial performance of the company over the past two to three years. This is best done by going through the annual report of the company. A reading of the annual report of the company you wish to invest in is a must. This coupled with the available analyst research reports not only helps understand the financials of the company but also places the business of the company in the context of its peers and the industry.

As the investor gets his head around the financials of the company, it helps to plot the basic data about the company in an excel sheet to enable further analysis. It is not required to plot all available information to the last detail as that may become a tedious exercise and divert the focus from the main picture. However, the major elements as discussed below, ought to be plotted since they would become the base for the investor to value the company.

2. STEP 2 - COMPANY'S SIZE, CURRENT VALUATION AND CAPITAL STRUCTURE

The starting point to understand the company's financials is to understand its size.

Take the number of equity shares in issue. Plot this on your excel sheet. Plot the current market price of the company's share to arrive at the current market capitalization of the company.

Plot the long term debt in the balance sheet of the company as well as the cash and current investments.

By adding the long term debt and reducing the cash and current investments from the market capitalization of the company we arrive at the enterprise value of the company in question.

The market capitalization and enterprise value of the company give you a flavour of the size of the company and its current valuation as pegged by the market, which are key figures to put all other financial metrics of the company in context. Surprising as it may sound to many newly initiated investors, the per share market price of the stock of the company does not of its own tell about the size of the company. Thus, a company with a stock price of INR 500 per share may yet be a smaller company than another company with a stock price of INR 20 per share as the latter may have a much larger capital base than the former. Hence, plotting of the market capitalization and enterprise value is the most important starting point in analysing its value.

In case the company is in the manufacturing segment, the current installed capacity of the company should also be plotted at this step. This will aid in determining the Enterprise Value of the company per tonne of installed capacity and give you a perspective on the unitary valuation of the company. In case the company is in mining or oil and gas production, the reserves held by the company as disclosed in its financial statements should be plotted. Similarly, the size of the company in other unitary terms may also be plotted.

3. STEP 3 – PAST OPERATING PERFORMANCE

After getting a sense of the size and value of the company, one should study the P&L of the company for the preceding two to three years. In case the company is in multiple segments of the business, the segmental accounts should be seen first to get a sense of the performance in each segment rather than on a consolidated basis. Of course, in case a segment accounts for a miniscule percentage of the overall revenues and profits of the company, then such a segment may be ignored by the investor for the purpose of the analysis, except in case such a segment is expected to play a major role in the future prospects of the company.

The revenue of each segment should be analysed as well as the gross operating margin.

The gross operating margin, and the trend in the same will indicate to the investor how the pricing power of the company is evolving in the competitive environment and whether the business of the company is becoming more challenging or more profitable over the preceding years. This also tells about the durable competitive advantage, which as per Warren Buffet, is the most essential element to be present in an investible company. A company with a durable competitive advantage would see a healthy growth rate in its revenues year on year and an expansion in its margins as well.

Apart from the gross margin, one should see the quantum of indirect costs or overheads or administrative expenses in the P&L of the company and the general trend of these costs in the preceding few years in comparison to the revenue. The quantum of fixed overheads is critical to the operating leverage of the company. A company that is able to keep its fixed overheads in check and is able to increase its revenues and gross margins would see a quantum jump in its profits and the return per equity share to the benefit of the shareholders. By deducting the indirect costs from the Gross margin figure you arrive at the EBIDTA of the company.

Once you have a sense of the turnover, the gross margins and EBIDTA of the company, you should study the depreciation and interest charges to the P&L of the company as well as the interest income the company earns on its surplus funds and investments. The depreciation charge should be compared with the fixed asset block of the company while the interest charge should be compared with the long term debt of the company. This will give the investor a sense of the level of depreciation charge and effective cost of debt of the company. This will also help the investor project the depreciation and interest cost figures of the company in the ensuing years based on the expected level of debt and fixed assets of the company. The interest income is a function of the available cash and investments of the company and can be projected for subsequent years by determining the cash the company would generate from it's operations as opposed to the cash spend on capital expenditure and loan raise/repayments.

By deducting the depreciation and interest charge from the EBIDTA and adding the interest income, you would arrive at the Profit before Tax of the company. It is worthwhile at this stage to plot and compare the EBIDTA and Gross Margin as a percentage of the Revenue in the preceding few years, in order to ascertain the trend in the EBIDTA margin and Gross margin of the company. An increasing or decreasing trend would signal how the business of the company is faring. A highly erratic pattern may, on the other hand, be a tell-tale sign of discrepancies in the financials or aberrations in the business which may detract from the long term viability of the company.

The PAT figure and the tax amount should be seen next. The tax as a percentage of the PBT should be plotted so that the investor has a benchmark percentage rate to apply to future projected profits of the company.

The above exercise would give you a fair idea of the contours of the income statement of the company with an assessment of the gross margin generated by each business segment, the indirect overheads, the EBIDTA with the EBIDTA margin and the PBT and PAT.

The purpose of this exercise, especially in the context of understanding the business of the company, is for the investor to understand, by plotting himself, how the business of the company translates to its P&L account and the cost and revenue structure. Furthermore, plotting the data for two to three years, enables the investor to review the trend in each of these elements, in the context of the macro-economic and regulatory environment which has prevailed in the corresponding past years. This will in turn help the investor in estimating the trends in the future performance of the company.

Once the investor has completed this step, he ought to take a step back and look at the past financials of the company with a fresh perspective especially putting these in the context of the size of the company and its business. By comparing the past financial performance trends of the company with how the business of the company looks, the investor will be able to tell whether the business of the company is in an uptrend or the company is struggling. In case the company is struggling, the investor will be able to tell whether this is because of the challenges to the product or service segment of the company, or its high financial leverage or other factors. Furthermore, on putting the profitability figures in the context of the size of the company the investor will get a sense of the relative size of the company to its earnings.

Last, but not the least, having already studied and understood the business of the company, the performance being seen in terms of numbers juxtaposed with the business environment will give the investor a proper perspective regarding the company rather than a typical analysis of financials in vacuum.

4. STEP 4 – PROJECTING THE PERFORMANCE

Once the above steps have been completed and the investor has a broad sense of the business of the company, its size and capital structure, as well as the structure of its P&L, one proceeds to the next and most critical step...

To plot the projected performance of the company for the ensuing two to three years.

The plotting of the performance of the company for the ensuing years requires a number of assumptions to be made as well as a fair understanding of the business of the company. If you reach this step but are not confident of plotting such projections, it is then recommended that you read more about the company including available research reports on the company as well as the industry it operates in. In case the company in question follows the practice of giving annual guidance as is done by companies such as Infosys, then the same may also be used as a basis for the projections and tweaked by the investor on the basis of his views on the prospects of the business of the company.

If despite an in-depth study on the business and prospects of the company, clarity on its projected earnings evades you, then it is best to abandon the company in question as an investment target and look at other candidates.

However, in case you have gained a fair understanding of the business segments of the company then you proceed with this step of plotting the earnings of the company for the ensuing years.

Broadly, this step would proceed with your estimating the revenue figure expected for each segment of the company based on the expected performance of the company in each business segment. This should be plotted having regard to the expected unitary sales and pricing of the product of the company, keeping in mind the trend in the recent years as well as the expected macro-economic factors, business cycle and changes to the product mix of the company.

Once the revenue figures are projected, the gross margin would need to be projected either based on the historical gross margin percentages of the company or based on the expected margins for each segment as may be estimated by the investor based on his analysis of the of the product mix of the company, raw material costs as well as the expected pricing pressures in view of competition.

The indirect overheads may then be projected based on past trends as a percentage of revenue or based on the growth rate seen in these costs in the past trends.

By deducting the indirect overheads from the Gross Margin figure you would arrive at the EBIDTA. The EBIDTA margin as a percentage of revenue can then be compared with the historical EBIDTA margin actually reported by the company to gain perspective.

The interest income and interest charge would be plotted based on the cost of borrowing as well as the rate of return expected to be generated by the company with respect to surplus funds. While computing these, the investor would plug in his assumptions on the expected trend in interest rates based on the macro-economic environment and the fiscal and monetary policy of RBI. The borrowing level would be estimated based on the expected cash to be generated by the company from its operations and whether the company will use the cash to pay down the debt or raise additional debt for funding the expected capex by the company.

The depreciation charge may be projected based on the fixed asset block of the company as well as expected capital additions and applying thereon the average rate of depreciation.

By deducting the Interest charge and depreciation charge from EBIDTA and adding the interest income, one would arrive at the PBT figure.

From the PBT figure, applying the expected tax rate, one would arrive at the PAT figure for the company.

Upon plotting the above figures in the projected P&L of the company, you would be able to decipher the trend in the company's performance in terms of Revenue, Gross Margin, EBIDTA, PBT and PAT.

Taking a step back and reviewing such a projected P&L with fresh eyes would give the investor insight on what the prospects of the company look like, how the earnings and other metrics are shaping up in view of the business prospects of the company and whether or not the prospects of the company translate to superior earnings for the shareholders.

Once the projected P&L of the company is in place, this can be compared with the actual quarterly performance results of the company as declared from time to time and based on such actual performance, the projected P&L assumptions can be tweaked.

As the years progress, the P&L for the succeeding years can be plotted and the preceding years can be changed from projected P&L to actual numbers. The investor would thus, be able to keep the valuation model so devised constantly updated without major difficulty and also be able to validate his assumptions and understanding of the business against the actual performance thereof. The continuous study of the quarterly results and tracking the business performance of the company vis-à-vis the developments in the business environment will progressively deepen the understanding of the investor of the business of the company and aid in greater refinement of his analysis over time.

5. STEP 5 – PUTTING THE VALUE OF THE COMPANY IN PERSPECTIVE

Using the output of the above steps it would now be possible for the investor to gain a perspective on the real value of the company.

This can be done by deriving a few key valuation parameters using the data plotted above.

By dividing the market capitalization of the company by the projected PAT figure for the ensuing years, one would arrive at the forward PE ratio of the company.

Similarly, by dividing the Enterprise value of the company by the projected EBIDTA figure you would arrive at the forward EV/EBIDTA ratio of the company.

Further, in case of a manufacturing or other similar company, by dividing the Enterprise value of the company by the installed capacity, you would arrive at the present per tonne valuation of the company and by dividing the future projected EBIDTA of the company by installed capacity the investor would be able to get a sense of the earnings generated by the company per unit.

Other ratios may also be computed such as return on capital (by dividing EBIDTA by the Enterprise Value), Return on Equity (by dividing the PAT by the Shareholder Funds i.e. Equity plus free reserves) and Interest coverage ratio (by dividing the EBIDTA by the interest cost).

A study of the above ratios in the context of the multiples prevailing for the broader market as well as the multiples prevailing for the peer companies, would in most cases give the investor clarity on not only whether the company in question is cheaply valued and worth investing in but also a sense of the upside it offers on investment. For instance, a company that quotes at a low PE ratio based on current earnings may be found to be adequately valued when the investor computes the PE ratio using the projected earnings which may be bleak. In contrast, a company that quotes at a high PE ratio based on current earnings may be found to be cheaply valued when compared with the high growth expected in its profits in the ensuing years. Thus in this manner the valuation ratios would be put in context of the business prospects and future earnings of the company as opposed to being seen on a stand-alone basis where they can yield unreliable inferences.

The investor would thus be able to arrive at a sense of the real value of the company and the extent of it's under or over valuation.

A sample of a projected P&L for a company engaged in the mining business, being plotted as per the above exercise is shown below for reference.

All figures in INR Crores except where indicated otherwise	2014-15	2015-16	2016-17	2017-18
GROSS TURNOVER	12,347	6,456	10,200	12,791
OTHER OPERATING INCOME	9	2	-	-
REVENUE FROM OPERATIONS	**12,356**	**6,458**	**10,200**	**12,791**
DIRECT COSTS	331	356	370	399
ROYALTY	1,390	883	1,530	1,919
ROYALTY %AGE	11%	14%	15%	15%
SELLING EXPENSES	1,168	417	659	826
SELLING EXPENSES %AGE	9%	6%	6%	6%
GROSS MARGIN	**9,467**	**4,802**	**7,641**	**9,647**
GROSS MARGIN %	**77%**	**74%**	**75%**	**75%**
EMPLOYEE COSTS	703	675	700	720
OTHER COSTS	999	946	900	940
EBIDTA	**7,765**	**3,181**	**6,041**	**7,987**
EBIDTA Margin %	62.84%	49.26%	59.22%	62.44%
DEPRECIATION	173	209	216	216
INTEREST INC	2267	1774	1,559	1,909
INT COST	0	65	71	71
PBT BEFORE EXCEPTIONAL ITEMS	9,859	4,681	7,313	9,609
EXCEPTIONAL GAIN/(LOSS)	-113	-184	0	0
PBT AFTER EXCEPTIONAL ITEMS	9,746	4,497	7,313	9,609
TAX	3,346	1,476	2,437	3,203
EFFECTIVE TAX RATE	34%	33%	33%	33%
PAT	6400	3021	4,876	6,406
EPS*	16.16	7.63	12.31	16.71
P/E	8	14	9	7
MARKET CAPITALIZATION	51084	43164	43164	43164
ENTERPRISE VALUE	32,748	28,548	24,265	16,485
EV/EBIDTA	4.2	9.0	4.2	1.7

*Calculated on the basis of the shares outstanding at the end of the relevant financial year

The above projected P&L and ratios of the company give a bird's eye view of the future of the company in question. After having understood the core business of the company in question when the investor would have populated the above P&L the investor would see that the company after having seen a dip in its earnings in the immediately preceding year due to declining commodity prices, is poised for a good growth curve both in terms of the revenue and profitability at the back of a favourable price cycle and higher production levels. The EPS and EBIDTA of the company are slated to grow exponentially in view of the high operating leverage of a mining business and in this context the forward EV/EBIDTA multiple and P/E ratio of the company are also reasonable.

By putting the business prospects of the company in the context of the macro-economic environment that the company operates in, the investor would thus be able to assess whether the growth prospects of the company are realistic and how the company compares with its peers.

A decision on investing in the company can thus be reached in this manner without resorting to detailed DCF or cash flow modelling. The key, of course, lies in understanding the business of the company and being able to ascertain its future prospects and projected earnings. The efficacy of the above method, however, turns totally on the assumptions of the investor about the future business of the company and it is thus of utmost importance that the investor obtain a proper understanding of the future business prospects of the company in the context of the various factors affecting the same.

Some case studies of real life Indian companies are presented below to help illustrate the above.

1. CAIRN INDIA

Step 1 – Understand the business.

Cairn India is engaged in oil & gas business. It has been operating in the upstream segment i.e. exploration & production with oil & gas assets situated in Rajasthan and other locations in India.

It is one of the few companies in the private sector in this segment of business in India.

Cairn has achieved tremendous success in its E&P business over time under the aegis of Cairn UK – the UK based independent oil & gas upstream company which promoted Cairn India.

After achieving exploration success in its fields in Rajasthan, Cairn commenced production of crude oil from these fields in early part of the century. The technical team of Cairn has shown perseverance in producing what is decidedly a more difficult variety of crude being highly waxy and difficult to produce. As an operator, Cairn went on to lay the requisite pipeline network to produce and evacuate the crude so produced and hit production levels of 175,000 barrels of crude oil per day.

As a business, Cairn has been present in a high risk business of oil & gas exploration. Its prospects have been promising after the development and production from its Rajasthan fields and the other assets acquired and under exploration by Cairn have also appeared promising. However, given the inherent nature of the oil and gas exploration business there are frequent write-offs or impairment of assets when oil wells drilled turn out to be dry or the reserves estimated in an asset need to be written down on the back of revised estimates. After having surmounted the initial risk hurdle of the exploration in Rajasthan and reached production stage from such fields the company has been churning out cash year on year with the help of the production from the fields with the infrastructure being in place.

There was a change of the promoter group when Cairn UK sold its stake in the company to Vedanta Group – an Indian promoter family group led by Mr. Anil Aggarwal.

The market capitalization of the company went up to INR 65,000 crores on the back of peak production and peak crude oil prices of USD 100+ per barrel.

However, in 2015, the prospects of the business of Cairn have been hit by the tremendous fall in crude oil prices in the international market which have slid from USD 100 per barrel to USD 40 per barrel in 2015.

An investor looking to invest in a company such as Cairn would thus need to understand the macro situation around the crude oil demand and supply as well as the prospects of various assets held by Cairn India, in India as well as abroad to determine the expected production profile of the assets and the per barrel realization.

Furthermore, understanding the business of a company such as Cairn would also require the investor to track the tax structure around production and selling of crude oil. While there has been a tax holiday around exploration and production of crude oil, there has also been levied a cess by the Government of India on crude oil which dents the profitability of Cairn.

A detailed study of the crude oil demand supply scenario around the world with policy stance of oil producing nations such as Saudi Arabia and other OPEC nations, an analysis of the expected crude oil prices in the near future and a study of each of the assets held by the company in India as well as overseas to determine the expected production profile and expenditure are some of the essential ingredients of understanding the business of Cairn in depth.

Step 2 - Company's Size, Current Valuation and Capital Structure

As discussed in Step 2 above, the size of Cairn India has been plotted in terms of the market capitalization, debt, cash and enterprise valuation thereof with reference to its consolidated balance sheet as on 31st March 2016 below. The unitary metrics i.e. the reserves have also been plotted as these are relevant in the case of a company such as Cairn India.

All figures in INR Crores except where indicated otherwise	2015-16
NO. OF SHARES	187
MARKET PRICE	150
MARKET CAPITALIZATION	28,050
SHAREHOLDER FUNDS	48,792
DEBT	0
CASH	17,385
NET DEBT	-17,385
ENTERPRISE VALUE	10,665
2P RESERVES (MN BARRELS)*	503
EV/BARREL (USD)	3.53

* Oil and Oil equivalent - net interest of Company out of gross reserves

Cairn India as a company has a share capital base of about 187 crore shares.

At the market price of INR 150 per share the company's market capitalization is INR 28,000 crores approximately.

The company does not carry any significant debt on its balance sheet. On the other hand, it is a cash rich company with cash and current investments to the tune of INR 17,400 crores.

Thus, the company has an Enterprise Value of INR 10,600 crores approximately.

Given the 2P (Proven and probable) reserves of oil and oil equivalent of 503 million barrels falling to the share of Cairn under the relevant production sharing agreements, as disclosed in their annual return, the company quotes at an enterprise value which is below USD 4 per barrel of oil available to be produced as opposed to the global benchmark crude price which quotes in the range of USD 40 to 50 per barrel.

Step 3 – Past Operating Performance

The operating performance of the company in financial years ending March 2014, 2015 and March 2016 is populated below.

All figures in INR Crores except where indicated otherwise	2013-14	2014-15	2015-16
GROSS TURNOVER	18,761	14,646	8,625
REVENUE FROM OPERATIONS	**18,761**	**14,646**	**8,625**
DIRECT EXPENSES	4,058	4,565	4,698
GROSS MARGIN	14,703	10,081	3,927
GROSS MARGIN %	78.37%	68.83%	45.53%
OTHER EXPENSES	1016	1557	610
EBIDTA	13,687	8,524	3,317
EBIDTA MARGIN	72.95%	58.20%	38.46%
DEPRECIATION	2,297	2,569	3,107
INTEREST INCOME	1,502	1,809	2,008
INTEREST COST	41	20	26
PBT	12,851	7,744	2,192

Equity:In

All figures in INR Crores except where indicated otherwise	2013-14	2014-15	2015-16
EXCEPTIONAL GAIN/(LOSS)		-2,633	-11,674
(TAX)/TAX CREDIT	-417	-629	-3
PAT	12,434	4,482	-9,485
EFFECTIVE TAX RATE	3%	12%	0%
EPS*	65.10	23.97	-50.72
P/E	5	9	n/a

*Calculated on the basis of the shares outstanding at the end of the relevant financial year

A study of the above would show that the revenue of Cairn India declined heavily from 2014 to 2015 and even further in 2016. A careful reading of the annual report of the company would reveal that the production of the crude oil by the company was more or less constant at about 175,000 barrels per day and the decline in the turnover was primarily on account of the decline in crude oil prices from USD 100 per barrel levels to USD 40 per barrel levels.

Consequently, the gross margin of Cairn has also declined from ~80% levels to ~45% levels and the EBIDTA margin from ~70% to ~40%.

The Earning Per share of the company has also declined from a healthy INR 65 per share to INR 24 per share in 2015 and a negative number in 2016.

The case of Cairn India is a classic case which demonstrates that the valuation ratios if considered in vacuum, could lead to disastrous results. Consider the case of an investor who may have looked at Cairn India in March 2015 at which time the stock was quoting at INR 220 per share.

On a stand-alone basis, Cairn India was still quoting at a PE ratio of about 9 at the end of FY 2014-15. To someone who would rely solely on such a ratio, Cairn would appear to be a lucrative investment candidate given that the company was quoting at a single digit PE ratio versus the broader market which was quoting in double digits. In fact the stock of Cairn would have also appeared to be a worthwhile investment given its decline from highs of INR 350 per share to INR 220 per share. However, a basic analysis of the above data i.e. the operating performance of the company tells a different story.

As a company, Cairn had been struggling in 2014 and 2015 not only on account of the decline in the crude oil price but also the fact that in 2015 it has an exceptional write-off of INR 2,600 crores i.e. INR 14 per share on account of the write-off of exploration expenses and impairment of asset. Such a huge exceptional loss occurred due to the company taking a write-off of expenses incurred by it for exploration of certain oil assets which have not resulted in oil discovery or have otherwise proven to be commercially unviable for production and have thus been abandoned. Such write-offs, while typical for an oil and gas exploration company, are exaggerated in a low crude oil price regime where certain oil assets or wells drilled, though showing oil reserves may not be economically viable to produce given the low crude oil price realization. Further write-offs in the industry also include write down of estimated oil reserve values due to the fallen crude prices.

In fact as the situation unfolded in 2015-16, the performance of Cairn India suffered even further with revenues declining and a further exceptional write-off of INR 11,000 crores i.e. INR 60 per share! This write-off led to Cairn India recording one of the highest ever losses in its history – a loss of INR 9,400 crores or INR 50 per share.

The consequential movement in the share price of Cairn Indian during this period is shown in the chart below.

A perusal of the chart would show that the stock price of the company performed in consonance with its business prospects and declined from INR 290 levels in March/April 2013 to INR 150 levels in March 2016. This clearly demonstrates the importance of the second criterion for picking an investment i.e. the business prospects of the company. A lay investor relying solely on financial information would have found Cairn India as an attractive investment in April 2014 given its high EPS, high cash balance, low enterprise value and low PE ratio. However, an investor who would have considered the future business prospects of Cairn in view of the sliding crude oil prices would have perhaps stayed away from the high risk stock rather than taking a position and ending up staring at a loss of 50% on his purchase price.

Step 4 – *Projecting the Performance*

Projecting the performance of a company such as Cairn, from March 2016 forward, requires analysing and forming a view regarding the quality of assets it holds, the expected production levels from the various fields, the Capex and Opex required and the expected net back from each barrel of oil that it would produce in the ensuing years. A view also needs to be formed regarding the crude oil price that would prevail in the ensuing years.

The projection shared below has been done on the basis of the main assets of Cairn India being in Cambay, Rajasthan and Ravva. The expected productions from these assets for the years 2016-17 and 2017-18 has been plotted and a view regarding the crude oil prices has been taken to arrive at the expected revenue. Based on the view regarding the crude oil prices, gross margin percentage has been taken and interest and depreciation plotted based on the fixed asset block and debt expected for the company.

The major elements which may throw the projected performance of the company off the track are, the underperformance or outperformance of crude oil prices as against the assumed levels, and the company incurring further major write-offs in the form of asset impairments or wasteful exploration expenditure.

The projection given below assumes a constant 'bottomed out' crude oil price of USD 40 per barrel and a declining production profile for the assets of Cairn India with no significant discovery of oil kicking in. At the same time it is assumed that capital expenditure being incurred by Cairn would be marginal, in view of recent impairments in exploration assets, low crude oil price and no major exploration program in the offing.

All figures in INR Crores except where indicated otherwise	2016-17	2017-18
GROSS TURNOVER	8,327	8,459
REVENUE FROM OPERATIONS	**8,327**	**8,459**
DIRECT EXPENSES	4,750	5,040
GROSS MARGIN	3,577	3,419
GROSS MARGIN %	42.96%	40.42%
OTHER EXPENSES	710	733
EBIDTA	2,867	2,686
EBIDTA MARGIN	34.43%	31.75%
DEPRECIATION	3262	3425
INTEREST INCOME	1,912	2,435
INTEREST COST	31	33
PBT	1,486	1,662
EXCEPTIONAL GAIN/(LOSS)	-	-
(TAX)/TAX CREDIT	-120	-165
PAT	1366	1497
EFFECTIVE TAX RATE	8%	10%
EPS	7.31	8.01
P/E	21	19
MARKET CAPITALIZATION	28,050	28,050
ENTERPRISE VALUE	5,917	829
EV/EBIDTA	2.1	0.3

A perusal of the above projections would show that with conservative assumptions Cairn India would end up doing an EPS of about INR 8 per share which would be a PE ratio of 19 pegged to the forward earnings of FY 2017-18. Furthermore, the rich cash balance and nil debt position of Cairn would yield a successively lower Enterprise Value.

Step 5 – *Putting the value of the Company in perspective*

The above analysis puts the position and prospects of Cairn India in perspective. An investor who studies the oil market globally would know that the demand supply situation does not look bullish insofar as the pricing of crude oil as a commodity is concerned. With the greater influx of supply, newer technologies for production and shift to alternative fuels, crude oil prices have declined and continue to stagnate in the USD 35 to 45 per barrel range. The major institutions including IEA do not project much higher prices. OPEC member countries are refusing to cut back on production and with the re-introduction of crude from Iran post the removal of US sanctions the supply situation has only worsened. As such, the prospects of crude oil recovering to previous highs of USD 100 levels seem remote.

In the case of a company such as Cairn, it has met limited success in its new exploration assets other than Rajasthan, which accounts for the bulk of its production. As a block, Rajasthan block of Cairn is reaching its peak production and appears to be set to start declining.

The low crude prices coupled with the stagnating/declining production does not bode well for the business prospects of Cairn India. Add to this the fact that the company also bears the brunt of write-offs of exploration costs and impairment in asset values due to lower crude oil price or downward revision of its reserve estimates.

The fact that the company has huge cash reserves does not by itself augur well for the company where it is not able to find profitable areas for deployment of such cash reserves. Moreover in the low crude oil price regime, the management of Cairn has been vocal about their intention not to aggressively pursue exploration activities having burnt its fingers with certain write-offs in the recent past.

All in all, even though the company quotes at low EV/EBIDTA multiple, the investor would not be encouraged about the long term prospects of the company given that the bulk of the PBT of the company is generated by way of interest income and not the operating profits of the company. Thus, the valuation of the stock would not appear cheap when considered in the above context. As such an investor would have reasonable clarity on Cairn India as an investment at the end of the above analysis. The investor, after having gone through this exercise and understood the financials and valuation of Cairn in the context of its underlying business, would be able to track the company's progress, and as and when any of the assumptions regarding crude oil prices, expected production levels or exploration successes changes, the investor would be able to ascertain whether the changed business prospects of the company merit an investment in the company by plotting these against the expected performance of the company.

2. ADANI POWER

Step 1 – Understand the business.

Adani Power Limited (APL) is a company owned and promoted by the Gautam Adani led Adani Group.

APL is in the business of setting up and operating merchant power plants in the thermal (coal based) power space. APL has set up and operates power plants in Gujarat, Maharashtra and Rajasthan with an aggregate capacity of ~10,000 MW. The thermal power plants have been set up using super critical technology and have been executed and commissioned on a timely basis. APL has further tied up the sale of part of its power generation output on long term basis by way of power purchase agreement (PPA) with state electricity boards (SEBs) of various states.

Adani Group entity, and a sister concern of APL, Adani Transmission Limited has also laid down transmission lines for transmission and sale of power to adjoining states.

Even though India has been a ripe contender for build-up of power generation capacities given the extreme gap between demand and supply and the peak load power deficits in the country, the business prospects of APL have been dented and performance affected by the adverse macro-economic and regulatory changes of the past few years.

The factors which have had an adverse effect on APL, as well as the other power generation companies, in the past few years include the non-availability of coal from Coal India Limited at the agreed local rates which are lower than imported coal price. This has caused companies such as APL to import coal from overseas at higher prices and generate power leading to a higher variable cost of generation of power. The second factor which has added to it's woes is the SEBs refusing to pay higher rates under the PPA owing to the higher coal cost which is typically a pass through to the buyer.

To add insult to injury, the dues of the SEBs, even on the agreed rates, have remained unpaid owing to the tight financial situation of such State Electricity Boards. As a consequence, the power companies including APL have continued to bleed and have been litigating for compensation of tariff by the buyers against the higher fuel cost on one end, seeking allocation of domestic coal on the other end and also paying high interest cost on borrowed funds due to non-realization of dues from SEBs to top it all.

The power companies have thus not made for a good investment option in the past number of years in India even though, in the first decade of the 21st century the power business was one of the most lucrative businesses drawing most of the business houses including Jindals, Jaypee Group, Adanis, Reliance, GMR and Lanco in the wake of the projected demand supply imbalance in the power situation in the country. In fact the Government of India was itself encouraging the setup of thermal power plants by providing tax holidays to companies setting up such plants. Little would anyone have known that the tax holidays are essentially redundant where the company bleeds losses due to governmental policies and inefficiencies and thus doesn't have any taxable income to enjoy the exemption in the first place.

Anyone looking to invest in APL or any other power company would need to study and understand carefully the future outlook of the power sector in India, including the projected demand and supply as well as the regulatory and commercial aspects of the power generation business.

While the business prospects of a company such as APL may prima facie, still appear very promising given the continuing deficit of power generation capacity and the existing on ground generation assets, nevertheless the true business prospects need to be seen after considering the expected resolution of the PPA tariff compensation and availability of cheaper coal.

Thus the second criterion i.e. business prospects of APL requires an in-depth analysis by an investor. Assuming a view is formed that the future does, in fact, look more promising for APL in terms of its business prospects, one would then move to the third criterion and embark on a valuation study of the company.

Step 2 - Company's Size, Current Valuation and Capital Structure

The capital structure and key metrics of APL as a company based on its consolidated financials of March 2016 is plotted below.

All figures in INR crores except where indicated otherwise	2015-16
NO. OF SHARES	333
MARKET PRICE	30
MARKET CAPITALIZATION	9,990
SHAREHOLDER FUNDS	7,376
DEBT	36,200
CASH	1,000
NET DEBT	35,200
ENTERPRISE VALUE	45,190
INSTALLED CAPACITY (MW)*	10,440

* Includes 1200 MW of Udupi Power plant acquired from Lanco Infratech during the year

APL as a company did an IPO at INR 90 per share in 2009 pegging its market cap at INR 25,000 crores approximately at the time. By 2015, the value of the shares of APL had significantly fallen to INR 30 per share pegging its market cap at INR 10,000 crores approximately. With a net debt of INR 35,000 crores in its balance sheet, the enterprise value of APL is INR 45,000 crores approximately.

The stock price movement of APL over the last five years is provided in the following chart.

Equity:In

As would be seen from a cursory review of the above chart, the stock of Adani Power has not made for a good investment in the last five years. This has been a reflection/outcome of the business performance of the company over the last five years.

Against the above said market capitalization, APL has a book value of INR 7,300 crores and an operating capacity of 10,440 MW of thermal power approximately. In effect, the company as at the end of March 2016 quotes at an enterprise value of INR 4.3 crores per MW. As per the industry norms, this is close to the replacement cost of a power plant on per MW basis.

Step 3 – Past Operating Performance

The operating performance of APL in the last three years is populated below.

All figures in INR crores except where indicated otherwise	2013-14	2014-15	2015-16
GROSS TURNOVER	15,463	18,823	25,231
REVENUE FROM OPERATIONS	**15,463**	**18,823**	**25,231**
EXPS (EXCL INT & DEP)			
POWER PURCHASE	330	291	190
FUEL COST	9305	11614	14726
FUEL COST %AGE	60.18%	61.70%	58.36%
FOREIGN EXHANGE LOSS/(GAIN)			

All figures in INR crores except where indicated otherwise	2013-14	2014-15	2015-16
GROSS MARGIN	5,828	6,918	10,315
GROSS MARGIN %	37.69%	36.75%	40.88%
OTHER EXPENSES	1000	1439	1435
EMPLOYEE EXPENSES	235	320	327
EBIDTA	4,593	5,159	8,553
EBIDTA MARGIN	29.70%	27.41%	33.90%
DEPRECIATION	1937	1818	2336
INTEREST INCOME	231	241	201
INTEREST COST	4162	4863	5964
PBT	-1,275	-1,281	454
(TAX)/TAX CREDIT	1080	0	34
PAT	-195	-1281	488
NON RECURRING GAIN (LOSS)	-95	466	0
PAT AFTER EXCEPTIONAL ITEMS	-290	-815	488
EPS (WITHOUT NON RECURRING)*	-0.67	-4.46	1.47

*Calculated on the basis of the shares outstanding at the end of the relevant financial year

As would be seen from the above, the turnover of the company has increased from INR 15,000 crores in 2013-14 to INR 25,000 crores in 2015-16 as more and more of the power generation capacity has been commissioned and the plant load factor (PLF) has increased. The execution track record of the company has been consistent with the power units being constructed and commissioned despite the head winds that have been faced by all the companies in this sector. Unlike the competitors, none of the projects of APL have been put on hold.

The company has also shown EBIDTA positive performance with the EBIDTA growing from INR 4,500 crores in 2013-14 to INR 8,500 crores in 2015-16.

However, at the PAT level the company has continued to bleed with the high interest cost and depreciation plaguing the financials. The compensatory tariff has not come through, nor has the cheaper domestic coal from Coal India. This has necessitated the company to operate on the basis of imported coal, which is reflected in the high percentage of fuel costs ~60%.

The non-recovery of dues has strained the cash flow position of the company with mounting debt and the interest costs have grown from INR 4,000 crores in 2013-14 to INR 6,000 crores in 2015-16.

Consequently, the company has recorded losses of INR 1,200 crores (before tax) in two of the three preceding years.

In view of the aforesaid circumstances, the inevitable question is whether or not APL constitutes a good investment at the current price levels, especially when the stock price quotes at near all-time lows.

A decision on this point requires the investor to analyse the future business prospects of the company and how these translate to the projected earnings of APL.

Step 4 – Projecting the Performance

Projecting the performance of APL requires a view being formed regarding the expected coal price in the future, the average per unit power sale price (whether or not the company would receive compensatory tariff) and the plant load factor (PLF) i.e. the level of capacity that the power plants of APL would operate on.

Moreover a view regarding the macro-economic scenario as well as the regulatory environment in which the company operates needs to be formed by the investor when considering the future business prospects of APL. While projecting PLF levels, the investor also needs to consider the effect of renewable power generation in the form of solar and wind power coming on-stream with the thrust on these being provided by the Government in view of surmounting international pressures on reducing dependence on coal due to environmental factors.

Once a view is formed regarding the above factors, the metrics can be plugged into the projected performance and the projected P&L of APL for the ensuing two years can be populated.

The NDA-led Government of India has taken various steps in 2014 and 2015 to alleviate the problems of the power generation companies. In 2014, the government resumed the coal blocks whose allocation had been cancelled by the Supreme Court and convened an e-auction of the blocks. The blocks were allotted on a transparent basis to captive users and the power generation companies have been able to secure rights over mines to help reduce the dependence on imported coal. Further, the Government has launched the Uday scheme under which the State Electricity boards are proposed to be re-capitalized using bonds and liquidity provided whereby the dues of the power generation companies can be paid and their financial tightness eased.

The CERC (Central Electricity Regulatory Commission) has also acknowledged the rights of the power generation companies to be compensated for the higher fuel cost owing to imported coal.

On the global front, the prices of imported coal have also tapered off with the reduction in global commodity prices.

All in all, the power generation companies, at least the ones which have completed the execution of their projects and have weathered the storm of the preceding few years seem poised for better times in view of the macro-economic and regulatory developments.

Moreover the ability of some of the companies to refinance their borrowings in USD terms or at lower rates in view of the lower interest rate regime should also reduce their interest cost burden.

However, the recent Paris Climate Change accord in 2016 whereby pledge was made by leading nations of the world to reduce dependence on coal as a source of energy, is poised over a medium to long term, to affect the business prospects of the company adversely and would necessitate companies such as APL to shift to alternative sources of fuel for the power plants in the long term.

In view of the foregoing factors, it is assumed that APL would be able to sell power at an average price of INR 3.75 per unit with a PLF of 72% keeping in view the renewable sources of power coming into play. The imported coal is assumed to be available at price of USD 58-60 per tonne (including freight). The interest rate and debt are assumed to be declining and there is no major capex expected to be incurred by the company in the forthcoming years.

A tentative projection on the aforesaid basis is provided below.

All figures in INR crores except where indicated otherwise	2016-17	2017-18
INSTALLED CAPACITY (MW)	10440	10440
AVERAGE SELLING PRICE/KWH	3.75	3.95
PLF	72%	74%
NUMBER OF UNITS PRODUCED KWH	65,84,71,68,000	67,67,62,56,000
AUX CONSUMPTION	10%	10%
UNITS SOLD	59,26,24,51,200	60,90,86,30,400
PROJECTED REVENUE	22,223	24,059
COAL GCV (KcAL/KG)	5500	5500
PLANT HEAT RATE (KcAL/KWH)	2250	2250
COAL CONSUMPTION (KG/KWH)	0.41	0.41
FOB COAL COST USD/TN	43.00	44.00
FREIGHT	15.00	15.00
LANDED COST USD/TN	58.00	59.00
LANDED COST INR/KG	3.83	4.01
FUEL COST/KWH	1.57	1.64
GROSS TURNOVER	22,223	24,059
REVENUE FROM OPERATIONS	**22,223**	**24,059**
EXPS (EXCL INT & DEP)		
POWER PURCHASE	210	220
FUEL COST	10,312	11,108
FUEL COST %AGE	46.40%	46.17%
FOREIGN EXHANGE LOSS/(GAIN)		
GROSS MARGIN	11,702	12,731
GROSS MARGIN %	52.66%	52.92%
OTHER EXPENSES	1510	1550
EMPLOYEE EXPENSES	350	360
EBIDTA	9,842	10,821
EBIDTA MARGIN	44.29%	44.98%
DEPRECIATION	2,350	2,300
INTEREST INCOME	0	0
INTEREST COST	4,279	3,810

All figures in INR crores except where indicated otherwise	2016-17	2017-18
PBT	3,213	4,711
(TAX)/TAX CREDIT	-1060	-1555
PAT	2152	3156
NON RECURRING GAIN (LOSS)	0	0
PAT AFTER EXCEPTIONAL ITEMS	2152	3156
EPS (WITHOUT NON RECURRING)	6.46	9.48
P/E	5	3
MARKET CAPITALIZATION	9990	9990
ENTERPRISE VALUE	41,688	40,231
EV/EBIDTA	4.2	3.7
EV CRORES/MW	3.99	3.85

Based on the aforesaid assumptions the company is conservatively expected to increase its gross margin to 52% and achieve an EBIDTA of INR 9,800 crores and INR 10,800 crores respectively in FY 2016-17 and 2017-18. The EPS expected is INR 6.50 per share and INR 9.50 per share.

Step 5 – Putting the value of the Company in perspective

Assuming the above performance metrics, the financials of APL give a clear view to the investor regarding the EV/EBIDTA multiple and PE ratio of APL based on forward earnings.

Pegged to 2017-18 earnings, APL would expectedly enjoy an EV/EBIDTA multiple of 3.7 and a PE ratio of 3. Further the company continues to quote at a price which is below the replacement cost of the power plants it operates.

More than the valuation ratios, the above metrics, in the context of the business positioning of the company as well as the developments in its business environment indicate that with every incremental improvement in the various factors such as power tariff, reduction in interest cost, cheaper coal, the gain in the company's performance would be exponential given that the company's operating assets and infrastructure are in place to capitalize on these. Add to this the share price of the company having fallen to all-time lows over the last five years, any improvement in the financial performance of the company, as has started to show from 2015-16 onwards, would compel a re-rating of the stock and generate possibly multiplier returns for the investor.

Further, put in perspective of broader market indices as well as peer power companies, the aforesaid valuation ratios of APL are on the lower side and would thus give the investor a perspective on the value of APL, as compared to the current market price. The expected intrinsic value of APL based on the aforesaid metrics being higher than the market price of APL the investor would thus be motivated to buy the stock.

However, in case the investor finds causes of risks or concern to the business prospects of APL which call for assumptions different than those illustrated above, the investor would need to provide for alternative assumptions factoring in such considerations and arrive at the revised projected earnings of APL which would then form the basis for determining the value of APL shares and a decision to invest or avoid.

3. DLF

Step 1 – Understand the business.

DLF Universal Limited (DLF) is one of the premier real estate companies in India. It enjoys the legacy of not only developing real estate projects in the National Capital Region of India but de facto settling the township of Gurgaon with major apartment projects as well as plots which DLF has provided to the residents of Gurgaon.

Apart from the aforesaid residential projects DLF has also set up major commercial buildings and centres in Gurgaon with DLF Cyber city being home to the major multinational corporations operating out of the National Capital Region.

DLF has also set up and operates many shopping malls which are the hub of high end retail and entertainment in many parts of the country.

The real estate portfolio of DLF is now a mix of projects being developed for sale and those which are held by DLF and leased out to quality multinational tenants for an assured lease rental.

For the foregoing reasons, as also the evergreen love that Indians have for real estate, DLF has always been viewed as a lucrative company to invest in, and when it did its public offering in the year 2007, the IPO was generously priced valuing the company at a market capitalization of INR 100,000 crores with the promoters divesting 10% of the company and raising INR 10,000 crores. The IPO was lapped up by the punters and investors alike.

DLF, as a company has continued its business operations post listing, in the various segments of real estate. Residential projects have continued to be developed and sold, with premium segment projects such as Magnolias and Aralias, commercial projects in the form of office buildings have been constructed and sold too in the heart of Delhi such as DLF Southcourt and in Gurgaon such as DLF Horizon Centre.

Additionally, DLF has established a leasing vertical wherein it is constructing, owning and leasing out spaces and building up a healthy rental income stream rather than selling the spaces outright. DLF has also established a retail presence with its malls including high end malls such as DLF Emporio as well as a movie exhibition business in the form of multiplexes housed in DLF malls under the brand name of DT Cinemas.

The company has also continued to build up its land bank and launch projects at regular intervals.

The stock price of DLF since the time of its IPO has not fared well and anyone who would have bought the company in the IPO would inevitably be sitting with huge losses in their portfolio on this stock.

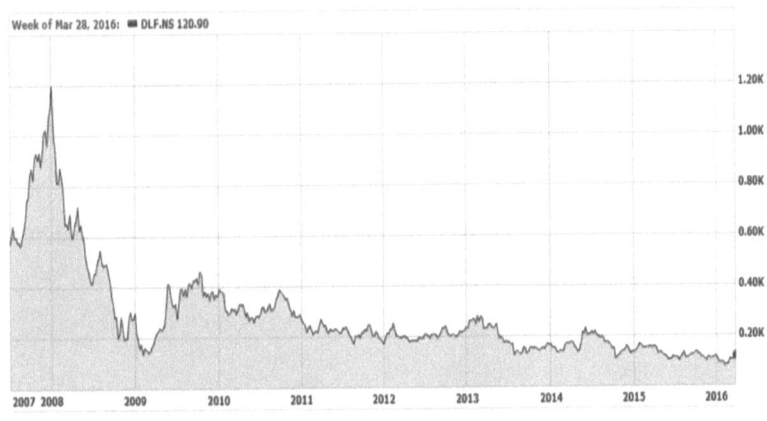

Equity:In

So what went wrong? And where does the DLF stock price go from here? For understanding this and for determining whether or not DLF makes for a good investment at current levels, one would need to proceed with a study of the past operating performance of the company and form a view of the projected earnings in light of the perceived future business prospects of the company.

The understanding of DLF's business is fairly straight forward and should not pose a challenge for most investors. However, what needs to be seen is the future business prospects of the company in the context of its size and past operating performance.

A view would need to be formed by the investor regarding the prospects of the real estate sector in the NCR region where DLF has its majority exposure. The investor would need to reckon the expected inventory liquidation by DLF and price level that may be achievable by DLF as a company.

Step 2 - Company's Size, Current Valuation and Capital Structure

The capital structure and key metrics of DLF as a company based on its consolidated financials of March 2016 is plotted below.

All figures in INR crores except where indicated otherwise	2015-16
NO. OF SHARES	178
MARKET PRICE	120
MARKET CAPITALIZATION	21,360
SHAREHOLDER FUNDS	27,360
DEBT	26,200
CASH + INVESTMENTS	3,466
NET DEBT	22,734

DLF as a company did an IPO in 2007 with a market capitalization value of INR 1,00,000 crores. The market capitalization has since fallen to INR 21,000 crores even below the book value of the company. The per-share price of the company has fallen to INR 120 per share and the net debt has mounted to INR 22,000 crores.

The enterprise value of the company thus, pegs at about INR 43,000 crores with the company boasting about 5.5 crore square feet under development and about 3 crore square feet being it's rented out inventory.

Step 3 – Past Operating Performance

The operating performance of DLF in the last three years is populated below.

All figures in INR Crores except where indicated otherwise	2013-14	2014-15	2015-16
GROSS TURNOVER	8,298	7,648	9,259
REVENUE FROM OPERATIONS	8,298	7,648	9,259
COST OF LAND/DIRECT COSTS	3880	3,284	4,050
GROSS MARGIN	4,418	4,364	5,209
GROSS MARGIN %	53.24%	57.06%	56.26%
EMPLOYEE COSTS	576	348	315
OTHER COSTS	1356	991	1028
EBIDTA	2,486	3,025	3,866
EBIDTA MARGIN	29.96%	39.55%	41.75%
DEPRECIATION	663	544	777
INTEREST INCOME	1491	519	559
INTEREST COST	2463	2303	2615
PBT	851	697	1,033
EXCEPTIONAL GAIN (LOSS)	-329	-67	-78
PBT AFTER EXCEPTIONAL ITEMS	522	630	955
(TAX)/TAX CREDIT	84	-158	-419
EFFECTIVE TAX RATE	-16.09%	23%	41%
PAT (after Minority Interest and prior period adjustment)	646	540	549
EPS*	3.63	3.03	3.08

*Calculated on the basis of the shares outstanding at the end of the relevant financial year

As would be seen from the above, the turnover of the company dipped in 2014-15 owing to a slowdown in the real estate market in the country. Not only did the area sold by the company take a hit, but there was a broad-based fall in the per square feet prices in the country both in the residential and commercial space.

In 2015-16, however, the turnover of the company has picked up while the gross margin has been more or less constant.

The EBIDTA of the company has also picked up from INR 3,000 crores to INR 3,800 crores owing to savings in employee and other costs. However the interest cost has risen owing to a higher debt level. The company continues to be strained in terms of its PBT and EPS which was a mere INR 3 per share in 2015-16.

DLF has struggled in its operating performance in the preceding three years much like most of the real estate companies. The company has not been able to sell inventories in the face of the real estate slowdown and the per-square feet realizations have also suffered. The debt of the company has continued to mount from INR 13,000 crore levels in 2013 to INR 23,000 crore levels in 2015-16. The company is thus faced with a mounting interest bill of INR 2,600 crores every year and is in dire need to improve its earnings and pare down the debt.

Step 4 – Projecting the Performance

Projecting the performance of DLF requires a view being formed regarding the real estate market in India (especially the NCR) in the forthcoming years including the effect of various governmental measures such as the Real Estate Regulation Act, an increase in circle rates and stamp duties as well as the seizure of black money.

One of the unique elements of the Indian real estate market is the fact that this sector has heretofore been the harbinger of black money and all real estate transactions have been known to have an element of black money or cash payment. In the case of listed companies, it is the wish of an investor that there are no cash transactions undertaken by the management of the company as there would be no way for an investor to track or forecast such cash based revenue flows.

The Indian real estate sector has also been largely unregulated and many real estate companies have gotten away with murderous malpractices including diversion of funds received from home buyers for a particular project to other projects, delay in construction and delivery of projects, alteration in layouts and project specifications to the detriment of the buyers. In fact in the case of DLF, the company has faced the levy of penalties by the Competition Commission of India to the tune of INR 600 crores on the ground that the company has misused its dominant position to the prejudice of customers. While this levy has been challenged by DLF the company continues to be plagued by such issues and its sales would somewhere be suffering on this account.

The law makers, to tackle the menace of malpractices by the real estate companies have enacted the Real Estate Regulation Act (RERA) which provides for the rules regarding utilization of proceeds from the sale of projects, changes in project specifications etc. The enactment of RERA is supposed to bring transparency and predictability in the working of real estate companies but will also affect their cash flows as proceeds of the sale of a particular project would need to be put in escrow and only used for construction and completion of such projects.

There has also been legislation which has been brought in permitting real estate companies to divest their rental portfolio into separate companies and sell stakes in such companies as Real Estate Investment Trusts/Companies. This has opened up the avenue for companies such as DLF to monetize their real estate rental book at good valuations with a view to generate cash flows to possibly pare down its high debt burden.

DLF has also consistently taken steps to sell off non-core assets including its investment in Aman Hotels and DT Cinemas, all with a view to ease over the tough financial times of the previous few years.

In view of all these developments, the investor would need to carefully study the position of DLF and determine how it is positioned in terms of its projects under development, its rental portfolio as well as its debt.

Once a view is formed regarding the above factors, the metrics can be plugged into the projected performance and the projected P&L of DLF for the ensuing two years can be populated.

A tentative projection in this regard is provided below on the basis of the segment wise analysis of the business of DLF in the ensuing years.

It has been assumed that the company would be able to sell 16% to 18% of its projects under development in the following years with an average realization of INR 6000 psf and cost of land and construction at INR 3000 psf. Regarding the rental vertical it has been assumed that the company would be able to increase its average realized rentals to INR 60 psf per month. The revenue from the other verticals i.e. maintenance and land sales has also been projected based on the assumptions regarding the annual growth rate in these based on the macro-economic growth and growth outlook for the real estate sector based on various real estate sector reports from consultants such as JLL and Knight Frank.

The company is also assumed to be retiring debt out of the cash flows generated to the tune of INR 1500 crores in the ensuing years.

Based on the projected revenue mix, margins and financials, the projected P&L as well as the segmental estimates of the company are plotted below:

All figures in INR Crores except where indicated otherwise	2016-17	2017-18
GROSS TURNOVER	10,079	11,014
REVENUE FROM OPERATIONS	**10,079**	**11,014**
COST OF LAND/DIRECT COSTS	4,004	4,408
GROSS MARGIN	6,075	6,606
GROSS MARGIN %	60.28%	59.98%
EMPLOYEE COSTS	347	381
OTHER COSTS	1079	1133
EBIDTA	4,649	5,091
EBIDTA MARGIN	46.13%	46.23%
DEPRECIATION	759	742
INTEREST INCOME	339	318
INTEREST COST	2964	2784
PBT	1,266	1,884
EXCEPTIONAL GAIN (LOSS)	-	-
PBT AFTER EXCEPTIONAL ITEMS	1,266	1,884
(TAX)/TAX CREDIT	-418	-622
EFFECTIVE TAX RATE	33%	33%

All figures in INR Crores except where indicated otherwise	2016-17	2017-18
PAT (after Minority Interest)	848	1262
EPS	4.76	7.09
P/E	22	15
MARKET CAPITALIZATION	18690	18690
ENTERPRISE VALUE	40,017	38,213
EV/EBIDTA	8.6	7.5
SEGMENTAL ESTIMATES		
SALE OF PLOTS		
LAND BANK (CR SFT)	30.8	30.8
PRICE/SFT (NET OF DEV COST)	3000	3000
TURNOVER	268.00	268.00
GROSS MARGIN %AGE	95%	95%
GROSS MARGIN	254.60	254.60
SALE OF FLATS		
SFT UNDER DEV (CR SFT)	5.55	5.55
AVG PRICE/SFT	6000	6000
LAND & CONSTRUCTION	3000	3000
ORDER BOOK	33300	33300
SFT SOLD	0.888	0.999
%AGE OF INVENTORY SOLD	16.00%	18.00%
TURNOVER	5,328	5,994
COST OF PROPERTIES	2,664	2,997
GROSS MARGIN %AGE	50%	50%
GROSS MARGIN	2,664	2,997
RENTAL		
RENTAL AREA UNDER DEV		
SFT RENTED	2.94	2.94
AVG RENT/SFT/ANNUM	700	750
TURNOVER	2,058	2,205
GROSS MARGIN %AGE	90%	90%
GROSS MARGIN	1,852	1,985

The above projections reflect that the company's gross margin is poised to improve to 60% levels on the back of improving turnover. The reduction in debt of the company would also aid in the company's PBT and PAT improving with the EPS going up to INR 7 by 2017-18.

Step 5 – Putting the value of the Company in perspective

The foregoing projections show that the financials of DLF would improve in case the assumptions regarding the real estate sector and the company's performance as plotted above pan out.

In such a case the company would tend to be valued at a multiple of 15 to the FY 17-18 earnings and an EV/EBIDTA multiple of 7. The investor, on comparing these multiples with those of other real estate players as well as the broader market, would be able to form a view regarding the investment worthiness of DLF.

The overall decision by the investor to invest in DLF or not would hinge on the perception of the investor regarding the future of the real estate sector and the risks to the operating performance of DLF in view of the macro-economic and regulatory developments as well as the execution track record of the company.

The investor would also need to form a view regarding the potential value unlocking of DLF's leasing business via the REIT model.

A continuous tracking of the development in the real estate sector on the ground level coupled with the actual sales and price realization of the real estate companies would give the investor a fair sense of the assumptions to be tweaked in projecting the future performance of DLF and a view regarding the intrinsic worth of the stock of the company.

4. M&M FINANCIAL SERVICES

Step 1 – Understand the business.

M&M Financial Services (MMFS) is a company that operates in the niche segment of providing credit to the rural population of India in the form of financing for tractors as well as other agricultural loans. The company started out as a finance arm of its sister concern Mahindra & Mahindra to finance tractor or other vehicles sold by M&M Motors. However, over a period of time the company was able to establish a deep seated network of distributors and financing channels in rural India so as to be able to finance third-party purchases as well.

The company thus represents a unique play on the economic prosperity trickling down to the rural sector in India.

The company has a straightforward business of lending to the rural population, primarily agriculturists and relies on its expertise of penetrating the rural market and building a book of solid loans around the rural population.

Anyone looking to invest in MMFS would need to understand the long term prospects of the rural economy in India as well as the quality of the assets held by the company in terms of its loan portfolio. Future prospects in terms of agricultural growth and the income pattern in the hands of the farmers would drive the growth in earnings of a company such as MMFS. On the other hand, poor agricultural growth, droughts, poor crops and lower realization in agricultural prices would inevitably lead to defaults in the loan obligations by the farmers and dent not only the earnings of MMFS but also its capital base.

Thus, an in-depth study of the rural economy in India, coupled with the trends in agriculture growth are an essential pre-requisite to determining the business prospects of MMFS.

Step 2 - *Company's Size, Current Valuation and Capital Structure*

The financial metrics of MMFS based on its consolidated financials as at 31st March 2016 have been plotted below.

All figures in INR crores except where indicated otherwise	2015-16
NO. OF SHARES	56
MARKET PRICE	290
MARKET CAPITALIZATION	16,240
NET WORTH	6,469
DEBT	21,265
CASH + INVESTMENTS	1,155
NET DEBT	20,110
ENTERPRISE VALUE	36,350

The above table indicates that the company has a share capital base of 56 crore shares with a market cap of INR 16,000 crores approximately. The company has a net debt of INR 20,000 crores which is primarily the deposits the company has taken to fund it's loan book. The enterprise value of the company is INR 36,000 crores.

A meaningful metric for the size of a company such as MMFS which is primarily engaged in lending or NBFC activities is the book value per share. The book value of the company's shares is INR 115 per share approximately as opposed to the market value of INR 290 per share.

Step 3 – Past Operating Performance

The operating performance of M&MFS for the past three years is populated below.

All figures in INR crores except where indicated otherwise	2013-14	2014-15	2015-16
GROSS INTEREST EARNED	5,275	6,021	6,554
OTHER INCOME	25	39	43
TOTAL REVENUE	**5,300**	**6,060**	**6,597**
INTEREST PAID	2,280	2,643	2,869
GROSS MARGIN	3,020	3,417	3,728
GROSS MARGIN %	57.25%	56.75%	56.88%
EMPLOYEE COSTS	495	567	704
DEPRECIATION	26	45	46
WRITE-OFFS	519	849	1098
OTHER COSTS	518	556	657
PBT	1,461	1,400	1,223
EFFECTIVE TAX RATE	34.02%	34%	36%
(TAX)/TAX CREDIT	-497	-475	-437
PAT	964	925	786
EPS*	17.21	16.52	14.04
EBIDTA	1,487	1,445	1,269
EBIDTA MARGIN	28.06%	23.84%	19.24%

*Calculated on the basis of the shares outstanding at the end of the relevant financial year

It would be seen that the performance of the company in the preceding three years has been robust with the gross interest earned increasing from INR 5,300 crores *to* INR 6,600 crores. This has been on the back of an increasing loan book of the company which has risen year on year, as has the company's reach through augmentation of its distribution network.

The net interest margin earned has also increased from INR 3,000 crores to INR 3,700 crores. The gross margin that the company has been earning, which is the interest spread it makes, has been stable at about 57%.

However, at the PAT level, the performance of the company has not shown similar pace of growth primarily due to write-offs and provisioning for non-performing advances (NPAs). NPAs being a bane of the banking and finance sector are an even more pronounced risk when dealing with rural or unorganized sector borrowers. The write-offs have increased from INR 500 crores to INR 1,000 crores and are a worrying indication regarding the asset quality and financial health of the loan book of MMFS.

As such, the PAT of the company has declined from INR 960 crores to below INR 800 crores in the last three years.

Step 4 – *Projecting the Performance*

For projecting the performance of the company over the next two years a view needs to be taken by the investor regarding the second criterion i.e. the future business prospects of the company. To evaluate this, a study needs to be undertaken regarding the rural sector's performance in the Indian economy with specific reference to the agricultural outlook. The disposable income of farmers is highly dependent on the performance of the agricultural sector which in turn depends on the crop yields, monsoons and the price realization.

The customer base of MMFS is thus sensitive to the above factors and the inherent asset quality is vulnerable to risks which may affect the above.

The investor would thus need to project the performance of the company based on a view formed on the above factors. The investor would also need to form a view regarding the loan book of MMFS, the spread of interest it is likely to earn in view of the interest rate regime as well as the quantum of write-offs expected in relation to the overall loan book of the company.

The investor would need to reckon the foregoing factors after taking into account management commentary regarding the loan book expansion and asset quality concerns. A view regarding the macro-economic interest rate trends and the monetary policy would indicate what the company is likely to incur as its cost of funds and the interest spread it is likely to earn in the future.

As we have seen in the performance of the company in the preceding three years, the write-offs can play spoilsport in years which otherwise see a robust financial performance by the company. Thus, careful determination of the asset quality of the company based on management commentaries and emerging trends is an essential element of the projection of the performance of the company.

A tentative projection for the next two years based on assumptions regarding the loan book, interest spread and other costs, is populated below.

All figures in INR crores except where indicated otherwise	2016-17	2017-18
LOAN BOOK		
NET WORTH OPENING	6,469	7,341
DEBT CLOSING	25,876	33,034
LOAN BOOK	31,345	39,374
SPREAD MARGIN	9%	9%
GROSS INTEREST EARNED	5,956	7,481
OTHER INCOME	50	55
TOTAL REVENUE	**6,006**	**7,536**
INTEREST PAID	2,588	3,303
GROSS MARGIN	3,418	4,233
GROSS MARGIN %	57.39%	56.58%
EMPLOYEE COSTS	750	775

All figures in INR crores except where indicated otherwise	2016-17	2017-18
DEPRECIATION	50	50
WRITE-OFFS	627	787
ADMIN OVERHEADS	690	715
PBT	1,301	1,905
EFFECTIVE TAX RATE	33%	33%
(TAX)/TAX CREDIT	-429	-629
PAT	872	1277
EPS	15.57	22.80
P/E	19	13
EBIDTA	1,351	1,955
EBIDTA MARGIN	22.50%	25.95%
MARKET CAPITALIZATION	16240	16240
ENTERPRISE VALUE	41,116	48,274
EV/EBIDTA	30.4	24.7
PRICE TO BOOK	2.21	1.88

In the foregoing projections, the loan book of MMFS has been projected on the basis of the available net worth, the write-offs of doubtful provisions made and the ability of MMFS to leverage the net worth. The gross interest earned and the net interest earned has been assumed based on the expected rate of interest that the company may charge from its customers as well as the cost of funds borrowed. It would be seen from the above that while the company's loan book is expected to grow, the gross margin would also likely hold up to previous levels. The main joker in the pack would be the extent of the write-offs the company would still be expected to take. While in the preceding two years such write offs have been as high as 5% to 6% of the loan book of the company, the write-offs at a 2% level have been projected in the above workings based on broader market trend and management commentaries.

Assuming the company achieves the above performance metrics in the ensuing years, it would do an EPS of INR 15 and INR 23 respectively and be quoting at a PE ratio of about 13 based on the projected FY 2017-18 earnings. Moreover the price to book ratio would be at about 2.

Equity:In

Step 5 – Putting the value of the Company in perspective

Evaluating the projected performance of the company over the next two years it would be seen by the investor that if the company is able to leverage its existing network of rural borrowers to grow its loan book, and is able to keep the NPA levels under check it would be able to deliver growth in the ensuing years.

Upon comparing the above numbers with the ratios of the broader market as well as the other peer banking and non-banking financial institutions in the background of the growth prospects of MMFS, the investor would thus be able to form a view regarding investing in the company.

An NBFC with the reach and monopoly of MMFS quoting at forward PE multiples of 13 and a price to book value of less than 2 would prima facie appear attractive as an investment proposition given the scale of the Indian rural market and the potential for growth given that the market remains largely unpenetrated.

However, a critical piece of the analysis would be the anticipated asset quality and write-offs since this would determine the real intrinsic value of the company. The investor would thus need to project the earnings of the company accordingly and thereafter evaluate the third criterion for determination of investment decision.

5. PVR CINEMAS

Step 1 – Understand the business.

PVR Cinemas is one of the foremost companies in India in the area of movie exhibition. Starting out with its flagship Priya cinema which garnered the lion's share of Hollywood movie exhibition revenues in Delhi in the 1990's, PVR has become a prime mover of the multiplex revolution and has grown to be one of the largest multiplex screen owners in the country with over 500 screens and presence in over 45 cities across India. The company has also developed unique movie watching experiences with PVR Directors cut, PVR Gold Class, PVR Icon and PVR Premiere category of movie halls.

The revenue streams of PVR originate primarily from movie exhibition i.e. ticket sales for multiplexes.

PVR also has revenues from F&B sales at its multiplex outlets. The unique proposition in this regard is the retail space that the company has been able to develop incidental to the multiplexes with 4.5 million square feet already existing and another 3 million under development. The substantial quantum of retail space has added a retail flavour to the company in terms of its earnings diversifying off movies tickets and including F&B sales and retail rentals, with F&B spends accounting for upwards of 35% of the ticket sale revenues for the company.

Additionally, the company has been able to build up a robust advertising revenue portfolio with leading companies advertising on its screens between shows, in the premises via sign boards and even ticket stubs.

While the understanding of the business of PVR is fairly straightforward, an investor should evaluate the business of the company in depth especially having regard to the competitive landscape in which it operates as well as the growth prospects of PVR's business. The growth prospects would, of course, be a function of the growth of the sector as a whole on the back of increased consumer spending, which is projected at upwards of 10% CAGR by industry reports, as well as PVR being able to retain and augment its market share in the movie exhibition space by offering distinctive movie going experiences. As of March 2016, the company boasted a market share of ~30% in Hollywood movies exhibition space and 20% in Bollywood movie exhibition space.

The ability of the company to augment its market share would basically depend on the number of screens that the company is able to add, as well as its branding, customer recall and quality of experience it delivers as opposed to its competitors.

In June 2015, with a view to augment its market position, PVR entered into an agreement to acquire DT Cinemas, the 39 screen cinema business of DLF in Delhi for an enterprise value of INR 500 crores.

An investor looking to invest in PVR cinemas would thus need to ascertain its business prospects by understanding the dynamics of the movie exhibition and retail segment in India, the competitive landscape of a company such as PVR and also the expected growth in the various segments in terms of consumer spends and margins. Further, the investor would also need to ascertain the regulatory framework within which PVR operates as well as the expected taxation structure given the high incidence of entertainment tax and VAT on ticket sales.

Step 2 - Company's Size, Current Valuation and Capital Structure

The capital structure and key metrics of PVR as a company based on its consolidated financials of March 2016 is plotted below.

All figures in INR crores except where indicated otherwise	2015-16
NO. OF SHARES	4.66
MARKET PRICE	850
MARKET CAPITALIZATION	3961
SH FUNDS	869
DEBT	636
CASH + INV	267
NET DEBT	369
ENTERPRISE VALUE	4,330
SCREENS	516
EV/SCREEN	8.39

PVR as a company has grown over time both in terms of its presence and number of screens as well as the market capitalization. The market capitalization based on its financials as at 31st March 2016 and its market price of INR 850 per share, was INR 4,000 crores. With a net debt of INR 370 crores, the company had a sizeable enterprise value of INR 4300 crores which translates to about INR 8 crores per screen.

The stock price of PVR has grown consistently over the last 3 years as can be seen from the chart below.

The company, in 2015, entered into a transaction to acquire 39 odd screens of DT Cinemas at a price of INR 500 crores i.e. 12.8 crores per screen. After going through the scrutiny of the Competition Commission of India, PVR was asked to leave out certain number of screens from the scope of the transaction and acquire the bulk of the business of DT at a revised price of INR 430 crores approximately.

Apart from the said transaction, the company is also expanding in terms of screen size organically.

Step 3 – Past Operating Performance

The operating performance of PVR in the last two years is populated below.

All figures in INR Crores unless indicated otherwise	2014-15	2015-16
NO. OF SCREENS	464	516
SEATS	1,09,253	1,18,124
FOOTFALLS (LACS)	592	696
SEATS/SCREENS	235	229
FOOTFALLS/SEATS/DAY	1.48	1.61
AVG TICKET PRICE	168	182
SALES PER HEAD	61	73
TICKET SALES REVENUE	824	1014
F&B SALES REVENUE	348	467
ADVERTISING REVENUES	168	206
OTHER REVENUES	47	78

All figures in INR Crores unless indicated otherwise	2014-15	2015-16
GROSS TURNOVER	1,481	1,874
REVENUE FROM OPERATIONS	**1,481**	**1,874**
OPERATING EXPENSES	1,276	1,539
EBIDTA	205	335
EBIDTA MARGIN	13.84%	17.88%
DEPRECIATION	117	125
INTEREST INCOME	4	24
INTEREST COST	78	84
PBT BEFORE EXCEPTIONAL ITEMS	14	150
EXCEPTIONAL GAIN/(LOSS)	-2	-6
PBT AFTER EXCEPTIONAL ITEMS	12	144
(TAX)/TAX CREDIT	-1	-23
EFFECTIVE TAX RATE	8%	16%
PAT	11	121
EPS*	2.65	25.97
P/E	234	33

*Calculated on the basis of the shares outstanding at the end of the relevant financial year

As would be seen from the above, the size of PVR has increased from 464 screens to 516 screens and the consequential turnover of the company has also increased from INR 1,500 crores in 2014-15 to INR 1,900 crores in 2015-16. The company has been able to increase the footfalls per seat as well as the average ticket price and sales of F&B per head. As a consequence, the EBIDTA margin of the company has expanded from 14% to 18%. The interest and depreciation charge not expanding proportionately, the PAT of the company jumped from INR 11 crores in 2014-15 to INR 120 crores in 2015-16.

All in all the company seems to be poised at the cusp of an upswing having overcome the hurdle of reaching a critical mass and the strong brand presence required to leverage itself into a larger geographical reach with economies of scale.

Step 4 – Projecting the Performance

Projecting the performance of PVR going forward requires the investor to form a view regarding the consumer spending growth in the context of the Indian economy. The investor needs to understand the competitive landscape of a company such as PVR and its ability or lack thereof to charge premium pricing from the customer for the tickets as well as the F&B spends by providing a distinctive cinema going experience. The investor also needs to form a view regarding the expected pace of growth in the company's screen portfolio as well as the margins it is expected to realize with the economies of scale.

The performance of PVR, for case study purposes has been projected for two years. To arrive at the projected performance an assumption has been made regarding the increase in the number of screens taking into account the DT cinemas deal.

Assumptions have also been made regarding the average ticket price and average spend per head, as well as the expected improvement in footfalls. Assumption has also been made regarding the increase in advertising and other revenues by the company.

The resulting projections are plotted below.

All figures in INR Crores unless indicated otherwise	2016-17	2017-18
NO. OF SCREENS	613	635
SEATS	140990	146050
FOOTFALLS (LACS)	849	933
SEATS/SCREENS	230	230
FOOTFALLS/SEATS/DAY	1.65	1.75
AVG TICKET PRICE	185	195
SALES PER HEAD	75	80
TICKET SALES REVENUE	1571	1819
F&B SALES REVENUE	637	746
ADVERTISING REVENUES	237	272
OTHER REVENUES	90	103

Equity:In

All figures in INR Crores unless indicated otherwise	2016-17	2017-18
GROSS TURNOVER	2,534	2,941
REVENUE FROM OPERATIONS	**2,534**	**2,941**
OPERATING EXPENSES	2,027	2,294
EBIDTA	507	647
EBIDTA Margin	20.00%	22.00%
DEPRECIATION	178	181
INTEREST INCOME	30	43
INTEREST COST	124	124
PBT BEFORE EXCEPTIONAL ITEMS	234	385
EXCEPTIONAL GAIN/(LOSS)	0	0
PBT AFTER EXCEPTIONAL ITEMS	234	385
(TAX)/TAX CREDIT	-77	-127
EFFECTIVE TAX RATE	33%	33%
PAT	157	258
EPS	33.60	55.29
P/E	25	15
MARKET CAPITALIZATION	3961	3961
ENTERPRISE VALUE	4,628	4,390
EV/EBIDTA	9.1	6.8
EV/SCREEN	7.55	6.91

With the increase in the number of screens to over 600 and a slight improvement in the average ticket price (ATP) as well as the spending per head (SPH) factors, the company is poised to see revenues upwards of INR 2,500 crores. With the increase in scale, the margins are also expected to improve to 20% in 2016-17 and 22% in 2017-18.

The depreciation and interest cost has been projected on the basis of the expected fixed asset block and debt levels of the company. As a consequence, the company is expected to do an EPS of INR 34 in 2016-17 and INR 55 in 2017-18. With such a healthy growth the company's PE ratio based on forward earnings of FY 17-18 is expected to be at 15 and the EV/EBIDTA multiple at 7. The company is expected to quote at an EV/Screen valuation of 7 crores.

Step 5 – *Putting the value of the Company in perspective*

Assuming the above performance metrics, the financials of PVR convey a healthy growth for the company, coupled with an expansion in its margins, a reduction in its net debt and leveraging of economies of scale for the company. The company represents a powerful proxy play on the Indian consumer demand growth story given its reach and presence in the niche segment to encash on the movie going love of large urban Indian population.

While on a stand-alone basis the PE ratio of 15 may appear high, when seen in the context of the strong brand the company is expected to build, its monopolistic presence in areas such as NCR as well as its reasonable valuation in terms of the EV/EBIDTA and EV/screen, the investor may find the intrinsic worth of the company to be better than its quoted price and may consider investing in the stock of the company.

The above case studies demonstrate how, once the investor has selected a company based on the first criterion i.e. suitable promoter group and has been convinced of the second criterion i.e. the future business prospects of the company based on the macro-economic environment, regulatory framework, competitive landscape and the company's business execution credentials, the investor would proceed with the evaluation of the third criterion for investment i.e. the valuation by projecting the performance of the company for the ensuing years. As discussed and illustrated, projecting of the performance of the company is a composite exercise which requires a detailed study and analysis of the past performance of the company, the future business prospects and assumptions regarding the company's performance based on the understanding of the business of the company.

Once the expected earnings of the company in view of its future business prospects has been plotted, the investor would be able to put the value of the company in perspective as compared with the multiples at which it trades, the expected multiples based on future performance as well as ratios such as EV/EBIDTA. The foregoing exercise would yield to the investor a sense of the valuation of the company.

If it is found that the company in question trades cheaper than the value it is expected to fetch in view of its future earnings growth, the investor would be convinced to proceed with investing in the company and in case it is found that the company in question trades costlier than the perceived value, the investor may take a call to avoid investing in the company or even shorting the stock in exceptional cases.

The application of the three basic criteria thus provides the investor with a conclusion regarding investment worthy companies and helps the investor reach a point where he is able to decide which company he should invest in and which ones he should avoid.

In fact, it is expected that, in the process of carrying out the three step evaluation of a company, the investor would not only develop an in-depth understanding of the company's business and its financials, but even before the end of the exercise, the investor would be able to arrive at a sixth sense instinct regarding the value of the company and whether or not it should be invested in.

The evaluation of the three main criteria by the investor is a continuing exercise, and even after the investor has undertaken a position in a company's stock, the investor needs to constantly follow the developments with respect to the company's promoters, it's business, and it's valuation in view of the quarterly earnings performance. The Investor needs to constantly update his analysis and projections in view of evolving dynamics of the regulatory and macro-economic environment and the actual performance of the company's business. Thus once the investor has taken a position in a company, he would need to constantly update and review the three main factors of investment in relation to the company to ensure the investment thesis continues to hold good and to re-assess the intrinsic value of the company with passage of time.

Apart from the three basic and main criteria for investment, there are certain secondary criteria for determining whether or not to invest in a company which should also be considered while evaluating a company. These secondary factors are discussed in the succeeding chapter.

CHAPTER 6

SECONDARY FACTORS

> *A company may fulfil the three main criteria and yet may not be suitable as an investment. This is where secondary factors come into play and ought to be tested before initiating a position in a company's stock.*

We have seen that the three criteria that are of main relevance in picking companies to invest in India are, the promoter profile, the business prospects of the company and the valuation of the company in question.

Once an investor identifies a company, he should start with profiling the promoter group and determining whether or not the promoter group is amenable to value creation for the minority shareholders and runs the company with the best practices in corporate governance. Once this criterion is fulfilled, the investor should take a deep dive in understanding the business of the company in question including the future growth prospects of the company as well as it's position of competitive advantage. This study and understanding of the business of the company is of paramount importance and precedes an analysis of the financials of the company. Once, and only once, the investor has gained a comfortable level of understanding of the business of the company and is convinced of the future growth prospects of the company, should the investor move to the third criterion i.e. valuation.

As we have discussed there are numerous methods of valuation of a company and there is no single right or wrong method. Each method has its merits and demerits and an investor should adopt the method which he is able to best understand and efficaciously implement. A method has been suggested in the preceding chapter which is meant to factor in the business prospects of the company while remaining relatively simple for a lay investor to adopt and implement.

Once the investor has arrived at a valuation, he would be able to form a view as to whether or not the company is cheaply valued in terms of the current market price of the stock and how much of an upside the company's stock holds.

We have also discussed in earlier chapters of this book that while picking stocks, there are certain factors which are not relevant and should not be the sole trigger for an investor to initiate a position in a company. These factors include corporate events, technical trends, regulatory events, entry or exit of major investors, novel ideas, promoter related news and mergers and acquisitions. As we have discussed, the taking of investment positions solely relying on such factors is fallacious and ought to be avoided even though we see the general practice in the market being in favour of such short-cut investment decisions.

At the same time, over and above the three main factors there are certain incidental factors which, though not a trigger for investing in a company, would nevertheless need to be taken cognizance of while initiating a position in a company. These factors can affect the performance of the stock price over the medium to long term and thus negate any thesis of returns built on the three main factors. While the incidental factors may be diverse and vary from sector to sector, some of the prominent incidental factors have been discussed below.

1. LEVERAGE

The level of financial indebtedness of a company is a material factor to be evaluated when taking an investment decision in a company.

A company, which may be managed by a promoter group with credible profile and having good future business prospects, may find itself cheaply valued in the current market due to a large debt overhang. High indebtedness of a company may be suppressing the earnings of the company on account of large interest burden. Further the cash flow position of the company may also be strained since the cash the business may be generating may be getting utilized for repayment of loans that may be maturing. As such the company may not be able to embark on meaningful capital expenditure programs to grow it's business undertaking.

Such a company may be avoided despite the fact that such a company would inevitably be quoting relatively cheap in the market. This is so, as despite the company's stock price quoting at low multiples the company is running the risk that the future earnings may not be able to grow adequately to service not only the interest burden but also the upcoming debt repayment instalments, leading to the company becoming a potential defaulter which would, in turn, precipitate margin calls on the company and on its shares which may have been pledged by the promoter group as collateral. As a consequence the stock price of the company may be driven successively lower and the investor may end up losing money on an ostensibly cheap stock.

In the Indian context, this risk becomes more exacerbated since the Indian economy has traditionally seen high cost of debt. As such, a highly leveraged company runs high risk of collapsing in case the earning prospects do not pan out as planned. The earnings of the company may also be affected by the macro-economic uncertainties in the country or by the regulatory events and the company would end up stumbling in its debt servicing efforts.

In fact, there have been many companies in sectors such as cement, infrastructure and steel which have leveraged the balance sheet to build the capital block for the company or to execute large project order books but have ended up seeing red in their P&L accounts as the business cycle has turned unfavourable or other business factors have not turned out as planned and the company has found itself in a debt trap. Some companies with high debt have also faltered due to the suboptimal execution of their intended business plans. Earnings of such companies, suppressed by the interest burden, see their stocks quote even below book value and may appear as a lucrative investment bet especially when one starts to eye the reversal of the commodity cycle on which these depend. However, some of these companies have failed to emerge out of the debt trap and have in fact been forced into liquidation, even though the commodity cycle may have turned in their favour subsequently.

One instance of such a company is Kingfisher airlines. A company that ran a credible and quality oriented airline operation but suffered under the adverse market conditions of high aviation fuel prices, low fares due to competitive price wars and high debt and interest burden.

The stock performance of Kingfisher Airlines is given below.

The stock continually languished and while in 2016 the airline industry was set to make a comeback on the back of lower crude oil prices and northward moving fares, the company did not sustain to see the light of such days and its aircrafts were grounded with the lenders moving the court for realization of their dues. The stock thus appearing to be cheaply valued ended up never performing for the investors while its competitors such as Jet Airways and Indigo have seen a reversal in their fortunes at the back of stronger execution and financial discipline.

Thus, a company with promising business prospects and appearing cheaply valued may yet be avoided in case of high leverage as this increases the risk of the company's failure with the slightest of things going wrong in its business plans.

Another example of a company which has suffered on account of high leverage is Electrosteel Steels Limited. Engaged in the business of steel manufacturing, the company with a capacity of 2.5 mmtpa found itself excessively leveraged with debt to the tune of INR 8,000 crores against an equity of INR 1,000 crores. When the steel cycle turned unfavourable the company was not able to service the debt burden or the interest of INR 500 crores. The stock price of the company has languished over the last many years below the par value of INR 10 per share and the company was one of the prominent companies which has been taken over by the lenders under the newly framed Strategic Debt Restructuring (SDR) scheme whereby the lenders are aiming for the turnaround of the company by seeking to divest the shareholding of the promoters in favour of an interested strategic investor. Thus despite the steel cycle turning favourable, a company such as Electrosteel has not been able to find it's footing and has succumbed to the pressure of excessive leverage.

2. STOCK PERFORMANCE

We have discussed that investment in a stock needs to be based on the systematic approach and common sense application of the three main criteria. However, it does not take away from the fact that the investor looking to initiate a position in a stock should nevertheless have a look at the chart of the stock in question for a period of the preceding 3 to 5 years. A look at the chart of the stock price in question is a very telling reading and may alert the investor to certain systemic problems with the stock in question.

The behaviour of a stock that has languished over a long period of time cannot be ignored.

A company that fulfils all the three criteria for investment but shows a stock price chart with little or no returns for the investor over medium to long term is a cause of concern. Unless the investor can study and identify concrete reasons for the stock not having performed in the past and such issues having been resolved in the present, it is best to avoid such a stock. At the end of the day, the returns of an investor are linked to the stock price and if the stock price does not move in tandem with the performance of the company, then all analysis and compelling investment factors are academic.

A prominent example of such a stock is Reliance Industries.

As a company Reliance Industries is not only the flagship of the Ambani group, it is also one of the largest companies in India in terms of market capitalization and turnover. Housing not only the largest single location oil refinery in the country i.e. the Jamnagar refinery with ~60 million tonnes per annum capacity, the country's largest petrochemical plant and also the upstream business which includes the prolific KG basin gas asset, Reliance has been considered to be a good investment pick by many brokerage houses over the last many years. Not only has the company been touted for investment on account of its promising business prospects, it has also delivered on performance with the execution of its plans for new areas of business such as retail. The turnover of the company has increased from INR 2,00,000 crores in 2009-10 to INR 3,40,000 crores in 2014-15 and the earnings of the company have increased from INR 16,000 crores in 2009-10 to 22,000 crores in 2014-15. Given the high base figures, such consistent growth is in itself a commendable achievement.

Yet the stock price of the company has languished. The market capitalization of the company has in fact reduced from INR 3,50,000 crores in 2009-10 to INR 2,40,000 crores in 2014-15. A chart of the stock price of the company from 2009-10 to 2015-16 is provided below.

Thus anyone who may have invested in Reliance Industries in 2009 would actually be a loser in terms of the stock value despite the company having performed well in terms of its revenues and earnings.

The reason for such underperformance in the stock can be manifold. It may be on account of certain perceived corporate governance issues around the stock, or regulatory risks overhang on the stock or even a bleak future outlook. The reasons are however of secondary importance. What is of primary import is the fact that the stock has underperformed in terms of it's stock price and the superlative earnings growth has not translated to the returns in its stock.

If the investor finds a stock consistently underperforming, it is best to avoid such a stock unless the investor has clear visibility on the reasons for such underperformance and is convinced that such reasons would not prevail in the future and the three basic criteria would take the stock to the level of its real intrinsic value, going forward.

Thus, in the case of Reliance, the investor may, as a result of the analysis of the three main factors, find the company to be a worthwhile investment. However the investor would still need to contemplate the reasons for the stock's underperformance in the past. If, and only if, the investor is able to find a credible reason for such underperformance and is convinced of the absence of such a reason in the future, should the investor proceed with investment in the stock of Reliance. It may well be that the stock price of Reliance has underperformed due to the company meeting limited success in its upstream business with the KG Basin and Shale gas assets not yielding the desired results for Reliance. Further, the intensive capital expenditure program of Reliance (upwards of INR 1,00,000 crores) in ventures such as Reliance JIO which have traversed many years without yielding any revenues, may also be a reason for the stock's underperformance. If, at the cusp of the launch of Reliance JIO, marking the end of the capital expenditure cycle for the company, the investor is convinced, that in addition to the main criteria being fulfilled, the aforesaid reasons do not subsist in the future and the company is set to benefit from the long capex cycle, the investor may consider taking a position in the company. Else, the stock is best avoided owing to the secondary factor of lacklustre stock performance over the years.

3. PROMOTER STOCK PLEDGING

Related to the point of leverage in the company's books is the pledging of the company stock held by the promoter group.

One of the prominent occurrences in the Indian equity markets is the pledging of stocks by the promoter group. The promoter group pledges equity held by them in their listed entity with lenders against amounts borrowed. While this does not directly impact the public float of listed equity shares, or the earning prospects of the company, it is nevertheless a relevant secondary factor to consider as it may affect the performance of the stock price of the company.

A promoter group may leverage its stock holding in the company for a multitude of reasons. They may do so to raise finance for any of their other ventures – whether unlisted or listed – but unrelated to the company in question. Similarly they may do so to raise finance for acquisition of any other company. Lastly, they may do so as an additional collateral to the lenders of the company itself where the lenders, apart from the collateral from the assets of the company, desire access to the promoter shareholding which they may seek to liquidate to recover their dues in case of default by the company itself.

Regardless of the reasons for the leverage of the company's stock by the promoter group, it is a red flag which ought to be factored in by the investor looking to take a position in the company. Pledging of the company stock by the promoter group can often devolve into a situation where the lenders resort to selling the stock so pledged in case of default in servicing of their loans. Moreover, where the price of the stock in question plummets due to market related movements, the value of the stock held by the lenders as collateral may fall below the required collateral cover of the lenders triggering margin calls. When the promoters fail to top up the margin calls, in cash or by way of further stock, the lenders would start selling the stock in the market leading to a further fall in the stock price, further margin shortfall and further selling thus leading to a spiralling crash in the company stock price purely on the back of the promoter group pledging which may or may not be related to the financial performance or the business of the company itself.

Thus, a company with high promoter pledged stock exhibits high beta to the stock market as its movements tend to be exaggerated as compared to the broader market.

An example of this is the performance of Bajaj Hindusthan stock in February 2016. Bajaj Hindusthan, as a company, has the promoter shareholding of about 29% and the entire shareholding has been pledged by the promoters. In February 2016, the Indian markets took a dive on the back of liquidity and other macro concerns. While the Sensex during that period fell 3%, the Bajaj Hindustan stock fell by more than 20% on account of pressure of margin requirements by the lenders. A chart of Bajaj Hindusthan for January and February 2016 along with the Sensex for the same period is provided below.

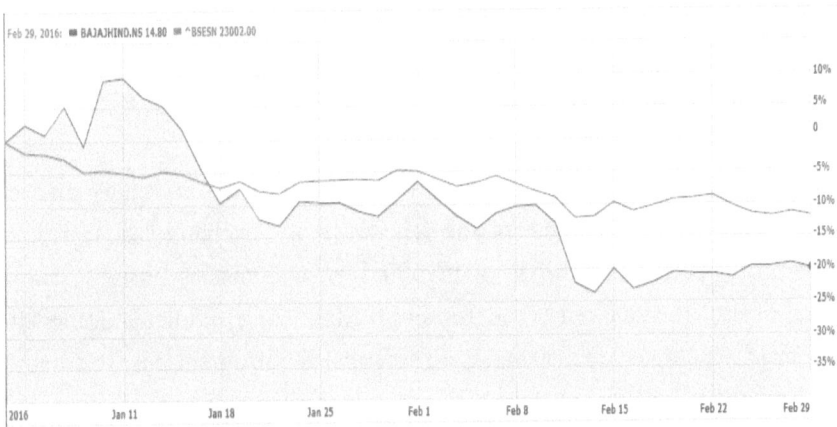

Thus, pledging of a large position of the stock by the promoter group poses a material risk for the investors in the company's stock insofar that the company stock may materially underperform even though the company per se may fulfil the three main investment criteria. As such, a look at the quantum of company stock pledged by the promoter group is a relevant secondary factor to be considered at the time of investing in a stock.

In this context, data regarding the extent of company stock pledged by the promoters has been made a mandatory disclosure requirement by SEBI. An extract of the quantum of shares pledged by the promoters of the top Nifty stocks is provided in the table below:

Company	% of Promoters' holding Pledged
Adani Port	33.11%
Asian Paints	13.19%
Aurobindo	3.15%
Bajaj Auto	0.06%
Hindalco	0.09%
M&M	5.10%
Sun Pharma	1.67%
Tata Motors	6.44%
Tata Power	5.10%
Tata Steel	9.00%
Yes Bank	3.62%
Zee	42.35%

Similar data is available for any and every other listed company and can be accessed from the website of the relevant stock exchange as part of the shareholding pattern of the company filed on a quarterly basis. A careful perusal of such data as well as the trend of pledging of promoter shareholding, whether increasing or decreasing, is an essential requirement post the analysis of the three main criteria.

4. LIQUIDITY

The purpose of all investment decisions is to generate a return on capital deployed. Generation of return on equities primarily arises by way of dividends and capital gains on liquidation of the holding of an investor. Liquidation of the holding presupposes a ready and liquid market for the stock in question. An illiquid market for a stock not only leads to difficulties in building up and winding down a position in the stock in question but also displaces the price discovery for the stock. For instance, a stock may appear to be quoting at a price of INR 100 however when the investor places an order to purchase a substantial quantity of the stock, he is not able to accumulate a position for that price and has to pay a price higher than the quoted price chasing trickling quantity of sell orders at higher and higher prices.

Similarly, when an investor seeks to liquidate a position in an illiquid stock that shows a price of INR 100, he would likely end up realizing a much lower selling price for his position owing to the lack of liquidity in the stock in question.

Of course, in all such cases, liquidity is to be reckoned relative to the quantum of the position that an investor seeks to build. For a retail investor a relatively illiquid stock would still be an investible option as the retail investor would be able to enter and exit the position without being bogged down by extreme price movements owing to the relatively smaller quantity he wishes to transact. However, even in such a case, caution would have to be exercised about the fact that the quoted price is not necessarily a real indicator of the price at which the position may be available to be accumulated or liquidated as the stock price may yet fluctuate wildly on any given day given the buy or sell action of large investors. Thus a stock quoting at INR 100 per share may really have sellers only at INR 105 and thus the analysis of the investor of the third main criterion regarding the valuation of the company, basis INR 100 per share would be somewhat fallacious.

Liquidity is thus a relevant factor that needs to be considered by an investor while initiating a position in a stock which may otherwise fulfil the three basic criteria for investment. A stock with a strong promoter group, good business prospects and cheap valuation may still need to be avoided as it trades thinly and cannot be amassed or liquidated by the investor without huge fluctuations in the stock price which in itself diminishes the valuation arbitrage existing in the stock in question.

Moreover, a relatively illiquid stock is also more prone to market speculative actions and wild price movements brought on by extraneous events which may distort the price correlation of the stock to the intrinsic value. For instance, if we consider the real estate space, we may take the example of two real estate stocks i.e. DLF and Ashiana Housing. While DLF is a stock priced at about INR 130 and sees average volumes of 1 crore shares on National Stock Exchange on a daily basis, Ashiana Housing which is a stock priced at a similar price range of INR 130 to INR 150 sees daily volumes of only about 25,000 shares on National Stock Exchange.

In such a situation even where an investor forms a view regarding Ashiana Housing as a stock fulfilling the three main criteria for investment, the investor may still find the stock not suitable for investment if the investment size of the investor is such that it cannot be comfortably transacted based on the average volumes of Ashiana of only 25,000 shares daily. In such a case the investment thesis of the investor assuming the current market price of Ashiana at INR 130 and finding it as undervalued would likely be fallacious as the price at which he would actually be able to accumulate the desired quantity of the stock may be 5% to 10% higher thereby being closer to the intrinsic value of Ashiana assessed by the investor.

Furthermore, if a regulatory event or another event occurs such as an adverse legislation or court order against real estate companies, such an event would likely disrupt the stock price of Ashiana Housing much more than it would disrupt that of DLF given the lower volumes in the former. Thus the quoted market price discovery and the alignment of the said price to the intrinsic value of the stock of Ashiana Housing would always be hamstrung by the liquidity factor and ought to be taken into account in addition to the analysis of the three main criteria by the investor.

5. REGULATORY UNCERTAINTY

We have seen that the regulatory environment in which a company operates is to be considered while evaluating the second criterion for investment i.e. the future business prospects of the company. For example, while evaluating an investment in a power company, the regulatory environment regarding the power companies in relation to the payment of power tariff by the buyers or the regulatory environment concerning the availability of coal as feedstock for thermal power generation companies are relevant to determine the future business prospects of the company in question.

However, in certain cases the regulatory uncertainty as an overhang may be of such an overarching nature that it may have to be reckoned as a secondary factor notwithstanding the company fulfilling the three primary criteria for investment. In such a case, the risk of regulatory overhang may outweigh the three main criteria and rule out a company as an investment despite it having favourable business prospects and cheap valuation.

For instance, an investor may evaluate an investment in a stand-alone oil refinery such as Essar Oil Limited and may find that the company fulfils the three main investment criteria in terms of the promoter group, the future business prospects and the valuation.

However, there may arise certain overarching regulatory uncertainties in the macro-economic scenario which would nevertheless need to be considered by the investor in addition to the three main criteria. An example of such uncertainty may be a possible regulatory disruption of the refinery sector by the Government such as a move to levy subsidy burden on private sector refiners. Such a regulatory event actually playing out would be difficult to anticipate and build into the financial projections of the company and thus such an investment would best be avoided notwithstanding it fulfilling the three primary criteria, at least until the uncertainties play themselves out.

Similarly, an investor looking to invest in a FMCG company, such as Nestle India may find the company fulfilling the three main criteria, i.e. the company having a credible promoter group, good business prospects and reasonable valuation, yet the events or regulatory actions may be playing out in a way that there exists higher than normal regulatory risk plaguing the company as we saw in 2015 when the food regulators in many states of India banned Maggi owing to alleged excessive lead content therein. In such a case, despite the three criteria being fulfilled the investor would be best placed to avoid investing in Nestle as the secondary factor of the regulatory uncertainty assumes overarching importance and should be negated before the investment position in Nestle should be taken. Even after the regulatory events have played out the investor should, with the benefit of hindsight of the nature and impact of the actual regulatory event, be able to reassess the business prospects of Nestle in light of the renewed regulatory setup and project Nestle's earnings in view of the same and then form a view regarding the valuation of Nestle and whether or not it still fulfils the three main criteria for investment.

6. MACRO-ECONOMIC FACTORS

Much like regulatory uncertainties, macro-economic factors affecting the business of a company are to be taken into account while evaluating the second criterion for investment i.e. the future business prospects of the company in question. However, there may be certain macro-economic or even global factors which may have over-arching effect on the investment decision, regardless of the company fulfilling the three investment criteria in question.

For example, an investor evaluating an investment in a bank may find the bank being run by a credible promoter group, having promising business prospects given the segments and geographies it is present in, and cheaply valued when evaluating the projected earnings of the bank and it's asset quality.

However, there may still be certain over-arching macro-economic factors which could dent the bank as an investment and thus cause reconsideration of the investment decision.

For instance, the bank in question may have high exposure and geographical reach to borrowers in a country such as Greece which is faltering in its debt servicing abilities. Such a factor would have to be considered and may cause the investor to defer the investment decision or avoid investing in the bank altogether till the macro-economic factors play out and the extent of the effect of such factors on the financials and business prospects of the bank become clear and measurable.

Similarly, an investor may be bullish on the prospects of airline stocks which may be looking favourable in terms of business prospects and earnings growth in view of the growth in fares, passenger traffic and lower cost regime in view of the benign crude oil prices. However, there may be certain global events which may be playing out that may have an overhang on the crude oil prices, for example, a geopolitical disturbance in the middle-east due to potential conflicts between two major oil producing nations which may disrupt crude oil supply and send crude prices spiking. In such a case again, the macro-economic factors assume overriding importance and ought to be considered in the investment decision even though the company in question may be fulfilling the three main criteria for investment.

Another example of the impact and reach of macro-economic factors was seen in January 2008 when the global financial crisis came to the fore at the back of the US Housing market meltdown. Companies in India, with the most promising business prospects also saw their prices getting affected as the entire market got sold off with major US and other foreign investors pulling out their money in a hurry.

Thus, a company such as Reliance Industries, which may have appeared to be fulfilling the three basic criteria, and had its stock quoting at INR 1,500 in January 2008 saw a meltdown due to the global crisis with its price falling below INR 1,000 levels in a matter of months and has since struggled to reclaim this price level and sustain above it.

Price chart of Reliance beginning January 2008 is provided below and amply demonstrates the overriding effect of macro-economic/global factors on a company's stock price despite the company otherwise fulfilling the three main criteria.

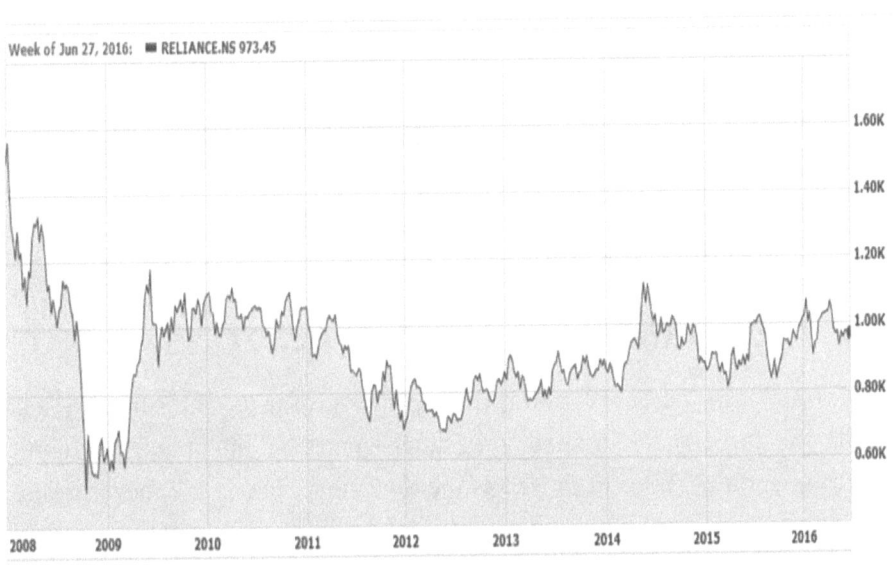

In June 2016, when the UK citizens cast a vote for Britain to exit the European Union (EU), i.e. the Brexit phenomenon, such a global development assumed importance in the business prospects of many companies. A bellwether such as Infosys took a hit on the back of Brexit concerns, i.e. that British customers would cut back budgets for IT spends to weather the Brexit storm and thus impact the revenue prospects of IT companies such as Infosys having a client base in UK. Such a global macro-economic event is thus a relevant over-arching factor in evaluating an investment in a company such as Infosys which may otherwise fulfill the three main criteria. A chart showing the impact of Brexit on Infosys is given below.

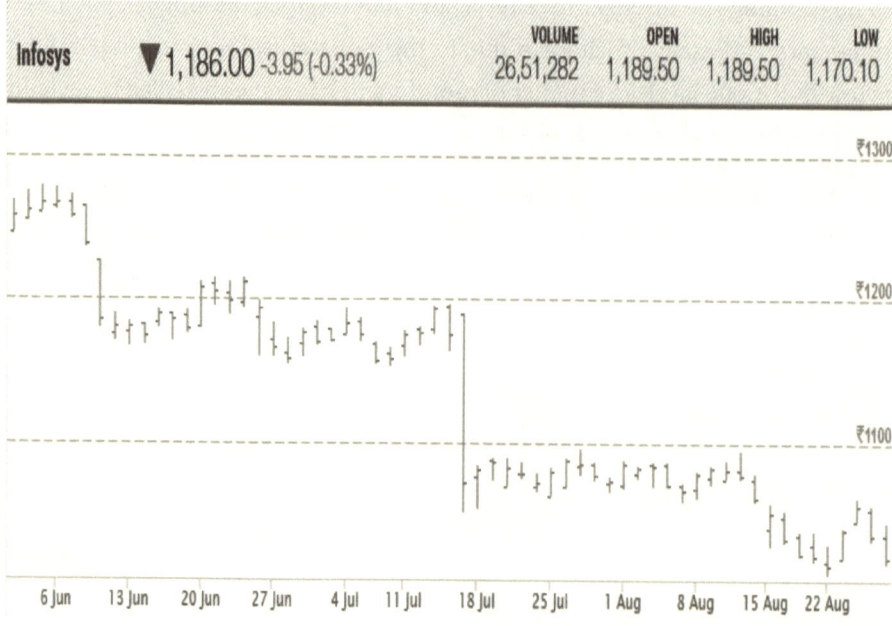

7. INORGANIC CORPORATE ACTIONS

An investor may be bullish about the business prospects of a company that fulfils the three main criteria, even after analysing the macro-economic environment it operates in as well as the regulatory framework, nevertheless, the inorganic actions being contemplated by the management of the company may play spoilsport on the prospects of the company nevertheless.

Inorganic corporate actions include actions such as the acquisition of another company or project by the company or branching out into a completely new and unrelated business vertical by the company or the company merging with another company. Such actions are generally carried out by leveraging the balance sheet of the company and straining the financials of the core business.

In case the inorganic actions of the company are of a scale that could potentially disrupt the core business and financials of the company, it would be a relevant secondary factor to be considered in evaluating the company's stock as an investment even though the company may otherwise fulfil the three basic criteria.

For instance, in November 2007, soon after its IPO, DLF as a real estate company, with its stock quoting at about INR 700 with promising business prospects, announced the acquisition of stake and entering into hotel segment by partnering with Aman Resorts founder. DLF acquired a stake in Aman Resorts for USD 500 million at the time. Such an inorganic move by DLF was disruptive of the earnings of DLF and even though initially the stock price reacted favourably, going up to INR 1,000 levels, the stock thereafter fell over a period of time. As things played out, Aman put major pressure on the financials of DLF with mounting losses year on year with DLF ultimately having to sell the chain with a view to pare down its mounting debt. In the meantime, the share price of DLF fell from highs of INR 1,000 to INR 150 per share.

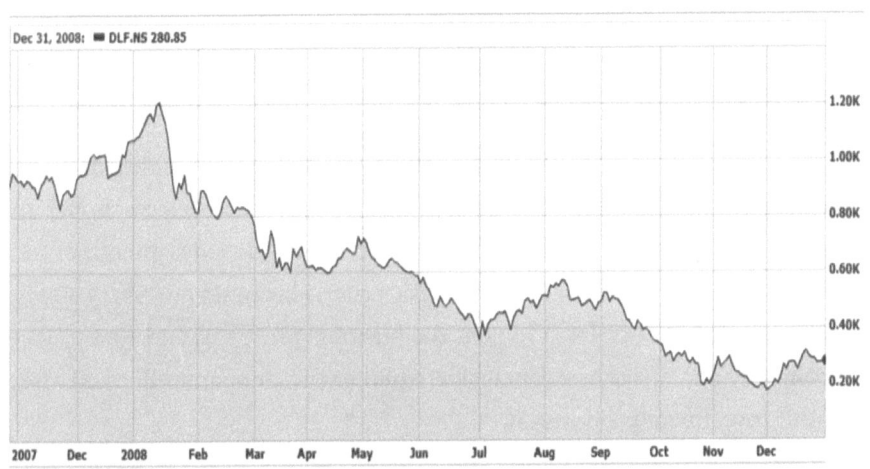

Similarly, in August 2016, when the Aditya Birla Group announced a scheme of restructuring whereby the group company Aditya Birla Nuvo would be merged with Grasim, the markets viewed this inorganic move to be dilutive of the shareholder value in Grasim's stock. Grasim which was traditionally viewed to be a company with exposure to cement and related businesses, now suddenly became exposed to completely unrelated businesses i.e. telecom, fashion and financial services. The market thus discounted the price of Grasim as a holding company of such businesses considering that the core earnings and cash flow of Grasim may be compromised to fund the other businesses by virtue of the merger. Consequently the price of Grasim's shares fell by almost 15% from INR 5,200 per share to INR 4,400 per share within the span of a few trading sessions, even though traditionally Grasim may have been viewed as a company fulfilling the three main investment criteria.

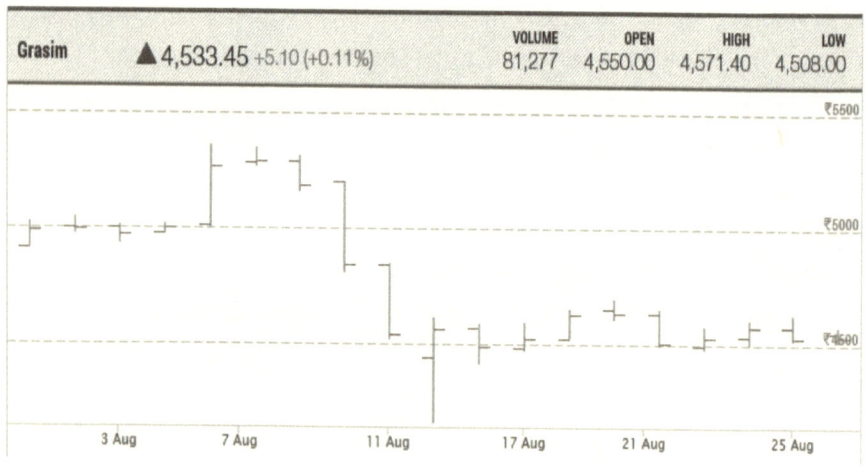

Thus the inorganic steps taken by a company having a material impact on its financials and or operations must be considered by the investor even though the company may otherwise fulfil the three basic criteria. As a consequence of such inorganic actions a review of the three basic criteria becomes necessary and the investor needs to take a fresh look at the business prospects and financials of the company and arrive at a conclusion whether the company still makes for a lucrative investment proposition.

There are thus multiple secondary factors which ought to be considered when factoring investment in a company and it is not recommended that a pedantic approach of only evaluating the three main criteria be adopted. The financial markets, especially equity market is a complicated and evolving one. There are many factors and aspects that touch upon every company operating in any business in India. While the three primary factors are the essential hurdles to be crossed by a company to make it investment worthy, there may still be certain secondary factors which may affect the investment decision in the company leading to the investment being avoided or deferred.

The list of secondary factors as provided here is illustrative and not exhaustive. There would be other secondary factors which would nevertheless be relevant in making a decision to invest in any stock which otherwise fulfils the three main criteria and the process of discovery and application of such secondary factors is an evolving one.

CHAPTER 7

TIMING YOUR ENTRY AND EXIT

> *Timing the purchases and sales of equity positions makes or loses you money. Yet, the timing of the purchases and sales should not be made the central theme of investing.*

Once a decision is made to invest in a stock the inevitable conundrum faced by every investor is how to beat the market by timing the purchase and sale in such a manner that the investor buys the stock at the lowest available price and starts registering market gains from the outset and sells the stock at the peak of the stock price to maximize profits.

The timing of the market to achieve the above goal is as pervasive a desire amongst investors as it is a daily pursuit of the traders.

However, the questions that inevitably arise are - Is there any formula or method to be able to successfully time the market? How to go about accumulating your position when you have decided to invest in a stock? How to ensure that you exit the existing position at the peak price of the stock?

The thrust of this book is to advocate an approach for investment in stocks with a medium to long term horizon. Once the method for evaluation of investments as propagated above has been followed by an investor and the stocks to be invested shortlisted, the premise remains that the stocks should achieve their intrinsic value in the medium to long term. Thus, in such a scenario the timing of the purchases of the stocks should typically not be of major relevance since gaining from intermittent price fluctuations is not the targeted outcome of medium to long term investment.

However, in the Indian equity markets, short term movements in the stock markets have been known to cause very large fluctuations in individual stock prices. Such movements have ranged as much as 20% or more in a span of one month. To be caught on the wrong side of such swings, in some cases, could lead an investor to lose more money on a position than the expected delta between the stock price and it's intrinsic value.

For instance, in January/February 2016, in a span of weeks, the stock price of most of the Indian equities fell drastically, only to recoup most of their losses by April/May 2016. Even Indian large cap companies such as Tata Motors and ICICI Bank fell more than 20%. Charts of the said companies during the said period are given below to help appreciate the extent and pace of the movement.

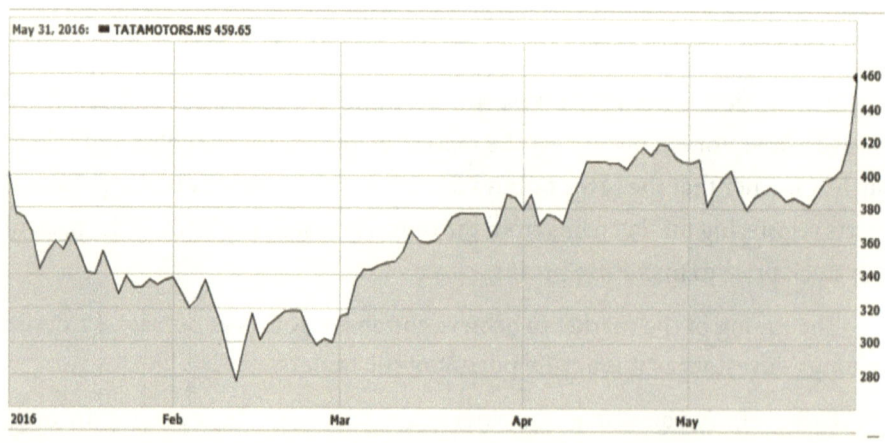

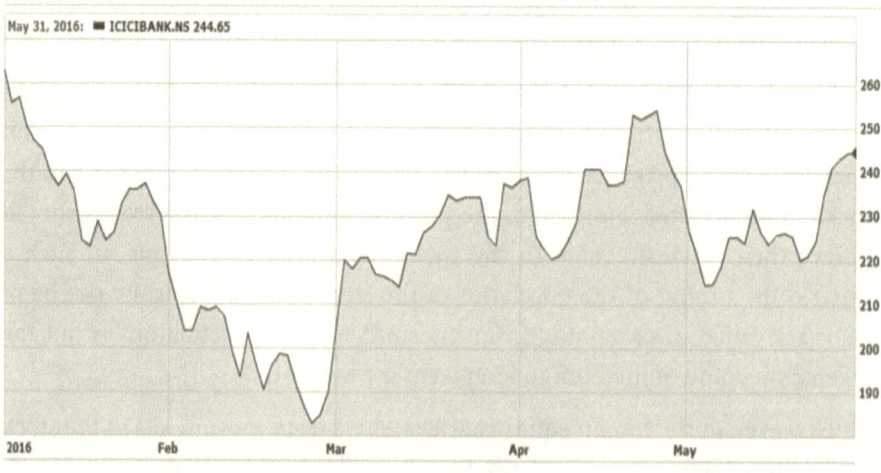

An investor looking to build or exit a position would have been in a dilemma as to what he should do in times of such drastic movement in the stock prices.

An investor looking to initiate a position in Tata Motors may have purchased the stock at INR 400 levels on the premise that the intrinsic value thereof is INR 480, only to see it fall below INR 300, thereby recording paper loss (INR 100+) of more than the intended gain as per his analysis (INR 80).

Similarly, an investor who may have invested in ICICI Bank at INR 220 levels with a perceived target value of INR 300, may not have exited the stock at INR 260 hoping for further upside, only to see their entire paper profits wiped out when the stock fell to sub-INR 200 levels.

As such, the timing of purchases and sales of stocks does assume some relevance, especially in the Indian equity markets which are susceptible to wide fluctuations and knee-jerk movements.

In view of the above, while the basis of investing remains the three main criteria and the method of identifying the stocks remains fundamental analysis, the question arises how an investor should react to price movements while building or liquidating a position in a particular stock.

There are different approaches to address this question. Some of these are discussed below.

1. THE ALL-IN APPROACH

This approach works on the premise that once a decision is made to buy or sell a stock the same should be implemented immediately and in its entirety.

For instance, an investor studies the stock of a company and finds it to be fulfilling the three main factors for investment. The investor thus decides to acquire the stock and build a position of 1,000 shares (say) in the stock in question. Under this approach, the entire quantity of 1,000 shares should be purchased by the investor immediately at the prevailing price given the fact that the investor has already seen in his analysis that the intrinsic value of the stock is higher than the prevailing market price. Thus, to realize the benefit of the differential between the current market price and the intrinsic value of the stock, the entire position would be initiated immediately and there lies no reason why the stock be allowed to run up and narrow the gap between the value and the market price, nor should the investor wait for an opportunity to enter the stock only when the stock price falls, as such an opportunity may or may not arise.

Conversely, where the investor has an existing position in a stock and the investor finds that the market price of the stock has outrun the perceived fair value of the stock, the time has arrived to liquidate the position and book profits. Under the all-in approach, the position is liquidated in one go on an immediate basis without waiting to test how much further upside may be left in the stock and without risking the stock coming off the current price and the investor losing out on converting the paper profits into real profits.

Thus, the all-in approach is a simplistic approach which does not attempt in any way to time the market and relies simply on the action being taken by the investor on an immediate basis given the arbitrage between the intrinsic value of the stock and its current market price.

The merit of this approach is that the mindspace and efforts of the investor are concentrated in this approach on evaluation of investments as per the fundamental approach and the investor does not expend energies in tracking short term price movements and trying to second guess them. Instead, the investor can concentrate energies on continually evaluating the business prospects of his investments especially in light of the ever dynamic business environment in which the companies operate.

2. THE AVERAGE OUT APPROACH:

The average out approach propagates buying a stock on its way down and selling the stock on its way up. The approach is a take on Warren Buffet's famous philosophy, that one should be greedy when the market is fearful (i.e. buy when the market is selling a stock and pushing it down) and fearful when the market is greedy (i.e. sell a stock when the market is greedy and pushing it up). Under this approach, it is suggested that the investor looking to build a position should commence by purchasing a fraction of the intended position size, say 20%, to start with.

Once this position has been initiated and the stock goes down from the current market price, the investor should add to the position by another 20% and keep on adding 20% on every down move of the stock till the investor has achieved the 100% holding desired. In the process the investor would have bought at successively lower prices and would thus end up holding the 100% position at a much lower price than what he would have achieved under the all-in approach had he purchased 100% in the first place. On the other hand, if after having taken a position of 20% or such other fraction of the desired exposure, the investor finds the stock move up, then rather than adding to the position, the investor should hold on to the fractional position and liquidate it at a higher price whence the stock nears the target, thereby booking a profit, albeit for a lower quantity of the stock than what was originally envisaged. A profit nevertheless.

Conversely, when looking to liquidate a position in a stock, this approach suggests liquidating a fraction, say 20% of the position when a price is achieved that is higher than the perceived value of the stock. After this, if the price moves further up the investor liquidates a further 20% at the higher price and so on until the entire position stands liquidated with the result that the average price for the sale of the 100% position is way higher than what the investor would have achieved under the all-in method by selling the entire 100% position in one go. On the other hand, if after having sold the initial 20% at a price the stock starts moving down and comes off below the perceived value of the stock, then the investor may buy back what he has sold at the prevailing lower price on the premise that the stock will again bounce back above its intrinsic value and thus the investor would make repeat profit on such fractional position.

Overall the 'average out' approach works on the premise that the intrinsic value of the stock remains unchanged and even if there are fluctuations in the stock price these do not affect any change in the investment decision which is guided purely by whether or not a stock is trading at above or below the perceived intrinsic value. The approach trumpets the fact that whether you are accumulating the stock or liquidating, you are able to achieve a lower cost or higher selling price by staggering out the purchase or sale action and are thus able to take advantage of short term market movements.

However, the approach does not consider the possibility that a concerted downward movement in the stock may be due to an altered premise of the business of the company and its intrinsic value actually depreciating. After all, the market knows and prices in much more than any individual investor. As such, if, while following this approach, an investor who has purchased a fraction of the intended position, finds that the stock continuously drifts downwards, such an investor ought to monitor the reasons surrounding the fall in the stock price. In case the fall in the stock is due to certain developments which have adversely affected the business prospects of the company, the investor ought to hold off adding to the position and reassess the basic premise of his investment decision.

Take the case of a stock, say Jet Airways, trading at a price level of INR 600 per share in May 2016.

Say the investor finds Jet Airways fulfilling the three basic criteria for investment and after the analysis of the stock considers the intrinsic worth of Jet Airways to be upwards of INR 700 per share. Given the delta between the current market price of the stock and the perceived intrinsic value, the investor decides to take a position in the stock.

Following the average out approach the investor acquires 20% position at INR 600, the stock moves down to INR 580, and the investor acquires a further 20% position and so on till the investor has accumulated 100% of the position at an average price of INR 575 per share by the time the stock has come down to INR 550 per share in June 2016.

What the average out method does not consider is the fact that while the position is being built, the stock has actually come off ~10% i.e. from INR 600 to INR 550 and whether there is something intrinsically wrong with the company's performance which ought to be relooked at and perhaps the intrinsic value of the stock is no longer INR 700 but a lower figure, even below INR 550. As such, a continuously declining price may provide the investor with a satisfaction of having achieved a lower accumulation cost for his position but that satisfaction may be short-lived in case the real value of the stock has declined, thereby causing the downward movement in the price.

It may be that the business prospects of Jet Airways have turned south on the back of higher crude prices or loss of market share or regulatory actions.

As such, the average out approach cannot be implemented in a vacuum without considering the nature and causes of the movement in the price of the stock itself and re-evaluating the company as an investment proposition in light of such movements. Assuming the business prospects remain intact, the investor may consider the average out approach towards building a position in the stock.

3. THE MARKET MOVEMENT APPROACH:

The diametrically opposite approach to the average out method is what we call the 'Market movement' approach. It is an approach that has been practised and propagated by many market stalwarts including Jesse Livermore who was one of the most successful traders of his time.

Under this approach, the overarching hypothesis is that the market knows best and you should follow the market rather than try to trade against the tide. Thus, if the price of a stock is rising, the market is showing you that the stock is going to perform well owing to undervaluation and thus you should be buying the stock. Conversely, if a stock is falling the market knows that there is some inherent deficiency in the stock or the underlying company which merits a fall in the stock price and thus you should be selling the stock. In other words, this approach advocates buying a stock when it is rising and selling it when it is falling, which is the opposite of the average out approach, which suggests adding to the position when a stock goes down and selling down a position when a stock rises.

In practice, this approach would require that an investor looking to build a position of 100 shares in a stock would first buy a fraction of this position at the prevailing price level and then wait to see how the stock behaves. If the stock starts to rise, it would indicate that the market is in agreement with the finding of the investor that the stock is in effect undervalued and merits a rerating in its price. Upon receiving confirmation from the market to this effect, the investor is then recommended to add to his position and so on and so forth at every up move till he has completed the purchase of this entire desired position at which point of time the investor is already sitting on a handsome book profit. On the other hand, if after having purchased the initial fraction the stock falls, the investor should hold on to his position and wait for the market trend to reverse before adding more quantity, in this way the investor does not end up adding to the initial fraction position which is already showing a loss, and in case, the view taken by the investor regarding the undervaluation of the stock is wrong, this approach insulates the investor from a much higher loss the investor would have incurred under the all-in approach or the average-out approach.

Similarly, in the case of selling of the position by the investor, this approach would require the investor to sell a fraction of the position. If the market thereafter moves down, it would indicate that the feeling of the investor is endorsed by the market and it is signalling that the stock has, in fact, reached its price potential. As such, on the way downwards the investor would continue to offload more quantity till he has squared up his position. On the other hand, if the stock after the selling of the fractional position shows an upward move, the investor would be advised to hold on to the position and wait till the market goes up and then reverses downwards to sell further quantities, in this way the investor would be able to maximize the profit on the position.

While the market movement approach is based on the sound premise of the market knowing and factoring in all the relevant aspects of a stock, it may not apply fully to Indian equity markets as our markets often experience wild gyrations in stock prices owing to knee jerk reactions borne out of non-recurring events which do not materially alter the intrinsic worth of the stocks in question.

As discussed above, a recent example of such wild gyrations is the movement of the market and the blue chip stocks in January/February 2016 when the Nifty fell almost 15% without there being any inherent trigger for revaluation of the blue chip stocks comprising the Nifty. As was seen subsequently, by May 2016 Nifty had made up these losses and so had the blue chip stocks comprising part of the Nifty.

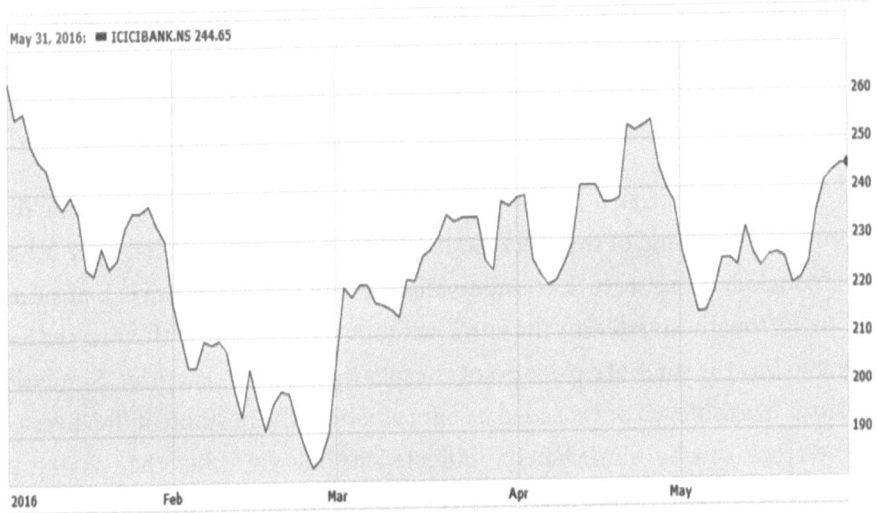

Thus someone following the market movement approach may have ended up liquidating his positions at market lows even though the intrinsic worth of the companies may not have changed, and then seen the market reclaim previous levels only to find that his initial analysis on the stock was correct but he ended up liquidating the positions at a loss while 'following the market.'

Apart from the above approaches, there are a plethora of other approaches to 'timing the market' that would be advocated by traders and chartists in the market.

The timing of the entry into and exit from a stock is a conundrum that not many have mastered, if at all anyone has. In fact, anyone who can master this would not need to worry about valuations of stocks in the first place. The timing of the market assumes more importance when you move from positional investing to trading and is thus, of marginal importance from a medium to long term perspective.

Nonetheless, the approach to take for building and liquidating one's position is one of personal preference and comfort. There is no right or wrong approach. Each approach has its arguable merits and demerits.

For the investor who is not seasoned at trading or reading market movements, it is suggested that the first approach i.e. the All-In approach may be the best approach to follow as it rules out the investor getting embroiled in a continuous exercise of timing the market and taking his attention away from tracking the business prospects, earnings and intrinsic value of the stocks in question.

The All-In approach is meritorious as insofar as it totally disregards the importance of timing of the markets. It moves on the premise that once it has been concluded that a stock is undervalued at the prevailing price, a position can be forthwith initiated in the stock without trying to 'time the market' i.e. trying to buy the stock at a price point cheaper than the current price. Similarly, if a stock has achieved or exceeded its fair valuation, the position of the investor in the stock can be immediately liquidated in one go rather than trying to second guess whether the price will rise further or not. Thus, this approach eliminates the issue of the timing from the investor's decision matrix and allows the investor to focus on the fundamental aspects of investing.

The average-out and market movement approaches on the other hand are meritorious insofar as these do not involve the investor taking or liquidating the entire position in one go. Rather the staggering of the purchases and sales under these approaches possibly allows the investor not only to curtail his losses and maximize profits but also enables the investor to continuously assess the market developments and adapt his stock position on the basis of the evolving scenario.

Notwithstanding the above, at the end of the day, every investor should adopt the approach to building and liquidating positions as they are most comfortable with, and more often than not, this is a function of the temperament of the investor in question than any other factor.

CHAPTER 8

PORTFOLIO ALLOCATION

> *Every investor has limited resources. How to divide available capital between the various appealing stocks is as pivotal to the investing exercise as is the art of selection of the stocks in the first place.*

You don't put all your eggs in the same basket. No matter how convincing or compelling may be the finding about the intrinsic value of a stock or it's undervaluation and the upside potential thereof, it would still be imprudent to put the entire capital into a single stock position. As such, it is a globally accepted investing principle that the available capital needs to be allocated between different stocks and sectors so as to diversify the position and hedge the exposure.

In the Indian context, this assumes even greater relevance given the susceptibility of stocks and sectors to a sudden shift in their fortunes at the back of regulatory changes and governmental actions. The Indian companies often see their prospects getting dented due to events which a typical investment analysis would not have revealed.

Financial Technologies (FT) is an apt example of an Indian company which exhibited promising business prospects but got affected by regulatory actions. FT, as a company was highly regarded as an upcoming contender in the IT space with its proprietary software solutions aimed at the financial services sector. Products and services of FT were used by the banking and financial services sector including major banks as well as stock exchanges, with the company enjoying a monopolistic advantage in its business. Additionally, the company was also the promoter and holding company of

Equity: In

two of the dominant exchanges in the commodity trading space in India i.e. National Securities Exchange Limited (NSEL) and Multi Commodity Exchange (MCX).

The company demonstrated growing earnings year after year and so did its stock price until July 2013 when there was a regulatory clamp down against its subsidiaries (specifically NSEL) on grounds of compliance irregularities, fraud, and embezzlement of funds of clients who were transacting on those exchanges. Over the course of next few months, things went from bad to worse and the regulators took drastic steps against the promoters of FT including the filing of criminal charges. The subsidiary, MCX was auctioned off to the highest bidder, Kotak, through a government managed auction process and the final nail in the coffin was an order mandating a merger of the beleaguered subsidiary NSEL with FT to the detriment of the minority shareholders of FT. As a result, the stock price of FT which once quoted upwards of INR 1000 tumbled down consistently and reached levels below INR 100 in a matter of a few years.

The case of FT is a classic example in the Indian context where betting on a single horse, which may be fulfilling the three main criteria, could lead an investor down a losing path that one may never recover from. The case for portfolio allocation thus emerges stronger than ever when investing in Indian equities.

Different sectors find favour at different points of time and thus a strong case is made out for sectoral diversification. While at a point of time, banking stocks may be in focus on the wave of the Government of India recapitalizing the public sector banks or on account of an enabling monetary stance, at another point of time, oil companies may be promising on account of deregulation of fuel prices or elimination of subsidy sharing or other initiatives of the Government.

Similarly, in the Indian context you may find the Governmental action dampening the sentiment attached to a particular sectors or stocks at a point of time. For instance, Governmental move to divest their stake in a public sector company at a discount to the prevailing market price may weigh down on the company's stock price or regulatory action to resume previously allotted coal blocks on the back of impropriety or corruption charges regarding the allotment process could kill the valuation of stocks of power companies.

It is thus prudent and recommended to carefully divvy up the capital amongst different stocks and sectors and thus build in an automatic hedge in the portfolio rather than having the entire exposure in a single stock or single sector.

Question thus arises - how best to allocate the portfolio in the context of Indian stock market peculiarities? There is no single best formula for portfolio allocation. It is more of a subjective exercise shaped by personal preferences and risk perceptions.

Regardless, certain guideposts which may shape the contours and components of a typical portfolio are discussed below.

1. NUMBER OF STOCKS

Having anything less than four or five stocks in the portfolio is a risky proposition as it could lead to a situation with the investor having the capital spread over too few stocks and being over exposed to particular companies or sectors. As seen above, the prospects of a company can be fatally dented with few regulatory events or judicial rulings or other events in quick succession and the investor may find a large percentage of his portfolio sinking into an irredeemable loss.

On the other hand, the number of stocks that an investor should have on the upper side is a function of the bandwidth available with the investor to track that many number of stocks and the companies in question.

Once the investor has taken a position in a company, he needs to continuously track the performance of the company by way of its quarterly result announcements, any changes in the business prospects of the company, regulatory actions having a bearing on the sector in general and the company in particular. The investor needs to evolve his view on the three basic criteria for investment into the stock of the company on an ongoing basis. Any actions or events affecting the promoter group of the company may adversely affect the decision to stay invested in the stock. Similarly, certain macro events or regulatory actions may adversely or positively affect the business prospects of the company at any given point of time. Lastly, valuation of a company may be adversely or positively affected by macro-economic or cyclical changes or the quarterly performance of the company may be a foretelling of leaner times to come. The constant tracking would, in turn, necessitate updating the projected earnings of the company in light of the changes and events. The updated earnings would, in turn, give a view regarding the valuation of the company in the context of the ever changing stock price and whether the company continues to be cheaply valued or has achieved the intrinsic value per share.

Thus, constant monitoring and follow up on the company and the sector is a *sine qua non* for any investor and the number of companies he can comfortably track based on available bandwidth is the determining factor in deciding the upper limit of the number of companies that the investor should have in his portfolio. For a typical investor with a day job and limits on bandwidth, five is an ideal number being not too low to over-expose him to particular companies and not being too high so as to make it onerous for him to track and value the company on a constant basis.

2. GOVERNMENT VERSUS PRIVATE SECTOR STOCKS

An appropriate diversification of the stocks in the portfolio of the investor with a view to diversifying exposure not only entails apportionment of the capital amongst number of stocks, it is also important that the investor is not overly exposed to government- owned stocks in the Indian context.

Indian markets offer a large number of Government companies as an investment option. It is easy to get swayed into investing in these to such an extent that the investor ends up with a portfolio which is dominated by such companies. This is more so for the reason that in India the Government owned companies operate in diverse sectors such as oil and gas, steel, shipping, mining and power generation.

A portfolio of an investor wherein the investor decides to invest in five stocks in diverse sectors such as oil & gas, banking may end up looking as below.

Stock	Sector	%age of Capital
Indian Oil Corporation	Oil & Gas	20%
NTPC	Power	20%
Steel Authority (SAIL)	Steel	20%
State Bank of India	Banking	20%
National Building Construction Corporation (NBCC)	Real Estate, Construction	20%

Prima facie, the above portfolio may appear to be a diversified and balanced portfolio, with possibly well-chosen large cap stocks which are leaders in their respectively sectors, such as SBI in banking space, Indian Oil in Oil & Gas space and NTPC in the power space. However, a closer perusal of the portfolio reveals the fact that the investor is over exposed to stocks belonging to the government promoter space. Over exposure to government companies may be a non-issue in other markets however in India it is a tenacious proposition. Given the unique political disposition in India on the back of the large democracy with multitude of regional parties, any changes of the government or even changes of portfolio of the minister where you suddenly find the minister for power being changed mid term from a representative of a liberal party to a person from a conservative party may change the fortunes of a state owned power generation company such as NTPC.

Similarly, a socialist government may pass on a greater burden of subsidies to the Oil companies of the state with a view to alleviate the inflationary stresses of high fuel cost on the population, thereby affecting the business prospects of companies such as IOC.

Again, a government which is excessively pro-business and growth may push the state-owned banks to bank roll risky business projects of companies which may default in future and lead to questionable asset quality of state owned banks such as SBI.

Furthermore, an unstable government at the Centre due to lack of majority in parliament, may cause frequent elections and lack of policy direction to PSUs which may bring an overarching cloud to bear on the business prospects of government-owned companies.

This is not to say that all government owned companies should be avoided in the portfolio altogether, but that the investor ought to have an appropriate mix of government and private companies to be able to balance the portfolio and avoid over exposure to government related risks.

3. PROMOTER DIVERSIFICATION

While it has been said that there be an appropriate balance of government and private promoter group companies in the portfolio of an investor, it also bears notice that amongst the private promoter group companies the investor needs to have a mix of promoter group companies rather than being overly exposed to a single promoter group.

This is not to question the reliability of a particular promoter group, for the unreliable promoter group companies are to be avoided as an investment option entirely as these would not qualify the first basic investment criterion. However, even for those promoter group companies that satisfy the first basic investment criterion, it is worthwhile to limit the number of the companies of the same promoter group in the portfolio.

Consider an investor who finds companies belonging to TATA group as companies satisfying the first investment criterion. Thereafter, the investor wishes to invest in five companies in his portfolio in different sectors and comes up with the following five companies which as per him fulfil the second and third criteria:

COMPANY	SECTOR
TATA CONSULTANCY	INFORMATION TECHNOLOGY
TATA MOTORS	AUTOMOBILES
TATA POWER	POWER
TATA STEEL	STEEL
TATA GLOBAL	CONSUMER PRODUCTS

While the above suggested portfolio may fulfil the three basic criteria and is also not a portfolio with over exposure to government-owned companies, yet the portfolio would be one which is overly skewed on account of being over exposed to a single promoter group. Any unforeseen events or developments affecting the single promoter group such as succession issues, regulatory action or adverse court orders may affect the entire portfolio of the investor and thus, the above would not be an advisable portfolio allocation.

An appropriate portfolio allocation would thus be one that diversifies amongst different promoter groups - whether they be private, government, family group, multi-national companies and so on.

4. SECTORAL DIVERSIFICATION

Building a portfolio of companies that fulfil the three basic investment criteria but fall in the same or related sectors is also not a good idea as it would leave the investor over exposed to the vagaries that may affect the sector in question.

Take for instance, an investor who allocates the portfolio into the following companies:

COMPANY	SECTOR
TATA MOTORS	AUTOMOTIVES
MOTHERSON SUMI	AUTO COMPONENTS
M&M FINANCE	AUTO FINANCE
SONA KOYO	AUTO COMPONENTS
MARUTI SUZUKI	AUTOMOBILES

While at first glance the portfolio may appear to be a reasonably diversified one with an appropriate mix of companies from private sector, including family owned promoter groups, large corporate houses and multinational companies, however, the portfolio still ends up being one which is skewed in terms of over exposure to automobiles in general and any fall out on automobile demand, adverse regulatory changes etc. would affect not only the automobile manufacturers in the portfolio but also have a cascading effect on the auto component makers as well as the automobile finance companies.

It is thus recommended to diversify the portfolio in terms of the sectors as well, so as not to have all the stocks in same or related sectors no matter how bullish an investor may be on the business prospects of a particular sector.

5. MARKET CAP DIVERSIFICATION

The size of the company being invested in is also a material consideration while building the portfolio. In the Indian context, you could find companies in the listed space with a market capitalization as low as INR 200 crores to companies with a market capitalization as high as INR 2,00,000 crores.

Blue chip companies typically have market capitalization nearer to the upper end of the spectrum. While it may be a relatively safer bet to build a portfolio comprising purely of blue chip large cap stocks, it may not be the best idea as the rate of return offered by a large cap stock would always be constrained by the large base/denominator of the existing market capitalization and sales and profit figures of the company in question. In other words, finding a multi bagger stock in a company which has a market capitalization of INR 2,00,000 crores + would require such a company to grow its sales and profit figures by multiples where such sales and profits figures are already in thousands of crores, which would be a time consuming process.

On the other hand, a small or mid cap stock, one having a market cap of say INR 500 crores, with sales of INR 500 crores and PAT of INR 50 crores could well be a multi bagger insofar as its PAT figure could quadruple to INR 200 crores in a matter of a few years.

Conversely, being over exposed to small or mid-cap stocks comes with its own pitfalls as such companies have other risk factors associated with them including high beta (fluctuation/susceptibility to market movements) as well as greater probabilities to falter and fall to deep discount to the current market price.

Thus, an appropriately diversified portfolio allocates the capital between different sized companies rather than being over exposed to only large cap or small or medium cap stocks.

We have thus seen that it is not only important to pick the right stocks that fulfil the three basic investment criteria but to also design a portfolio that has the appropriate diversification. The examples of portfolios shared above demonstrate the pitfalls of over concentration in particular sectors or promoter groups even though each of the companies may be fulfilling the basic investment criteria and be a good investment candidate in their own right.

Having a portfolio that is too skewed would be detrimental to the potential returns an investor may generate and would thus be counterproductive to the entire exercise of investing insofar as the investor may be saddled with subpar returns despite following the appropriate investment approach.

Given the high susceptibility of stocks in the Indian markets, portfolio allocation becomes an important exercise, an exercise as important as picking the right stocks in the first place. The portfolio should thus be developed by an investor keeping in mind his personal risk appetite and the appropriate diversification as discussed above.

CHAPTER 9

REGULATORY FRAMEWORK

> *The Indian Regulatory Framework not only acts as an automatic entry barrier for companies seeking to transact business but also for investors who can decipher the investments in its backdrop versus those who cannot.*

We have seen, in the context of the Indian markets, the three basic criteria for the selection of equity stocks by an investor. We have further seen the secondary factors that also have a bearing on stock selection and may sometimes trump the three basic criteria in determining the stock selection or rejection.

An important secondary factor that we touched upon with regard to stock selection pertained to the regulatory uncertainties surrounding a particular company or stock. The regulatory framework is an aspect of importance in any country but of particular significance in India, given the uniquely complex nature of our country's regulatory canvas. The regulatory events in India can be far reaching insofar as these can affect or even demolish the business prospects of a company or an entire sector. These can even affect an entire promoter group and their companies. These can also alter the competitive landscape of a company in a single instance. It is thus the purpose of this chapter to discuss the broad contours of the Indian regulatory framework such that an investor may be able to appreciate and comprehend the same and factor a proper study of the regulatory framework in his analysis.

The factors that set India's regulatory framework apart are:

1. FEDERAL STRUCTURE

Indian constitution has provided for a federal structure of government in the country. This translates to a government at the Centre and one at the State level for each of the respective states. The areas of legislations are also divided between the Centre and the State within the Constitution itself in the form of the Centre list, State list and the Concurrent list (matters on which both Centre and State can legislate).

Moreover the legislature of states is divided into the lower house and the upper house, same as the Centre. The members of the lower house of the Central legislature – Lok Sabha – are elected by the people directly while the members of the upper house of the central legislature – Rajya Sabha – are elected by the legislatures of the states.

The federal structure in India is thus a complicated one and thus poses its own unique challenges in our country. This is more often than not compounded by the fact that the government at the Centre and the State level need not be formed by the same political party.

Any investor looking to invest in a company would thus need to not only understand the scope of the legislative and governance powers of the State and Central Governments but also the particular Central and State laws having a bearing on the business of the company.

For instance, an investor looking to invest in a company such as Vedanta Limited which is engaged in the mining of iron ore in Orissa would need to understand not only the laws of Orissa in relation to mining but also the laws made by the Centre in relation to environmental aspects such as pollution. Similarly, the investor would need to understand the fiscal laws i.e. excise, VAT, entry tax etc. to determine the fiscal regime surrounding the activities of the company. Moreover, a company such as Vedanta which also has operations in crude oil via its subsidiary Cairn, in the state of Rajasthan, is also affected by laws relating to crude oil exploration and production of the Centre as well as the myriad fiscal laws in relation to production, transportation and sale of crude oil expounded by the State and the Centre.

This is not to say that an investor needs to be a legal expert to be able to invest in Indian companies. However, a basic understanding of the prevailing regulatory framework is important, both at the Centre and State level as a company which faces a benevolent regulatory framework for its business at the Centre may still face headwinds and bottlenecks at the State Government level of the state that it transacts business in or vice versa. The taxation and legal regime can materially affect the P&L account and balance sheet of the company as well as its business prospects and thus affect the investment thesis built on the three basic criteria.

2. COMPLEXITY OF LAWS

Apart from the laws being divided into Central and State laws, the Indian regulatory framework is also symbolized by a complex array of legislation and subordinated legislation.

Any law is typically enshrined in the form of an act and further fleshed out with rules, notifications and circulars. Add to that the judicial pronouncements on the law which sometimes have the effect of negating or significantly altering the effect of the law in operation. The resulting maze of legislation is not only complex but also voluminous and mired with legalese and cross references.

While an investor may not be expected to understand all the laws touching upon a company in depth or to delve into the minutiae of the above texts, if he does decide to invest in a company, it is recommended that he gain a general working knowledge of the laws touching upon the sector in which the company operates and thereafter follow the developments in these laws closely as these tend to have significant impact on the operations and business prospects of the company in question.

For instance, a company in the power space such as Tata Power would be affected by a suite of laws touching upon the power sector including the Government's policy on coal import, duty levied on imported coal, environmental laws on coal mining and power projects, the Government policy on payment of dues and honouring of Power Purchase Agreements by the State Electricity Boards and the pronouncements of the Central Electricity Regulatory Commission on tariff to be levied by the power companies and any compensation to be paid to them owing to any fluctuation in their fuel costs.

An investor looking to invest in any company in the power sector would thus need to gain a basic understanding of the policies of the government affecting the business of the power generation companies including those outlined above and thereafter follow development and changes in these laws and policies through the media and news reports as well as a reading of the source documents such as the amendments, notifications, and judgements, to be abreast of critical changes which may affect the business prospects of the investee company.

For example, in 2015, the Government of India under Mr. Narendra Modi has launched comprehensive reforms in relation to the power sector. This has included auctioning of the coal mines to captive users via a transparent e-auction process. Further, the UDAY scheme has been implemented with a view to replenish the cash flows of SEBs so that they may release dues of power generation companies. Around the same time, there have been orders of the regulatory and appellate authorities regarding the compensatory tariff to be paid to the power generation companies. Add to this, the WTO protocol signed by nations including India on the reduction of dependence on coal. An investor looking to invest in the power sector would need to have a basic understanding of the above regulatory landscape and a sense of the direction in which the winds are blowing as these will impact the business prospects of the power companies on an ongoing and material basis.

While some changes such as the UDAY scheme and the reallocation of coal mines may be positive, there may be negative implications of the WTO protocol. The nature and extent of the impact of each of such developments needs to be factored in by the investor in his investment thesis of the power company in terms of the business prospects and the future earnings of the company and a revised conclusion regarding the valuation of the company would need to be drawn.

3. DIVERSITY OF POLITICAL IDEOLOGIES

The regulatory framework of India, whether it be at the Centre or State level is also highly dependent on the ideologies of the political party in power.

Given the democratic diversity in India, we are confronted with a whole host of political parties with differing ideologies. With political parties which are left oriented having a conservative, non-business centric, pro-labour view point such as the CPI-M or TMC in West Bengal, to liberal, pro-business parties such as BJP.

Based on the geographical area of operation of a company's business as well as the scope of the business, it is likely to be affected by the political ideologies of the political party in power in the respective State as well as the Centre.

For instance, a company in the business of mining may face hurdles in its operations in case the mines are located in a State where the ruling party is pro-environment and legislates onerous obligations on the company in terms of its mining activities or disposal of effluents.

Similarly, a pro-labour Government may support trade union activities in the State and increase the cost of doing business in the state for the company transacting business in such a state.

An oil marketing company having high retail level exposure in a State may be affected in case a populist political party comes into power and seeks to fund its welfare activities via revenues by augmenting the VAT or entry tax on petroleum products to fund its populist initiatives.

Thus, a general sense of the regulatory framework surrounding a company in the context of the political party in power in the State of operation of the company gives a good indication to an investor on the potential pitfalls and commercial down sides associated with the company's business prospects. The investor thus needs to keep abreast of elections and political changes in the Centre and States where the investee companies have business operations.

Moreover, in case of coalition governments, especially at the Centre, regard should be had to the constituents of the coalition and the particular minister holding the portfolio relevant to the company, as the diverse parties forming part of the coalition often times affect the policies of the government and even hold back the hand of the dominant party inasmuch as the least confrontational path of governance is adopted by the coalition leader and the business oriented reform or agenda is compromised.

One of the prominent examples of the political ideologies playing on the business plans of a company in the recent history of Indian corporates is that of Tata Motors. When in 2008, Tata Motors sought to set up manufacturing facilities for Tata Nano in Singur, West Bengal, they ran into headwinds at the hands of the Mamata Banerjee led political party which championed the cause of the villagers in Singur in its pro-poor anti-business rhetoric. Recognizing the onset of difficulties and the bearing that the political ideologies prevailing in the state would pose for the operations, the Tatas took a decision to shift the project out of the State altogether and went on to set up the facilities in Gujarat under the then ruling Narendra Modi Government which was pro-business and expeditious in their approach to welcome the business of Tata Motors.

4. MULTITUDE OF AUTHORITIES AND APPROVALS

Another distinguishing feature of India's regulatory framework is the multitude of authorities and approvals applicable to any company and its business. Of course, there are some businesses which attract greater regulation than others in general. For instance, food and pharma businesses are subjected to greater regulation than road construction or real estate businesses. Nevertheless, it is a unique aspect of the Indian economy and Indian companies that conducting business in India requires dealing with multiple levels of regulatory authorities at different stages of the business.

The policies and decisions of a regulator can affect the sector in general and specific companies in particular, and thereby influence the business prospects of such companies.

For instance a company operating in the telecom space has to, inter alia, deal with the Telecom Regulatory Authority of India (TRAI). In case the TRAI, operating under a stricter mandate starts cracking down on issues such as operational efficiencies of the telecom companies or any decision of the TRAI regarding spectrum allocation is adverse to a particular company, it could affect the business prospects of the telecom companies in general or a company in particular.

Similarly, an environmental ministry which goes slow on clearance of projects would adversely affect the business prospects of infrastructure companies.

In 2015, the stringent crack down by the Food regulatory authorities spelt doom for Nestle when one of Nestle's staple products Maggi was banned across states and caused Nestle to withdraw the product from the market and destroy inventories on alleged adulteration charges. The stock price of Nestle took a beating by more than 20% falling from INR 7,500 levels in the month of April 2015 to INR 5,800 in the month of June 2015.

Further, the institution of new authorities for hitherto unregulated businesses also casts a cloud on the business prospects of the concerned companies. For instance the proposal to institute a real estate regulator by the Government of India would affect the real estate companies and any person looking to invest in this sector would need to evaluate the policies and regulations which would be coined by such an authority on its coming into existence.

Similarly, a regulator such as Competition Commission of India (CCI) which is mandated to regulate and check monopolistic practices by companies can also have a bearing on a particular company which is going in for an acquisition. For instance, in 2015 CCI sought clarifications from PVR Limited regarding its proposed acquisition of DT Cinemas from DLF, thereby affecting the transaction and casting a shadow on PVR's strategy for inorganic expansion. Even when the CCI did ultimately approve the acquisition it was after carving out certain theatres from the deal which in turn necessitated a re-negotiation of the valuation of the deal between PVR and DLF and also affected the business synergies for PVR stemming out of the acquisition.

The numerous regulatory bodies in India thus, have a role to play in the regulatory framework and their actions and policies ought to be borne in mind in determining the business prospects of a company that the investor may be looking to invest in or which the investor may have already invested in at a given point of time.

5. FREQUENT CHANGES BY LEGISLATORS AND JUDICIARY

The Indian regulatory landscape governing the businesses of the companies is not only characterised by the complex legal system with a plethora of regulators and approvals, it is further affected by frequent changes and events precipitated by legislative and judicial action.

A company operating in a given sector has to deal with the nuances of the regulations prevalent at a point of time as also changes which may be announced from time to time in these.

Thus an investor has to keep his eyes and ears open to the happenings in the regulatory landscape and be able to track the changes which materially affect the business prospects of a company that he has invested in or looking to invest in.

For instance, in late 2015, the National Green Tribunal announced an order banning registration of new diesel vehicles in the National Capital Territory. This order of the quasi-judicial authority had a direct bearing on automobile manufacturers such as Mahindra and Mahindra and Tata Motors which bank heavily on the sales of their diesel automobiles in the market. In fact the ban impacted the companies to such an extent that many of the automobile companies had to go in for a redesign or reconfiguration of their car models to comply with the engine size and type restrictions.

Similarly, an order of the Competition Commission of India alleging cartelisation and price fixation by a group of cement companies in early 2015 and again in mid-2016 also affected the financials of the named cement companies insofar as they were levied substantial penalties by the CCI.

A change in law such as the mining policy in a state, or the Supreme Court of India banning mining in certain regions altogether are also examples of changes that would affect the business prospects of the mining companies and would affect investment decision in these companies.

Again, a change in law allowing for additional coverage or construction on land parcels in a particular state would benefit the real estate players operating in that state and thus improve the business prospects of such companies.

We have thus seen that the regulatory framework is a material factor in evaluating an investment as well as continuing to stay invested in a company. In fact it is one of the most significant external factors that can affect the business prospects of a company in India.

Given the complexity of the regulatory framework, especially in the Indian context, an investor is well advised to have a reasonable understanding of the regulatory landscape governing the business of a company while evaluating criterion two, i.e. the business prospects of the company and while plotting the projected earnings of the company as part of criterion three.

Moreover, having invested in a company, the investor needs to constantly track any material changes in the landscape which may have a positive or adverse effect on the company and amend his investment thesis to factor in the effect of such changes on the business prospects and earnings of the company.

CHAPTER 10

INFORMATION BASED INVESTING

> *The temptation to make a quick buck on the back of 'credible and confidential' information about a company is a temptation that almost everyone has succumbed to, at one point in time, or another.*

One of the most popular and seductive approaches to trading and/or investing is doing so based on 'tips' or information regarding a company obtained through market rumours, media or grapevine.

While trading on the basis of inside information is a criminal offence in India as much as it is in any other developed country, many investors and traders often trade on the basis of information which need not necessarily be falling strictly within the four corners of the definition of inside information as espoused by SEBI regulations. As such, traders and investors often resort to taking positions based on tips or market rumours or even speculative media reports, thereby remaining within the bounds of law yet trying to make quick gains induced by the market price movement of a particular stock on the back of such information.

While the thrust of this book is to enable an investor to develop a medium to long term portfolio based on a systematic approach enshrined in the implementation of the three basic criteria for shortlisting investments, it is nevertheless relevant to discuss the treatment of various pieces of information that an investor may encounter, especially where such information touches upon a company that the investor is looking to invest in or is already invested in. While an investor may not trade on the basis of such information, it is nevertheless relevant for the investor to evaluate and process such information within the four corners of his investment thesis for that particular stock.

To better understand the approach to be adopted in tackling bits of information which may touch upon companies that an investor is interested in, it would be worthwhile to break down such information into various categories.

1. INFORMATION REGARDING EARNINGS

One of the most rampant pieces of information or rumours in the stock markets, found or heard in every nook and corner of the market grapevine, is the potentially superlative or inferior results expected of a company's earnings for the quarter or year. With the quarterly results calendar firmly in place, the rumour mills begin churning with the onset of every quarterly earnings cycle and one would hear of earnings forecasts of not just analysts but also the 'people in the know.'

While it is best to ignore such rumours and information bits, it even otherwise does not make sense to take a position in a company or to short the stock or to divest a pre-existing position based on information regarding a positive earnings surprise or a negative earnings rumour. More often than not, the news of the earnings upside or downside is already priced into the stock.

For instance, in the quarter of July 2015, Reliance Industries gave a positive earnings surprise declaring a PBT figure of INR 8,200 crores, higher than analyst estimates. However, the stock price of Reliance had already run up from INR 890 in June 2015 to INR 1,050 in July 2015 and on declaration of the quarterly results the stock price fell to INR 890 levels by August 2015.

As such, anyone looking to trade on the basis of the information would have either lost money or would have made only marginal gains.

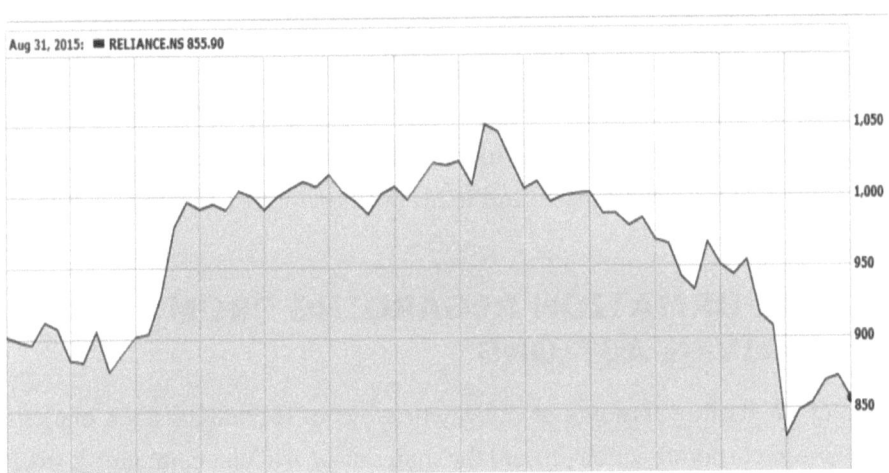

The only relevance and use of the information of such nature is for an investor to factor such information into his analysis of the company that he is looking to invest in or already invested in once such information plays out.

A positive or negative earnings surprise may signal a directional change in the forecasted performance of the company or may be symptomatic of a longer term upside or downside in the business prospects of the company. As such, the investor should analyse the earnings and the reasons for the change and if need be, amend the business performance forecasts built by him as part of the third basic criterion. Based on the revised forecasts, the investor should then form a view regarding the intrinsic value of the company and take a decision whether to take a position in the company or not, and in case where he is already invested, whether to continue with the position or liquidate.

In July 2016, Infosys declared lower than expected earnings for the quarter of April to June 2016. This was on the back of the loss in value of British pound and concerns regarding impact of Brexit on Infosys's revenue pipeline. The stock price of Infosys, as a result took a dive from its previous highs of INR 1250 to INR 1075. Any investor who may have already been invested in the stock of Infosys, ought to have processed the information of the dampened quarter by revising his investment thesis including the projected earnings of Infosys in the ensuing quarters and years. If on the basis of the analysis the investor would conclude that the intrinsic value of the stock stands altered due to depressed business prospects, the investor would consider liquidating the position. If on the other hand, the investor would have found that the prospects of Infosys remain intact and that the lower than expected quarterly earnings were in fact a temporary blip, the investor ought to have used the opportunity of the drop in the stock price to add to his position in the company.

2. INFORMATION REGARDING PROMOTER DRIVEN ACTIONS

One of the darling rumours or information bits of the Indian stock markets pertains to corporate action around the shares of a particular company. A stock of a company attracting an open offer at a premium to the market price, or a delisting offer at a premium juices up the interest in the counter and brings in the punters looking to make a quick buck.

While this bit of information also falls within the ambit of inside information if sourced from anyone in the know of the company, there may still be people looking to legitimately play in a stock based on such information when such rumours and speculations are reported in media or otherwise become public domain information.

An open offer for the shares of the company in question is generally triggered by a transaction involving the acquisition of substantial quantity of the shares of the company under the Takeover code of SEBI. Such a transaction triggers an obligation on the acquirer of the shares to make an open offer for the shares of the company to the public at the recent average market price of the company's shares or the acquisition price whichever is higher.

A delisting offer is made by the promoters of the company wherein they are looking to buy back the shares of the company from the minority shareholders and in the process delist the company from the stock exchanges. In the case of a delisting offer, the buyback price is determined on the basis of the average of the recently quoted market price of the company's shares and the price at which the shares of the company are tendered by the maximum number of shareholders to the promoter under the reverse book building scheme.

In either of the above cases, it is evident that an investor looking to build a portfolio of companies with the medium to long term perspective should not look to play on these information bits, since these may or may not turn out to be correct and even where these do turn out to be accurate, the scope for actual profit on the table may be minimized by front runners and speculators who would have driven the stock price up well ahead of such an action.

For instance, in December 2015, the promoters of Essar Oil launched a delisting offer for the company with the floor price of INR 146 per share. However, in anticipation of the delisting, rumours of which had been doing the rounds in media for many months, the stock price had already run up to INR 240 by December 2015 and the delisting went through at INR 262 per share being the price at which the maximum shares were tendered. Thus, any person who may have purchased the stock on the basis of the delisting information in December 2015 would have at best made marginal gains on tendering the shares in the delisting offer.

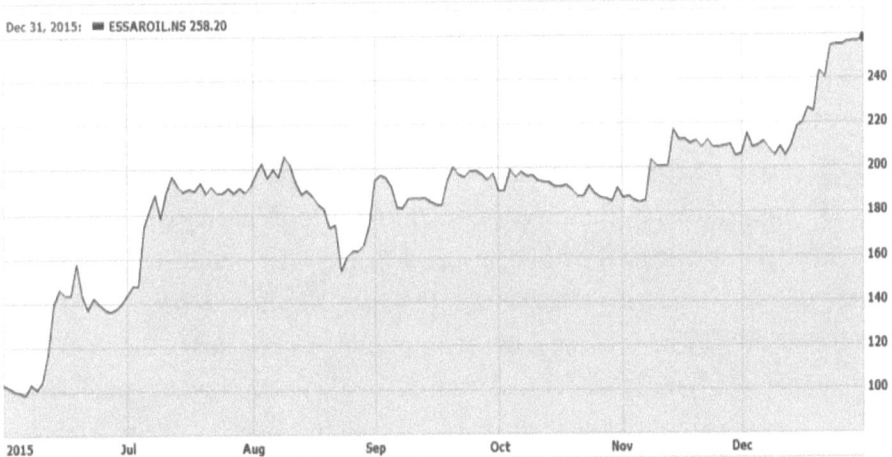

Similarly, in the case of the acquisition of MCX by Kotak Bank in July 2014, the share price of MCX had already run up from the lows of INR 250 in August 2013 to INR 850 by July 2014, on the anticipation of an open offer by Kotak at a much higher acquisition price. However the actual acquisition took place at INR 600 per share. Thus, any person who may have acquired the stock of MCX in the months preceding the acquisition on the hopes of an upside would have seen the stock not react to the acquisition as the acquisition in fact came in at a price lower than the then prevailing market price.

Thus, information regarding open offers or delisting should not be used for trading in stocks. Nevertheless, any information regarding corporate action such as a delisting or open offer should be factored into the analysis by the investor to consider implications thereof to the investor's position in a company.

In case of a delisting offer being made for a company in which the investor already has a position, the investor would need to evaluate whether or not to tender the shares held by him in the delisting offer and at what price he would consider tendering the shares in the offer. Needless to say, the purpose of investment may be defeated if the investor remains invested in the stock and the company ends up being delisted from the market as the investor may not be able to monetize his holding with ease subsequently. As such, any information regarding the delisting action and the anticipated delisting price would thus be relevant to an investor insofar as his decision to exit the holding that he may have in the company in question.

Similarly, in case of an open offer the investor should evaluate whether or not he should tender the position held by him in the open offer in case the price at which the open offer is being made is in the vicinity of the fair value of the stock as ascertained by the investor. At the same time, an open offer is more often than not triggered by a change in management control of the company and this should trigger re-evaluation by the investor of the first basic criterion i.e. the promoter group of the company. In case the company is going into the stable of a promoter group that does not meet the first basic criterion, then again the investor should consider exiting his holding in the company regardless of the offer price in the open offer.

For instance, in case of MCX, an investor who may have been looking to invest in MCX for its business prospects but would have avoided it on account of the controversies surrounding its erstwhile promoter group, may consider investing in the company post its acquisition by Kotak as he may find the first criterion for investment fulfilled.

Thus, information regarding corporate events may not be the trigger for trading but is nevertheless required to be processed and factored into the analysis of the investment in terms of the three basic criteria for investment.

3. INFORMATION REGARDING ACQUISITIONS BY A LISTED COMPANY

Acquisitions of businesses and other companies by Indian companies have always been in vogue vis-à-vis Indian companies. More so, with the liberalization of the foreign exchange regime in India there has been a spurt of acquisitions by the Indian companies overseas.

This includes acquisitions of both, companies as well as assets, by the Indian companies, and are typically aimed at inorganic growth or diversification by the company in question.

Some of the notable acquisitions in the Indian landscape in the recent past include the acquisition of Jaguar Land Rover by Tata Motors, Ssangyong by Mahindra & Mahindra, upstream oil assets by ONGC Videsh Limited and BPCL, Australia port project by Adani Group, acquisition of cement business of Jaypee by Ultratech Cement, and acquisition of DT Multiplex cinemas by PVR from DLF.

The Indian market often reacts positively to news of such acquisitions on a purely sentimental basis. We often see the acquirer company's share price run up on the back of such information or news even though the acquisition may be earnings dilutive for the acquirer or may even end up resulting in a loss in terms of the price paid.

When encountered with news or information regarding an acquisition being made by a company, the investor needs to understand the nature and scope of the acquisition and its implication for the business prospects and projections of the company. Thus, criteria two and three need to be re-evaluated in light of the acquisition.

Furthermore, in view of the price being paid by the company for the acquisition in question, the investor should also get a handle on whether or not the acquisition translates to a value accretion to the company's shares.

As such, while the news or information of acquisition on its own should not be a trigger for initiating a trading or investment position, the analysis of the effect of such acquisition on the business prospects of the acquirer may trigger an investment decision in the stock.

For instance, information regarding PVR Limited acquiring the DT Multiplex cinema chain from DLF for an agreed valuation in consideration for cash, would need to be evaluated in terms of the benefit of the acquisition to the business prospects of PVR i.e. basic criterion two. Further, the investor would need to evaluate the projected financial performance of PVR in light of the acquisition of the additional screens portfolio and geographical presence of DT Cinemas. Also, given that it is an all cash deal, the investor would need to consider the net cash or net debt position of PVR post the acquisition and compare the resultant projected EBIDTA of PVR against the Enterprise Value of PVR to ascertain whether the stock of PVR retains value as compared to the prevailing market price. Last, but not the least, the regulatory headwinds in the Indian context, that PVR may attract in the form of scrutiny by Competition Commission of India (CCI) or other regulatory authorities ought also to be reckoned in the review of the second criterion for PVR as a result of the acquisition.

In this case, the business prospects of PVR on acquiring DT Cinemas from DLF did in fact improve and this has reflected in the stock price of the company, which went up from INR 740 levels in April 2016 to INR 1,000 levels in June 2016 post the completion of the acquisition.

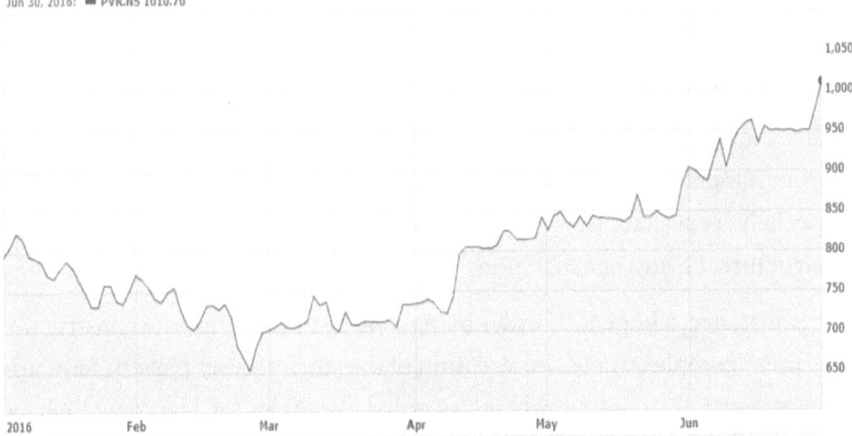

Often times in anticipation of the acquisition, the stock may have already run up and the market price may be factoring in or over valuing the benefits of the acquisition purely on account of positive sentimentality or speculative position build up. In such a case also the investor who already has a position in the company would need to evaluate whether the value targeted by the investor for the stock of the company has been achieved and there is the impetus to exit the holding on the back of the run up.

In some cases, acquisition of a company by another is by way of share swap, as was done by Kotak Mahindra Bank in 2015 while acquiring ING Vysya Bank. Kotak issued its own shares to the shareholders as consideration for acquiring from them the shares of ING Vysya. Thus, the merged entity under Kotak had a much bigger capital base with larger scale of operations, branch networks, revenues and bottom line. In cases such as this one, the investor looking to build a position in Kotak Mahindra Bank would need to evaluate the business prospects of the consolidated entity in view of the geographical presence and other synergistic benefits to Kotak bank by the acquisition of the business of ING Vysya. When revising the projections of Kotak bank as a consolidated entity as part of the exercise for evaluating the third basic criterion, the investor would need to then divide the revised financial metrics by the expanded capital base to arrive at per share values and determine whether or not the stock price of Kotak as a consolidated entity is fairly valued, undervalued or overvalued by the market post the acquisition.

4. INFORMATION REGARDING ORDERS OR CONTRACTS

Another recurrent theme of information churned out of the rumour mills is the procurement or award of major contracts or orders to companies. This is especially prevalent in companies operating in certain sectors such as Infrastructure, IT and construction.

For instance, a huge EPC order being awarded to L&T for the construction of a refinery complex draws the attention of the stock market players. Similarly, a road infrastructure company being awarded a contract for a national highway project also excites the market. Again, large size orders from clients of IT companies also draw market interest.

What is not reckoned by the market speculators before jumping on the bandwagon of the stock, at the back of such information, is whether or not the order or contract is value accretive to the company in question.

In the years 2007 and 2008, in the case of infrastructure and construction companies, we have seen the stocks rallying on the back of orders and contracts, with companies such as those in the road sector outbidding each other to build the portfolio of road projects under the public-private partnership (PPP) scheme as well as the construction companies trying to outdo each other in building large order books, many a times multiple of the revenues of such companies. However, as the story played out from 2008 to 2015 the Indian infrastructure and construction companies' bubble burst. What emerged was that the orders and contracts were secured at highly uncompetitive rates leading to losses and financial distress for these companies in the course of execution. Many projects remained unexecuted and those companies that had executed the orders had to go in for restructuring to pull themselves out of the debt burden. A tell-tale sign of such an impending bubble has always been a rat race amongst the competitors to grab orders at any cost, something which is now being witnessed in the e-commerce space in India.

Thus, buying a stock merely on the news or information of major orders or contracts is a fallacious strategy. Any major development of this nature needs to be evaluated in terms of the expected profitability of the order in question and the effect thereof on the business projections of the company. Only if the finding of such analysis is favourable should the investor consider building or adding to the position in the stock of the company on the back of such information.

5. INFORMATION REGARDING REGULATORY ACTION

Information or rumours regarding certain regulatory actions or developments, most of the time adverse to the operations of the company, are another trigger for frequent market speculation by the players in the Indian market.

For instance, rumours of cancellation of coal blocks auctioned to the companies by the Government of India created a furore in the market in 2014 and brought the stocks of many of these companies tumbling down.

Purported action by the investigative authorities such as CBI against Mr. Kumaramangalam Birla in 2014 again brought the prices down for the Birla group companies.

Action by US FDA against Sun Pharma in 2015 by way of warning letters issued against its facilities affected the Sun Pharma stock price.

Action by the regulators against alleged excessive lead content in Maggi led to the crash of the stock price of Nestle India in 2015.

It has been seen that most of the time, the effect of such information or rumours on the stock price of the companies is transient and it does not take long for the stock to regain its previous price level.

For example, in the chart below you would see that prior to the information on the issue of warning letter by US FDA in December 2015, the stock price of Sun Pharma was prevailing at INR 800 approximately and on the onset of the news it tanked to INR 750. However, soon thereafter the company stock regained the price level by recouping the losses triggered by the adverse regulatory news.

Similarly, the price chart of Reliance Industries reacted to news of ONGC and the Government of India proceeding against Reliance for alleged theft of gas reserves from the ONGC field in the KG Basin. As you would see from the chart below, the stock price of Reliance corrected from INR 990 to INR 940 at the back of this news in December 2015, but regained its feet and recouped the losses soon thereafter.

Thus, for the large part, the news of adverse regulatory developments have temporary effect except for the cases where the regulatory action is likely to materially impair the basic business structure of the company in question. As such, in most cases, the decline in the stock price should not be a trigger for an investor to liquidate his position in the company. On the contrary, the investor should look to build on the existing position at the back of the price slump or initiate a position in a company once the investor is convinced that the regulatory action is not likely to have a major or sustained effect on the earnings of the company in the medium to long term and that the reduced market price offers an upside in terms of the delta between the intrinsic value of the company and said market price.

However, as we have seen, in certain cases, the regulatory action may impair the basic business structure of the company to such an extent that it necessitates a re-evaluation of the investment thesis in the stock and a possible liquidation of position as was seen in the case of Financial Technologies in July 2013.

Thus, information regarding regulatory action should be considered and evaluated as a secondary factor and should not on its own be considered as a trigger or basis for creating positions by an investor.

We have thus seen that information churned out by the market grapevine and rumour mills, including speculative news reported by the media should not be considered as a basis for taking positions in stocks of companies. Apart from the fact that trading based on information secured from inside sources is illegal in India, same as in other countries, even information which may not qualify as 'inside information' but is in the nature of market rumours or media reports ought not to be relied upon as a trigger for the investor to take a position or liquidate an existing position. However, as and when the information does play out, the investor ought to consider the effect of the information on his evaluation of the three basic criteria and accordingly take a decision regarding the liquidation of existing position, or building up of a position in the company's stock in light of the developments and in light of the change in the market price of the company's stock as triggered by such information or rumours.

CHAPTER 11

TECHNICAL CHARTING AND TRADING IDEAS

> *How do you feed the penchant for short term gains? Is there any merit to the daily chatter on business news channels, of the market experts giving ideas for trading or technical chartists propagating quick gains to be made?*

Regardless of all the theoretical and practical merits of a concerted medium to long term approach to investing as championed by the likes of the great Benjamin Graham, Warren Buffett and many others, the fact remains that the natural human urge, borne out by the DNA in the age of instant gratification and limited attention span, is to make quick gains and benefit by short term spurts in prices of stocks translating not only to monetary gains but also the thrill and excitement befitting the spoils of the internet age. It has thus been a natural tendency on the part of every player in the stock market, whether in India or abroad, at some point in time or the other in their investing lifespan, to be tempted by the lure of trading and making quick gains in the process.

We have already seen in the preceding chapter, the pitfalls of trading on the back of market information and rumours and how, this may not only be illegal, it is even otherwise not recommended as a strategy for the reasons explained.

Apart from the trading based on information, typically the schools of trading can broadly be divided into two categories: technical charting and trading ideas.

While it is not the thrust of this book to advocate trading on a short term basis, the above schools are briefly discussed in this chapter to shed light on the pitfalls and advantages of these approaches so that a learned investor may make use of these approaches selectively in certain cases as elaborated below.

1. TECHNICAL CHARTING

Technical charting and trading based on how the price charts read is an entirely different approach to stock markets than the fundamental financials based approach advocated in this book and by most of the famous investors globally.

Technical charting as an approach bases its premise on the principle that the stock prices follow certain patterns in their movement and these patterns are bound to repeat. This premise regarding the pattern being followed by stock prices is rooted on the psychological behaviour of the market players who would tend to buy a stock around certain levels and sell it at certain levels.

By virtue of there being a pattern to the movement of the stock prices, technical chartists tend to read the historical price charts of stocks for significant levels and on the basis of the stock prices trading above or below a level, recommend a buy or sell trade in the stock in question. For anyone looking to be clued in on technical chartists' tips or recommendations, you don't have to look far beyond internet websites and business news channels in India such as CNBC or NDTV Profit. There are plenty of technical chartists who recommend trades in stocks on a daily basis pre-market opening and during market hours. In fact it is a unique aspect of the Indian stock markets that persons with no certification or oversight by any regulator are allowed to dole out advice on television channels as experts, on a daily basis.

A typical technical trade works in the following manner. A technical chartist studying the pattern for say, Tata Steel sees it close above INR 250 level in the month of October of 2015.

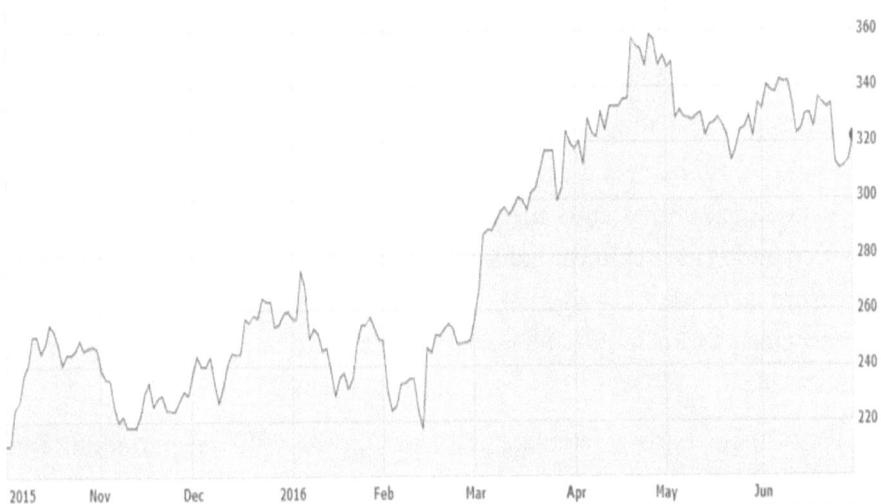

Jun 30, 2016: TATASTEEL.NS 321.95

The chartist regards this as a significant level given the patterns shown by the stock in the past. As such the chartist recommends a buy on Tata Steel with a stop loss of INR 240 and a price target of INR 300 (say) which would be a resistance level for the stock price as demonstrated in the past behaviour.

In such a situation, an investor (using the term loosely) would take a position in Tata Steel at the 250+ levels and look to make a quick gain on the stock running up, having closed above the critical level of INR 250. However, if the call of the chartist proves to be incorrect and the stock moves below INR 240, the stop loss would be triggered and the investor would exit the position at a loss. It's an entirely possible scenario that soon after the investor exiting the position at say INR 240, the stock moves up beyond INR 250 again and goes on to register gains.

As would have actually played out in the above case, viewing the chart of Tata Steel from October 2015 to June 2016, the stop loss of the investor would have gotten triggered causing the investor to exit his position in the stock by November 2015. Yet by June 2016 the stock of Tata Steel rallied and made new highs upwards of INR 340.

As you would see from the above illustration, taking of positions and making profits or losses in stocks under the technical approach does not in any way consider the fundamentals of the company or the business prospects or any other factors. It relies purely on the price movement.

While it is easy to ignore the approach of technical chartists and stay on the course of fundamental investing, it does merit a mention that typically all stocks, commodities and other markets do follow a pattern of movement where up moves are not linear but interspersed by bouts of down moves where selling/profit booking comes in and similarly down moves are not linear but are interspersed with bouts of up moves at the back of buying or profit booking by short sellers.

Thus, there exists a rationale and merit in the fundamental premise of technical charting. What is questionable however is the quality and efficacy of a particular technical call. As has been the experience of many, short term trading more often than not ends up being a zero sum game or even a loss-making proposition, and tempting as it may be, is best avoided in favour of fundamental medium to long term investing.

Having said the above, in case an investor is looking to build a position or add to a position in a stock on the basis of fundamental analysis or exit a position in a stock based on the valuation of the stock having been reflected in the market price thereof, and such an investor does have a strong handle on technical charting or believes in the reading of the technical charts by any particular expert, then such an investor may look to buy or sell as the case may be, based on the significant levels in the price chart of the stock and thus make use of technical charting as a supplemental tool to his investing.

2. TRADING IDEAS

Apart from technical charting, there are many other avenues for a person to take on positions in stocks with a view to making short term gains. As an investor spends more and more time in the market, even while practising the art of medium to long term investing and in the process keeping abreast of developments in the stock market as well as the economy in general, he would many a times stumble upon ideas, which though short lived, may make a compelling argument for a position in a stock, whether long position or short position.

The question thus arises whether the investor should pay heed to such ideas and delve into a position in the stocks to test the ideas.

While it is not the objective of this book to discuss short term trading or arbitrage ideas in detail, some of these are discussed in this chapter in brief to give a flavour of the nature and diversity of such opportunities with the intent that an investor may be able to filter the meaningful opportunities or ideas from the risky ones and be able to take the benefit of some trading ideas to supplement the long term portfolio accretion with short term gains, more so in the context of the Indian stock markets which are prone to drastic up and down moves in short spans of time.

a. Currency Re-Rating

As an investor in equities, while understanding the business prospects of various investee companies as well as the general macro-economic scenario, the investor would be clued into the happenings with the currency market as well as the policy action by the central banks of the various countries including India.

The monetary policy and the fiscal policy of the Reserve Bank of India as well as the Federal Reserve of USA determine the movement of INR and USD respectively.

Similarly, the policy action of Japanese Central Bank determines the movement of the Japanese Yen vis-à-vis the global major currencies, including the INR.

The movement of the currencies is in any case useful to be tracked as it would have a bearing on the earning prospects of companies in export and import as well as companies having foreign exchange exposure in terms of loans or assets or subsidiaries, and thus require the investor to consider the effect of such movements on the projected financial performance of the companies i.e. the third basic criterion.

At the same time, in certain instances, a significant re-rating of a particular currency may also provide a short term trading opportunity.

For instance, 2015 witnessed a significant and sustained devaluation of the INR against USD, when INR depreciated from INR 60/USD levels to INR 66/USD levels on the back of expected higher interest rate regime by the US Federal Reserve and the lowering of interest rates by Reserve Bank of India. In such a case, companies exporting goods or services to the United States of America, or otherwise having dollar denominated revenues would see a direct gain to their bottom line on account of the currency re-rating. Thus, in such a case, the investor could consider taking a short term position in stocks such as Infosys, Tech Mahindra or other IT services companies to capitalize on this currency re-rating even though it may be a one-time event.

Thus, an investor may consider the price movement in the stock such as Infosys coupled with his investment thesis factoring in the higher revenues due to the currency gain. In case, the currency re-rating has not been factored into the price already, it would be fairly reasonable to assume that the up-side on the back of higher revenues would directly add to the EBIDTA margin of the company and thus result in superior earnings in the current year and possibly the ensuing years as well. In such a case, a short term position in the stock without necessarily taking a long term position, may be considered to capitalize on the up move in the stock price in the short term.

b. Short Selling Opportunities

A medium to long term investment thesis as recommended in this book mandates long positions. Short positions, where the investor short sells a stock in expectation of it's price going down, are typically taken with a short term perspective.

It may occur, in the course of the analysis of investments vis-à-vis the three basic criteria as well as the secondary criteria, that the investor may be confronted by cases of compelling over valuation. A company analysed by the investor may reveal weak business prospects or a stock valuation which is not justified by the projected financial performance of the company.

Similarly, the investor may come across certain regulatory changes or other secondary factors which are likely to adversely affect the business prospects of certain companies where the investor does not have a position.

In cases such as the above, the investor could consider taking a short position in the stock in question by selling the stock in the futures segment with a view to buy back the stock on its decline and make a profit in the process.

For instance, the price of crude oil declined from USD 110 per barrel in June 2014 to USD 30 per barrel levels by the end of 2015.

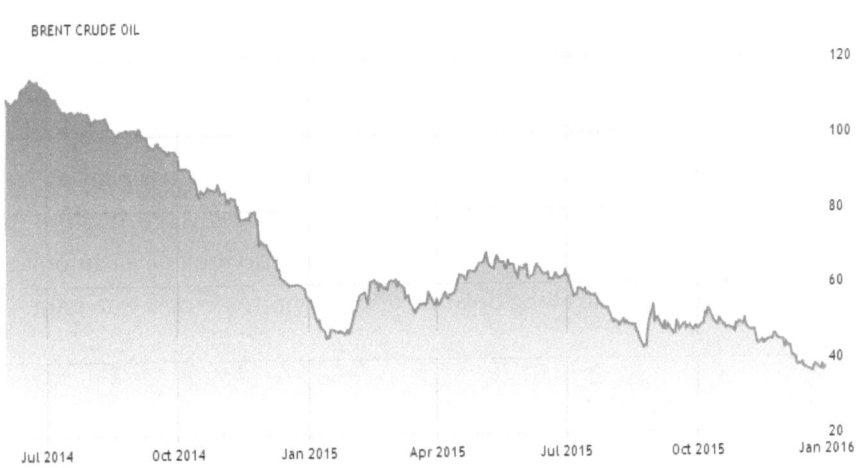

While an investor may not have been invested in a company such as Cairn India which derives its revenues primarily from crude oil sale pegged to the international benchmark crude price of Brent Crude Oil, the steep fall in the crude oil price in the international market would have provided a short selling opportunity to the investor nevertheless. As would be seen from the price chart of Cairn India below, the stock price slid down at the back of Brent crude falling and thus, would have yielded a short term profit making opportunity to the investor.

While short selling opportunities are high risk and generally ought to be avoided, nevertheless, in situations where the investor has a handle on the prospects of the company owing to his study of the fundamentals of the company as well as the macro-economic factors, the investor may consider venturing into the short selling trading strategies especially since these also provide an automatic hedge to the fundamentally long position oriented portfolio of the investor.

c. Ipo Proxies

In a market which is doing well, it is inevitable to see a flurry of Initial public offerings by companies looking to raise funds.

In India, IPOs have for the most part been celebratory events with a chance for quick gains as the stocks of the companies getting listed have traded at a premium to their issue price, notwithstanding the fact that the IPO may itself be priced at a high valuation to the company's underlying financials.

As a general rule it is not recommended to play for the short term pop of IPO listings as these may or may not materialise owing to speculative overhang. An IPO should only be considered from a long term position perspective by the investor evaluating the company for the three basic criteria and in case the IPO price is found to be lower than the perceived intrinsic value, the investor may consider subscribing to the IPO of the company.

On the other hand, IPOs present a meaningful trigger for the investor in assessing the stocks and taking trading positions in those which are already listed in the market and may present a proxy play to the IPO.

To elaborate, in the course of the analysis of the three basic criteria by the investor across various companies, the investor may arrive at a view regarding the valuation of certain companies operating in particular sectors. The investor may not be convinced regarding taking a position in such a company as the investor may view the company to be fully valued. However, if thereafter, there is an IPO by another company operating in the same sector and such IPO is priced at a higher multiple than that being accorded to the already listed company, then it may trigger a case for the investor to re-evaluate the already listed company as an investment or trading prospect. This is especially relevant in view of the fact that if the company going for the IPO has a stellar response to the IPO and its stock is listed at a premium to the issue price, it would merit a re-rating of the stock price of the already listed peers operating in the same sector, to the higher multiples and thus lead to a short term price jump.

In 2015, Indigo Airlines went in for its IPO. It priced the stock at INR 765 per share valuing the company at INR 27,000 crores. The IPO received sound response, being subscribed over 3 times. Within months of listing, the stock moved from the issue price of INR 765 to INR 1,200 per share.

As a proxy to Indigo, Jet Airways as a stock was quoting at the time of Indigo IPO at INR 330 per share. On listing of Indigo, the price of Jet was also re-rated with the stock rising to INR 440 per share. Chart showing the relative movement of Jet Airways and Indigo below.

Equity:In

Thus an investor who may have evaluated Jet Airways as a stock for the three basic criteria but may have given a pass to the stock on account of its valuation, would have done well to re-assess the value of Jet stock on the back of the valuation of Indigo in its IPO. A high valuation being given to Indigo in the IPO may necessitate a re-rating of the Jet stock and trigger a short term or long term position by the investor in Jet Airways as a proxy play on the Indigo stock.

As would have turned out, the investor would have made some short term profit on such a bet.

d. Writing Options

Put and Call options are part of the derivatives segment in the Indian stock markets. These options are available for both the indices as well as individual stocks. The primary purpose of put and call options is to hedge the current position of an investor against volatility and temporary movements in the markets.

For instance, an investor who is invested in say Reliance Industries with a medium to long term perspective, may consider buying Reliance puts where he anticipates that due to market volatility or down trend there may be temporary fall in the market price of Reliance stock even though the long term business prospects remain intact. As such, by buying the put options of Reliance, the investor would be able to hedge his position and make a profit on the put option on the fall of Reliance stock price thereby neutralizing the loss on his medium to long term position.

Use of put and call options for hedging the position built by an investor requires a sophisticated approach to investment which is not devoid of risk and transaction costs.

However, there may also be short term trading opportunities in 'writing' put and call options. This is the case where the investor finds the market going through excessive rounds of volatility owing to temporary blips or external events. For instance a market wide volatility in India may occur at the back of certain national events such as elections, terrorist attacks or other such occurrences. Similarly, the market may also fluctuate violently at the back of global events as has been seen in 2015 in the case of Greek debt crisis. In such times, while the medium to long term oriented portfolio of the investor may not be at risk so long as the overall business prospects of the companies remain intact, yet the market volatility may affect the value of the portfolio significantly.

For instance, from January 2016 to April 2016, there was high volatility in the Indian markets with the BSE Sensex gyrating over 10% in both directions from 26,000 levels to 23,000 levels and back to 26,000 levels. Even more exaggerated was the movement in the stock prices during this period with even large market cap frontline stocks moving over 20% in both directions.

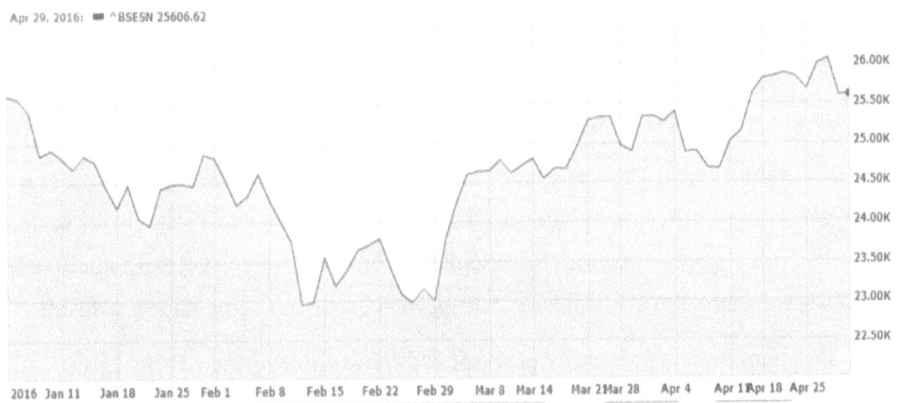

In such cases, so long as the investor is convinced that the volatility and the resultant fall in the market is of a temporary nature, the investor may consider selling put options or in other words writing put options at the index levels. This would imply that the investor is taking a long position at the market index level and betting on the assumption that the fall in the market is temporary and the losses would be recouped. The options are built to expire within a time-frame and with the passage of time, the value of the option depletes significantly thereby resulting in a gain to the seller of the option.

Such short term trading based on the writing of options is again a risky trade and though not part of the core philosophy of this book, may yet be explored by an investor where the ongoing market study of the investor bears out an understanding that the volatility in the market is short lived and any losses are bound to be recouped when the volatility settles.

e. Pair Trades

Over the course of analysing companies under the three basic criteria for purposes of building up the portfolio, the investor would often stumble upon apparent anomalies in the market. Two companies, operating in the same sector - one overvalued, the other undervalued. There may be a tangible reason for such difference in valuation of the two companies, such as inferior promoter group in one or poor business prospects of one versus the other. Or it may be a case where one company is genuinely undervalued while the other one is overvalued.

In such a case, instead of taking a bare long position in the undervalued stock the investor may consider initiating a pair trade whereby he goes long on the undervalued stock and short on the overvalued stock.

For example, in the case of airline space, if the investor finds that a Jet Airways is relatively undervalued while Spice Jet is overvalued, the investor may consider going long on Jet and short on Spice Jet. Typically such pair trades are executed on a rupee neutral basis, i.e. for the same rupee amount.

The benefit of a pair trade, as opposed to a solitary long or short position, is that the pair trade also has the effect of counter balancing market movements which may otherwise ruin a correctly judged long position.

Thus in the above example, in case the investor would have only gone long on Jet Airways on the basis of the analysis of relative undervaluation of the Jet Airways stock and the market sentiment goes overall negative which leads to a major decline in the broader market, the investor may see the holding come off his purchase price and lead him to a loss position which may not improve in the medium term in case the broader market sell-off is due to macro-economic or systemic issues. However in the same situation, in case the investor would have initiated a pair trade with short selling of Spice Jet in addition to the long position, the investor would see a profit in the Spice Jet short position in case of the market sell-off. In fact the fall in the spice jet stock price may be more accentuated than that in Jet Airways in case the fundamental analysis of the investor is true and in fact Jet Airways as a stock is undervalued as opposed to Spice Jet.

As such the investor, by having initiated the pair trade would have managed to hedge his long position in Jet Airways and would have mitigated the short to medium term loss in the Jet Airways position by way of a gain in the Spice Jet short position.

Pair trades are very specific and require greater conviction to pull off as the investor is taking diametrically opposite view regarding two stocks mostly in the same sector. Thus it would more often than not play out that one position would show a profit and the other would show a loss. As such the pair trade as a whole would make a profit for the investor only where the profit on one stock is more than the loss in the other stock.

Accordingly, pair trades should be executed only by a seasoned investor at the back of detailed analysis of two companies which convinces the investor that the play off of the pair would yield positive results.

f. Holding Subsidiary Arbitrage

Many listed companies, especially those belonging to family promoter groups in India are organized under a typical holding-subsidiary structure.

Under such a structure, the group 'flagship' company is the holding company in which the promoters own the majority shareholding. This group flagship company, in turn, controls one or more subsidiary companies which house the operating businesses. In many such cases, the holding company is not simply one that houses shares of the subsidiaries but also houses one or more operating businesses of the group itself.

A recent example of such a structure is the proposed restructuring by the Aditya Birla Group under which Grasim would become the group flagship company with shareholding in Ultratech Cement, Idea, Aditya Birla Financial Services and Aditya Birla Fashion. In addition Grasim would also continue to transact business in its own entity in VSF and chemicals space.

In a typical situation where the company being considered for purposes of investment by application of the three basic criteria for investment is a subsidiary of a holding company which is also listed, it would benefit the investor to also analyse the valuation of the holding company as part of his analysis.

In the instant case for example, where the investor looking to invest in the cement business finds Ultratech Cement, as a company to be undervalued and having favourable long term business prospects, the investor may also evaluate Grasim, which as the holding company of Ultratech, may be even cheaper in terms of valuation. So long as the cheaper valuation of Grasim is not owing to any systemic or financial issues in the balance sheet of Grasim or negative business prospects of any of the businesses housed in Grasim itself or of any of the other subsidiaries of Grasim, then the investor may consider investing in Grasim as a proxy for his call to invest in Ultratech and try to benefit from the holding company discount while at the same time also spreading out his risk in terms of businesses he is exposed to as a shareholder of Grasim versus as a shareholder of Ultratech. The holding subsidiary arbitrage trade moves on the premise that over a period of time the holding subsidiary valuation discount would narrow or subside.

However, a play on the holding subsidiary relationship is fraught with risk where the holding company imbibes multiple businesses as part of itself and also holds shares of multiple subsidiaries. In such a case it may turn out that while the investor's call regarding the particular subsidiary may prove to be correct, this may get offset by the losses or poor performance of the other businesses/subsidiaries of the holding company in which case the investor would lose out on making any money in the process, even though his fundamental call on the particular subsidiary may have been correct all along.

Moreover, a holding subsidiary structure is also often affected by the first basic criterion for investment i.e. the promoter group. Promoter groups of holding subsidiary structures have a strong hold on all the group companies and have often been accused of carrying out related party transactions such as movement of funds or payment of royalties from subsidiary to holding company thereby stripping out the value of the subsidiary company in an unjustifiable manner.

Thus, the play on holding subsidiary arbitrage ought to be attempted by an investor only in case the holding company presents a significant discount to the subsidiary and such discount in valuation is not on account of adverse factors surrounding the promoter group or the holding company's other businesses/ financials.

g. Stock's Inclusion In Benchmark Indices

At the end of the day, all movement in stock prices is a function of demand and supply. A stock where the demand outstrips the supply, sees an uptick in its prices and conversely a stock where the supply outstrips the demand sees a down-tick in its prices.

The fundamentals based approach as advocated by this book works on the hypothesis that the stock of a company that is undervalued as compared to its business prospects and financial projections would inevitably see buyers gravitating to purchase it and the demand would thus outstrip the supply leading to the price of the stock moving up towards the intrinsic value thereof.

However, there may be certain stocks which do fulfil the three basic criteria and still do not see the demand from investors such as large institutional investors owing to the stocks being smaller in terms of market capitalization or not being liquid enough in terms of volumes or otherwise not being in the radar of the large investors.

One eventuality which does change such a situation is the inclusion of the stock in any of the major indices of the market or other basket indices of major brokerage houses.

Thus, the inclusion of a stock in the Nifty 50 index of NSE, or in the Nifty midcap index or in the Nifty Bank index for instance would automatically bring the stock into the radar of many institutional buyers and furthermore lead to mandated purchase of the stock by institutions and mutual funds which are investing in index only stocks or whose portfolio is index linked.

Similarly, the inclusion of a stock in the basket of a brokerage house, such as the Morgan Stanley Index or Goldman Sachs would also attract institutional interest in buying the stock, especially by foreign investors.

A typical example of the Morgan Stanley index for India for two different time periods is provided below.

MSCI as at 31st March, 2014 (Top 20 Companies)

Name	Weight (%)
INFOSYS LTD	9.9268
HOUSING DEVELOPMENT FINANCE CORP.	8.6159
RELIANCE INDUSTRIES LTD	7.9192
TATA CONSULTANCY SERVICES LTD	6.6016
ITC LTD.	5.1585
HDFC BANK LTD.	5.007
LARSEN AND TOUBRO LTD	2.637
HINDUSTAN UNILEVER LTD	2.5861
SUN PHARMACEUTICAL INDUSTRIES LTD	2.3505
HCL TECHNOLOGIES LTD.	2.2391
WIPRO LTD	2.2036
TATA MOTORS LTD	2.0108
MAHINDRA AND MAHINDRA LTD	1.9886
STATE BANK OF INDIA ORD	1.886
ICICI BANK LTD	1.7981
DR REDDYS LABORATORIES LTD	1.7232
KOTAK MAHINDRA BANK LTD	1.6203
OIL & NATURAL GAS CORP. LTD.	1.6156
UNITED SPIRITS LTD.	1.518
VEDANTA LTD	1.288

MSCI as at 31st March, 2016 (Top 20 Companies)

Name	Weight (%)
INFOSYS LTD	11.4731
HOUSING DEVELOPMENT FINANCE CORP.	8.4947
RELIANCE INDUSTRIES LTD	6.9401
TATA CONSULTANCY SERVICES LTD	6.1081
SUN PHARMACEUTICAL INDUSTRIES LTD	4.0452
ITC LTD.	3.782
HINDUSTAN UNILEVER LTD	3.3748
HCL TECHNOLOGIES LTD.	2.3492
MAHINDRA AND MAHINDRA LTD	2.3121
BHARTI AIRTEL LTD.	2.1559
MARUTI SUZUKI INDIA LTD.	2.0138
LARSEN AND TOUBRO LTD	1.9745
DR REDDYS LABORATORIES LTD	1.8309
WIPRO LTD	1.7856
LUPIN LTD.	1.6732
TATA MOTORS LTD	1.5951
STATE BANK OF INDIA	1.5458
AXIS BANK LTD	1.3543
ICICI BANK LTD	1.3388
ASIAN PAINTS LTD	1.2807

As would be seen from the above, a stock such as Asian Paints got included in the MSCI in 2016, while the weightage of Infosys increased from 2014 to 2016. This would have necessitated buying into Infosys and Asian Paints by major investors as also the funds which have their portfolios designed around the MSCI.

As such, the inclusion or exclusion of a stock in any of the indices may be considered by the investor, and where the investor finds a stock which otherwise fulfils the three basic criteria, being included in the index, the investor may consider it to be an opportune trigger to buy into the stock or add to the existing position of the investor in the stock in question.

For example, an investor looking to invest in the stock of Ashiana Housing may find the company to have the right promoter group, good business prospects in its real estate space and be undervalued as a stock given the growth prospects of the company. However, the investor may be hesitant to invest in the stock owing to the low liquidity of the stock as shown below:

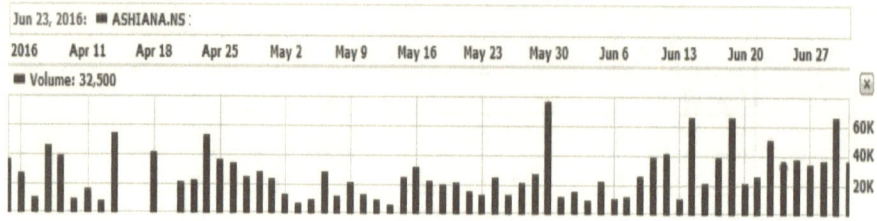

However if the stock of Ashiana gets included in one of the indices referred above, this may suddenly bring the company on the radar of the large investors and add liquidity to the stock. This may in turn bring in buying interest and cause re-rating of the stock thereby aligning the stock price to its intrinsic value. Thus, the inclusion of the stock in the index would be a good trigger for the investor to take a trading or even a long term position in the stock.

h. Dividend And Bonus Stripping

Dividend stripping and bonus stripping are conventionally considered as tax planning exercises, rather than trading strategies.

Dividend stripping involves a person buying a stock which is cum-dividend i.e. dividend has been declared by the company and the record date for payout of the dividend is yet to occur. In such a case, the person buys the stock with a view to receive dividend thereon which is tax-free in the hands of the shareholder. Thereafter the stock, which is now ex-dividend is sold by the shareholder at a loss and such loss is set off against other investment gains of the investor thereby saving him income tax on the investment gains.

For example, in March 2016 Hindustan Zinc quoting at INR 185 per share declared a special golden jubilee dividend of INR 24 per share. In such a case the investor would buy HZL cum-dividend at INR 185 per share, receive the dividend of INR 24 per share and thereafter when the stock goes ex-dividend and quotes at INR 161 per share or lower, the investor sells the shares at a loss of INR 24 per share which is set off against the other portfolio gains of the investor. In the process, the investor pockets tax free dividend of INR 24 per share and also uses the notional loss of INR 24 on sale of the HZL stock to save tax on other realised gains in his portfolio.

In the case of bonus stripping, the investor buys a stock of a company that has declared a bonus issue of shares. Once the bonus shares are credited to the account of the investor, the investor sells off the original shares of the company which are now ex-bonus thereby incurring a notional loss on these shares, which loss is set off against portfolio gains made by the investor thus saving tax for the investor.

For example, Kotak Mahindra Bank declared bonus issue of 1:1 and the stock of Kotak quoted cum-bonus at INR 1,300 per share. The investor looking to carry out bonus stripping would purchase the stock of Kotak at INR 1,300 per share and hold the stock till the ex-date for the bonus. Once the stock goes ex-bonus, it would likely quote at INR 650 i.e. half the price or lower. The investor would thus sell the original shares at a loss of INR 650 per share and this loss would be set off by the investor against investment gains appearing in the books of the investor so as to save tax for the investor. At the same time, the investor would receive bonus shares into his portfolio which would be at a cost of nil and would be held by the investor with a view to ride the capital appreciation on the stock in the medium to long term.

In our view, insofar as Indian markets are concerned, it has often been seen that stocks which go ex-dividend or ex-bonus may initially trade at a price which strips out the dividend or bonus element from the price as illustrated above, however where the stocks in question are intrinsically sound and fulfil the three basic investment criteria, such stocks gradually bounce back to higher levels. Thus, the investor may not incur a notional loss but in fact end up gaining from having taken a position in the cum-dividend or cum-bonus stock.

Thus, in the above examples, in the case of HZL, if the investor is convinced that the stock does fulfil the three basic criteria, he would do well to hold on to the stock even after it goes ex-dividend and trades at ex-dividend price of INR 161 per

Equity:In

share as it would inevitably start clawing back above the cum-dividend purchase price of INR 185 per share and the investor would end up with tax free dividend income of INR 24 per share as well as not be saddled with a loss on sale of the stock.

This did in fact come to pass in case of HZL, as would be seen in the chart below, where within months of going ex-dividend in April 2016, the stock clawed back above INR 185 levels by July 2016 owing to the business prospects of the stock looking favourable at the back of rising zinc price in the international markets.

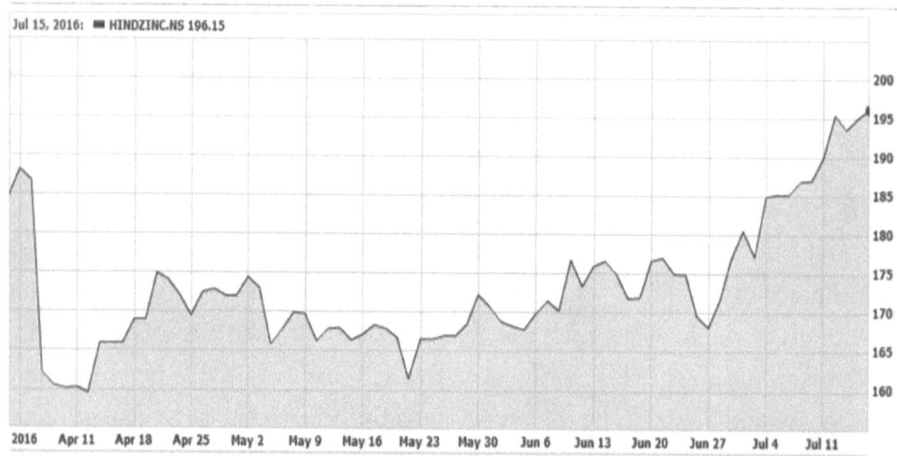

Similarly, in the case of the bonus stripping, the investor, if he is convinced that the stock of Kotak Mahindra Bank fulfils the three basic criteria, the investor may consider not selling the stock even after it goes ex-bonus and it may likely play out that ex-bonus the stock of the company trades higher than INR 650 per share, say INR 700 per share, in which case the investor would in effect be sitting on a consolidated gain of INR 100 i.e. INR 50 per share multiplied by two shares of Kotak Bank.

Thus, resorting to positions in stocks which are cum-dividend or cum-bonus and also fulfil the three basic criteria may be a recommended trading strategy not only from tax planning perspective but also from the perspective of short term trading or medium term gains.

i. Index Hedging

It often plays out that an investor has carefully studied various sectors, promoter groups and companies and by application of the three basic criteria, selected stocks and built up his portfolio which he expects to yield capital appreciation over a medium term horizon.

However, given the multifarious factors, domestic as well as global that affect the capital markets on an almost daily basis, it is but expected that the ride from the time the investor takes a position in the stocks to the time he expects the appreciation in values to happen, would not be a smooth one. In fact, it is never the case that any stock or portfolio of stocks would see a linear rise notwithstanding the underlying financials or performance of the companies involved.

More so, in India, which has conventionally been a high beta market, the broader market often takes a nose dive owing to negative sentiment, broad-based selling or international uncertainties. In such situations, the investor often finds the value of his portfolio stripped down even though nothing may have changed in terms of the business prospects of the companies involved.

While typically an investor should not be fazed about such movements, and so long as the basic fundamentals of the investee companies remain intact, any down-turn should be considered as an opportunity to add to the positions in the stocks in question, however at certain times, the investor who is seasoned and clued onto the broader market movements, may consider undertaking a trading position on the benchmark index to hedge against losses on his portfolio.

Given that the fundamental portfolio is by definition a long position, a hedge at the index level involves shorting the benchmark index, whether by way of selling the index futures or by buying put options or by selling call options on the index. When the investor undertakes such a trade and the index does, in fact, fall on the back of broad based selling, the investor would see a gain on his short position which would offset the unrealized loss on his long portfolio and thus act as a hedge for the investor.

Index hedging is a risky trade and should be done by an investor only in situations where the investor, based on his reading of macro-economic and international developments is fairly certain that a fall in the broader market is inevitable.

j. DVR Trades

Indian stock markets have started to mature and the evolved regulatory framework has allowed the concept of equity shares with 'differential voting rights' or DVR. While all companies can now have DVR equity shares, there are only a few companies in India, at present which are listed companies and have DVR shares listed as well.

Some examples of Indian listed companies also having listed DVR shares are Tata Motors and Future Enterprises Limited.

A DVR share by definition carries lower voting rights in terms of the say of the shareholder in the management of the company or other governance issues. On the other hand the DVR share ranks pari passu (on the same footing) as ordinary equity shares when it comes to financial rights, i.e. the right to receive dividends or right to receive assets of the company on liquidation.

DVR shares have typically quoted at a discount to the ordinary shares of the companies. Such discounts have varied from 20 percent to 40 percent plus. This is due to the voting rights which are vested with the ordinary shares as opposed to the DVR holders.

Nevertheless, in the analysis of the three basic criteria, if a stock is found to be satisfactory, the fact that the particular equity share does not carry requisite voting rights would not make much of a difference as the investor in question would anyway not seek to derive the value of his holding by proactively exercising voting rights or control over the investee company. As the proposition of the investment in this book already factors in the fact that the company should have the appropriate promoter group controlling the company, a company fulfilling this first basic criterion would thus be worth investing in, even if the investor does not carry any significant voting rights via the equity instruments he holds.

Thus, where an investor shortlists an investment in a company, say Tata Motors, which fulfils the three basic criteria, the argument for investment in the DVR instead of the ordinary shares would be even more compelling as the discount of the DVR to the ordinary shares of Tata Motors would make the undervaluation of Tata Motors even steeper. As such, in such a case the investor may consider investing in the DVR not only on the basic investment premise but also on the additional trading play that the discount of the price of DVR to the ordinary shares would ultimately narrow and yield an additional return to the DVR holder.

This has, in the case of a stock such as Tata Motors, been seen to be true as can be seen from the charts of Tata Motors ordinary shares and DVR below, where the DVR has outperformed the ordinary shares.

We have thus seen that in addition to or to complement the basic fundamental oriented medium to long term investing approach prescribed by this book, there are a number of trading strategies that may be adopted by an investor. Trading positions by their very definition, are riskier and ought to be undertaken only by an investor who is sufficiently clued in and convinced regarding the outcome of such position. It is often seen that the temptation for quicker gains promised by trading or technical strategies outstrips the concerted value investing approach and many an 'investors' end up negating all the gains they may make on their value investing portfolio by the losses on the trading positions.

While resorting to risky trading positions is not the thrust of this book, these have nevertheless been discussed as during the course of the detailed analysis of stocks, and keeping abreast of market developments, the investor may come across the ideas for such trading plays in actuality and the proposition may be too compelling to ignore or pass up.

CHAPTER 12

CLOSING SUMMARY

This chapter presents a bullet point summary which is designed to serve not only as a summation of the main propositions and points of discussion taken up in this book, but also as a ready reference to the investor regarding the various principles to be adopted and practised where there arise any doubts during the ongoing investment activities of the investor in the Indian equity markets.

1. India is an exciting market to invest in equities, more so, given the stage of Indian economic development, growth potential, and the flow of capital to the country's equity markets at the back of a pro-business government at the Centre.
2. Indian equity markets have exhibited unprecedented growth and returns in the last 15 years. The stage of economic development and activity that we stand on today provides the platform for fervent growth in corporate earnings and promise for the Indian stock markets to outperform its global peers. Probably, there is no other country in the world which today promises the high growth rate projected in India on as high a base GDP as India's.
3. Well known and established approaches to investing, applicable to western markets may not necessarily work with Indian companies as Indian markets exhibit unique characteristics such as lack of depth, complicated regulatory framework, federal political structure, rampant tips and speculation, diverse promoter group categories and high sensitivity (beta) to local as well as global developments. Thus the need for an investment approach adapted to the Indian markets.
4. In view of the unique features of Indian stock markets, this book presents an India specific approach to investing in equities. The approach recommended by this book has been developed keeping in mind the peculiarities of the Indian markets and takes into account certain unique features such as the diverse promoter groups, difficulties of conducting business in India and how different companies are valued in India.

5. In the Indian markets, it is as important to know what factors not to consider as the trigger for investing in a stock, as knowing what factors are to be considered. Some factors which by themselves should never be the sole basis of making an investment in an Indian equity, even though one would commonly find the Indian market players relying on such factors, include:

    a. Tips on earnings and other price sensitive information
    b. Mergers and Acquisition
    c. Promoter related news
    d. Corporate Events
    e. Regulatory development vis-à-vis the company
    f. Novel ideas regarding why a company presents a lucrative investment proposition
    g. Entry of a major investor into a stock
    h. Technical charts

6. This book recommends that any company, so as to be considered investment worthy, must fulfil three basic or main criteria.

7. The three main criteria, which any company must fulfil, as recommended by this book, are to be tested sequentially. If a company does not fulfil the first criterion, it ought to be rejected. If it does fulfil the first criterion, only then the investor should evaluate the second and then the third criterion. Only a company which crosses these three sequential hurdles must be considered investment worthy.

8. The three main criteria for investment as recommended by this book are:

    a. Promoter group profile
    b. Business Prospects
    c. Valuation

9. The first and perhaps the most important criterion in the selection of an investment worthy stock amongst the Indian equities, is the promoter group profile. A company may present itself as having a most promising business with its stock price being undervalued to a compelling degree, it

would still not be worth investing in if it is controlled by a promoter group that is not known for fair and transparent management of the company's affairs and following the proper corporate governance principles.

10. Indian corporate diaspora has its unique categories of promoter groups including family promoter groups, government-owned companies, multinational corporations and companies without any identifiable promoters. The presence of such diverse types of promoters makes it even more pertinent that the investor be certain about the promoter group profile of the company he is looking to invest in.

11. There have been many instances in the Indian corporate history where family promoter groups have been found to be violating principles of corporate governance and stripping out the financials of the listed company for their personal benefit and lifestyle, to the detriment of the minority shareholders. Practices such as drawing excessive remuneration, parking personal assets in the listed company using the latter's funds, construction contracts, delisting, preferential allotment of shares to themselves, and related party transactions have been misused by the promoter groups to siphon off funds of listed companies.

12. In the case of government-owned companies, the funds of the listed companies have been misused for public policy and welfare initiatives. Listed companies have been made to sell their products at subsidized rates for the welfare of the poor thereby totally obfuscating the profit earning structure of such companies. Corporate governance and transparency has been lacking in such companies and often times, the key managerial positions have been filled by babus and favourites rather than the most competent personnel. Such companies have also been used as government's go to vehicles for fulfilling diplomatic initiatives such as investing in foreign countries to boost bilateral ties even though such investments have not been aligned with the business objectives of the companies.

13. Multinational promoter companies, while for the large part seen to be fulfilling the first main criterion, ought to be reviewed in terms of the related party transactions such as royalty or technical fee being remitted by the Indian subsidiary to the parent.

14. Companies without any identifiable promoter group ought to be assessed for the first main criterion by considering the management team at their helm.

15. In the context of the above pitfalls surrounding the promoter groups of Indian companies, it is the first and necessary condition that the company must have a promoter group that is known for transparency, good corporate governance and fairness in dealings, especially keeping in mind the welfare of the minority shareholders. Only a company which has the appropriate profile of promoters ought to be evaluated for the other two main criteria for investment.

16. It thus bodes well for the investor to generally research the promoter group profile as well as instances of any past controversies touching upon the promoter group. Some tell-tale signs which shed light on the quality of the promoter group include:

    a. Share price performance of the company over the years

    b. Earnings growth trajectory of the company, whether the company has shown growth in earnings in the prosperous business cycles or the earnings have been stripped out by the promoters for their personal benefit even when the going has been good

    c. Whether the promoter has a professional management team or the upper echelons of management is crowded with family members

    d. Whether the promoter group has web of privately owned companies and there are host of related party transactions between these companies and the listed company

    e. Whether the promoter group has been mired in litigations

    f. Whether the personal lifestyle and private investments of the promoter group is commensurate to the earnings of the promoters via remuneration and dividends

    g. General background of the promoter group as culled out from various sources.

17. Once the investor has determined that the company in question fulfils the first main criterion, i.e. it has a promoter group that operates the company with the best governance practices, the investor proceeds to the second criterion i.e. the business prospects of the company.

18. It is not enough that the company prima facie appears to be cheaply valued or the stock price of the company has been demonstrating a good run. It is more important for the investor to first determine whether or not the company in question has promising growth prospects for its business. Only a company whose business is slated to grow year on year represents a stock that should be considered for investment.

19. To determine whether or not a company has favourable business growth prospects, the investor first needs to understand the exact nature of the business that the company is engaged in. In case the investor is not able to properly comprehend the business activities of the company in question, it is best for the investor to avoid investing in such a company altogether rather than be attracted to invest in the company only because it is in the favoured sector or appears to quote at a low multiple.

20. Understanding of the business of the company requires in-depth understanding of the company's revenue model, competitive landscape, cost structure as well as the regulatory framework under which the company operates, the effect of political ideologies of the government in power both at the Centre and the State on the business of the company.

21. Once the business of the company has been understood by the investor in-depth, the investor needs to evaluate its future business prospects by ascertaining whether the revenue and the net earnings of the company are slated to grow with some visibility in the near future. Factors to be considered in the future growth of the business include:

    a. Market or consumer base expansion
    b. Business cycle/commodity cycle
    c. Competitive landscape and market share of the company
    d. Changes in regulatory framework
    e. Geographical or product expansion
    f. Product diversification or expansion
    g. Inorganic growth initiatives such as acquisitions, mergers etc.

22. A company that has an appropriate promoter group and promising business prospects, fulfils the first two main criteria for investment. In such a case, the investor should proceed to ascertain the intrinsic value of the company which is the third main criteria.

23. There are numerous methods for valuation of a company. These include:

   a. Price Earnings Ratio – The PE ratio is an oft used measure for the valuation of a company. However, the fact remains that a high or low PE Ratio on its own does not indicate whether a company is cheaply or expensively valued.

   b. Price to Book Value – P/BV ratio is used to value banks and financial companies. However, this ratio also does not always give a clear picture of valuation of the company when considered in a vacuum.

   c. EV/EBIDTA ratio – This ratio measures the multiple of the enterprise value of the company to its EBIDTA. A high or low EV/EBIDTA ratio, does not in itself conclusively indicate whether or not a company is worth investing in at a certain price point.

   d. Discounted Cash Flow – DCF method is the most comprehensive method of valuation of a company as it involves making a number of assumptions and projecting the future cash flows of a company as well as its terminal value and discounting these to determine the present value of the enterprise of the company. While the DCF method yields a systematic estimation of the business growth of the company as well as the intrinsic value of the company, it is not feasible for every lay investor to develop detailed DCF models or to constantly update these on the basis of the earnings of the companies or to factor in changes in various factors and variables affecting the business of the company.

   e. Unit related valuation methods such as valuation of a company by ascribing a value per unit of its manufacturing capacity or a value per unit of its reserves is also a well-recognized method of valuation of companies, albeit restricted in its application.

   f. Sum of the Parts – It is a method of valuation which is used in case of companies having diverse business verticals, where each vertical is valued separately and added to arrive at the value of the company as a whole.

24. For the third criterion evaluation, this book recommends a simplified amalgam of the various valuation methods imbibing the investor's understanding of the business of the company, its growth prospects and putting this in the perspective of the company's size and its peers.

The steps to apply the third main criterion and to determine whether a company is overvalued or undervalued are as follows:

a. Understand the business of the company and translate this understanding to its financials. What are the key revenue drivers, the margins, investment in assets, regulatory framework, and global product cycles?

b. Understand the past business performance of the company and how the same is reflected in the company's revenues, cost matrix, gross margin, EBIDTA margin, the cost of borrowing, depreciation and taxes.

c. Ascertain the size of the company in terms of its share capital base, its current market capitalization, the net debt and the enterprise value ascribed to the company by the capital markets.

d. Project the expected future revenue and P&L of the company, for at least two to three years, in terms of the revenue growth, based on how the business of the company is poised to grow in view of the investor given the understanding of the business of the company, it's operating metrics, product mix, as well as the margins and other elements of the P&L of the company.

e. Determine key ratios of the company based on the future performance, such as PE Ratio, Price to Book Value, EV/EBIDTA, and Unitary valuation. Compare these ratios with those of its peers and the broader markets to get a sense of whether the company is overvalued or undervalued.

25. Upon carrying out the analysis of the third main criterion, the investor would, even before concluding the entire exercise, have a fair sense of the value of the company and whether or not the price at which it's stock currently trades is higher or lower than the intrinsic worth of the company. Based on such findings, the investor would be able to take a decision whether or not to invest in the company in question.

26. Apart from the three main criteria for investment decision in a stock, there are certain secondary criteria, which though by themselves are not the primary drivers of an investment decision in a stock, need to nevertheless be considered by an investor in addition to the evaluation

of the three main criteria when deciding whether or not to invest in a stock or where the investor is already invested in a stock, whether to remain invested in it or not. These include:

   a. Leverage. Excessively leveraged companies with a high amount of debt on their balance sheet have an uphill battle to achieve growth in the earnings available to their equity shareholders and are susceptible to default even though they may otherwise fulfil the three main criteria.

   b. Stock performance. A company may fulfil the three main criteria and yet may not exhibit commensurate performance in its stock prices. The cause for the lacklustre performance in the company's stock then needs to be evaluated as non-performance of the stock means the investor would not make any returns on his shareholding notwithstanding the three main criteria.

   c. Promoter Stock Pledging. High level of promoter stock being pledged tends to bear down on a stock when the markets are in a negative cycle or the company's performance is under pressure. Thus, a company may fulfil the three main criteria and yet find its stock getting sold off due to margin calls on promoter pledged stock.

   d. Liquidity. Stocks that have poor liquidity in terms of average traded quantities are not only difficult to invest in or liquidate, the quoted price of such stocks is often misleading as that may not be the real price on which the stock is available to purchase or sell in large quantities. Thus, the analysis of the relative undervaluation or overvaluation of such stocks is misleading and may not reflect the correct level of upside available on the stock.

   e. Regulatory uncertainty. Too much regulatory uncertainty surrounding the business of a company or its promoter group does not augur well for the company's stock price performance even though the company may otherwise fulfil the three basic criteria. This is so since, the risk reward ratio would not be commensurate with the level of undervaluation of the company.

   f. Macro-economic factors such as global economic crisis or a debt default by certain countries may cast an overarching cloud on the company and its stock price even though the company may be worth investing in on the basis of the three main criteria.

g. Inorganic corporate actions such as the company acquiring another company in a different business segment, or acquiring another company at a very high valuation thereby straining its balance sheet, ought to be evaluated as these can bring down the stock price of a company even though the company may otherwise fulfil the three main criteria for investment.

27. Once the investor has determined the stocks to invest in, he needs to decide the approach to adopt for buying or selling such a stock. While in the medium to long term, timing the market is not a critical consideration, nevertheless every investor adopts a particular approach to building up or exiting their positions. Some of the approaches which are commonly followed are:

a. All-in Method – in this approach, the entire position in a stock is taken by the investor in one go on the premise that since the current market price of the stock is lower than the intrinsic value as borne out by the analysis of the three main criteria, the investor should buy entire position of the stock in one go rather than speculate on the movement of the stock price in the short term. Similarly at the time of exiting the position the investor liquidates the position in one go on the premise that since the market price has hit or exceeded the estimated intrinsic value, it is no longer justifiable to hold the position in the stock and continue the risk of such a position for upside which is not justified by the intrinsic valuation of the company. The All in Method thus does not rely on timing the market at all.

b. Average Out Method – in this approach, the investor takes part of the position and waits. In case the stock after taking of the position moves down the investor buys more thereby averaging out his cost of acquisition while in case the stock moves up the investor holds the position and liquidates on its achieving the target price. Similarly while liquidating a position, the investor sells part of the position and sells more if the stock moves up. This approach thus attempts to 'max out' the selling price by staggering the sales while liquidating the position and 'average out' the purchase price while building a position.

c. **Market Movement Approach** - in this approach, the investor takes partial position and waits. In case the stock after taking of the position moves down the investor does not add to the position on the premise that the market knows more and is not rating the stock as highly as the investor's analysis leads him to believe. On the other hand, if the stock after taking of the initial position, moves up, then the investor adds to the position on the premise that the market is also agreeing with the investor's analysis of the stock being undervalued. Similarly while liquidating the position, the investor sells part of the position and waits. If after selling, the stock moves up the investor waits on the premise that the market does not believe that the stock has reached its fullest potential. On the other hand if after selling part of the position if the stock starts moving down, the investor liquidates the balance position. This approach thus follows the market rather than work against the current trend of the market.

The approach ultimately followed by the investor in entering into and exiting positions in a stock is dependent on the preferences of the investor as each approach has its pros and cons.

28. **Portfolio allocation:** No investor ought to put all the available capital in a single stock. The portfolio needs to be diversified so as to hedge the risk and maximize the profitability. While this is a well-known and acknowledged fact in any investment practice, when it comes to an Indian portfolio certain guidelines for portfolio diversification are as follows:

    a. Number of stocks should be sufficient as to provide adequate diversification and yet not be too many as the investor won't be able to monitor and continually study and update himself with respect to developments regarding the business, earnings, regulatory framework, promoters and corporate events touching upon each of the companies in his portfolio.

    b. The portfolio should have an adequate balance between government and private promoter group stocks. A portfolio that is overly skewed in favour of government stocks, especially in the Indian context, is a sitting duck for a beating in case there is a change of government and the new Government has a diametrically opposite view or philosophy in the conduct of the management of the affairs of state-owned companies.

c. The investor should diversify the portfolio between different promoter groups and not be overly skewed with stocks of a particular promoter group as overly depending on a single promoter group in the Indian context can be fraught with risk as any promoter group can come under the cloud of regulatory action or other factors that may upset the performance of their companies.

d. The portfolio should have an adequate spread of companies from diverse sectors. No matter how optimistic the investor may be with respect to a particular sector's prospects, it would not justify the investor holding stocks of companies in that single or few sectors. It is always possible, especially in an Indian context, that the prospects of a sector get adversely hit by sudden events or policy changes. Thus a diversification of the portfolio in terms of the number of sectors is essential.

e. The portfolio should have an appropriate mix of large, mid and small-cap stocks as opposed to being comprised of all stocks of one size. While a large cap stock ensures stability of earnings and lower risk, the multiplier returns are generally earned in the small cap stocks which bring with them much higher risk profile. An appropriate mix of large, mid and small cap stocks thus balances the risk and returns for the investor.

29. An in-depth knowledge of the regulatory framework is of the utmost importance for any person who wishes to invest in the Indian equity markets. The unique features of the Indian regulatory environment include federal structure, differing political ideologies of the different political parties, coalition politics mandated by the diverse democratic framework, frequent changes in legislation, complex legislative framework in terms of laws, circulars, notifications, a multitude of authorities and approvals, and overriding judicial activism. Any change in the regulatory environment can materially affect the business prospects of a company, so can the change of the government at the state or central level. An ongoing study and tracking of the regulatory framework affecting the overall business environment or the specific

business of the company is thus essential for the investor to undertake in the Indian context.

30. Information in the form of tips, rumours, corporate gossip are commonplace in India and although trading on the basis of inside information is patently illegal in India in as much as any other country, coming across information and tips is commonplace nevertheless. An investor actively present in the market would not be able to avoid coming across snippets of information even if they tried. While information-based trading is not recommended as a strategy in this book, information would nevertheless need to be processed by the investor as and when one is confronted with it. Some relevant information types include:

   a. Information regarding earnings – should be considered for updating the projected earnings of the company in the analysis of the valuation of the company by the investor and to determine whether the analysis of the investor regarding the business prospects of the company and its projected earnings is on or off the mark.

   b. Information regarding promoter actions such as open offer, delisting, ought to be considered in determining whether the investment in the company is worth continuing or an exit is in order, especially after considering the price on which the corporate/promoter action regarding the company's shares is taking place.

   c. Information regarding acquisitions by a company ought to be factored into the business prospects of the company and the impact of such acquisitions in terms of synergies in business, the financials of the company including the leverage, the cash flows and the incremental EBIDTA of the company owing to the acquisition ought to be considered.

   d. Information regarding regulatory actions should be evaluated for their impact on the business earning structure of the company and its business prospects as estimated by the investor.

   e. Information regarding any new or major orders or contracts should be factored into the company's projected earnings.

31. Technical charts and trading tips based on the interpretation of price charts of the stocks by technical analysts should not be made the basis

of investment positions and at most a person confident of charting tips may adopt these to time his entry and exit in stocks that he may have otherwise concluded as investment propositions based on the analysis of the three main criteria for investment. Pure trading based on technical charts is an extremely risky proposition and ought not to be resorted to by an investor except where the investor has a first-hand understanding of chart reading and interpretation.

32. Some trading ideas which may be adopted to supplement the investment positions taken by an investor on the basis of the approach recommended by this book include:

   a. Where an investor forms a view regarding the re-rating of a foreign currency, the investor may consider building a position in a stock for a short period where the currency re-rating materially impacts the earnings of the company to alter its P&L structure or where currency re-rating significantly alters the asset or liabilities of the company having exposure to foreign currency.

   b. Where during the course of the assessment of the three main criteria for investment, an investor finds a stock to be patently overvalued, the investor may consider short selling the stock on the premise that over a period of time the market would correct the price of the stock to the lower level of the intrinsic value of the company.

   c. Taking a position in a stock as a proxy to an upcoming IPO where the investor finds the already listed company better valued than the IPO company after considering the earnings of the IPO company and the multiple on which the IPO has been subscribed.

   d. Writing options i.e. selling put or call options where the investor finds excessive volatility in the markets owing to external factors, in such a case the investor would inevitably be able to encash the premium in-built in the call or put options so long as the investor has a view that the market or the particular stock would not move out of the range.

   e. Pair trades such as buying a stock which the investor believes to be cheaply valued and selling another stock in the same sector which the investor believes to be overvalued as a result of his analysis of the three main criteria. This enables the investor to not only encash the upside on the undervalued stock but also the downside on the overvalued one. At the same time, it makes for an automatic hedge against secular downward movement in the market.

f. Playing on the holding subsidiary arbitrage where the holding company is cheaply valued owing to holding company discount and thus, makes for a better proxy investment as opposed to investing in the subsidiary company which fulfils the three main criteria, so long as the holding company does not bring with it the baggage of other verticals or subsidiaries which have a negative effect on the valuation of the holding company.

g. Investing on the basis of the re-rating of a stock on account of its inclusion in one of the benchmark indices which induces greater liquidity and buying interest in the stock, especially by foreign investors, institutions and mutual funds.

h. Bonus or Dividend stripping are strategies adopted not only for tax planning but also to earn profits where the premise of the investor is that the stock will inevitably regain price levels existing at the cum bonus or cum dividend stage due to its fulfilling the three main criteria.

i. Hedging the overall portfolio of the investor against expected short term down movements in the broader market by short selling the index, especially in times of excessive volatility or global or political disturbances.

j. Investing in DVR shares versus ordinary shares to arbitrage the discount in DVR shares owing to the limited voting rights these carry, even though the intrinsic value attributable to each DVR share on a purely financial valuation of the company ought to be at par with the ordinary shares. Thus an investor finding a company worth investing based on the three main criteria may take a position in the DVR shares in addition to the ordinary shares to augment the gain since the differential between the perceived intrinsic value and the quoted price would be more accentuated in the case of DVR shares.

33. Investing in any equity market requires extreme discipline, avoiding temptations and sticking to one's approach and methodology. Moreover, in the Indian markets which are ever changing and react swiftly to changes, effective investing requires the investor to continuously keep himself updated with the multitude of events and factors affecting the company and its business prospects.

A systematic and disciplined approach followed by an investor adopting the recommendations prescribed in this book with a medium to long term holding, even if restricted to a few stocks, ought to benefit the investor in the exciting domain of the Indian equity markets which are poised on the cusp of an exciting growth cycle at this juncture.

ACKNOWLEDGEMENTS

First and foremost, I would like to thank my wife and companion of more than twenty one years, Rashmi Khanna, without whose constant love and support this book would not have been possible. Her unwavering faith in me and her encouragement are solely responsible for my converting this long standing aspiration into reality. I could not have asked for a better companion to traverse the journey of life.

I would like to thank my sister, Neha Khanna, for her valuable inputs on the content of this book as well as her steadfast support in many other respects.

I would also like to thank my parents, parents-in-law, family, colleagues and friends as they have all, in their own unique ways, helped shape me into the person that I am today.

My gratitude to Mr. Santosh Gadia, my senior partner, who has been a source of knowledge, wisdom and learning for many years. And to my partner, Chaitanya Gadia for his support and help.

Special thanks to Arvind Kapahi, for his assistance with the book, including proof-reading, editing, graphics and other valuable comments. Arvind's experience in the Indian stock markets has invited many insightful conversations between him and me over the years.

Thank you, to my teachers from high school, college, CA and law school as well as my seniors in different organizations, as I have learnt a lot from all of them at different stages of my life.

A special mention for Jayesh Sheth, my stock broker, who has been a dedicated companion in my stock market adventures over the years.

Acknowledgements

A big vote of thanks to the stock market itself, as it remains the biggest teacher when it comes to investing or trading in stocks, for any and every person.

Last but not the least, I would like to thank my children, as they are God's gift of shining light in my life.

And ultimately, I would like to thank God almighty for his being there for me through the hardest of times.

www.ingramcontent.com/pod-product-compliance
Lightning Source LLC
Chambersburg PA
CBHW020633220526
45464CB00001B/132